THE RATTLE BAG

THE RATTLE BAG

edited by
Seamus Heaney
and
Ted Hughes

ff
faber and faber

First published in 1982
by Faber and Faber Limited
3 Queen Square London WCIN 3AU

Printed and bound by CPI Group (UK) Ltd,
Croydon, CRO 4YY

A CIP record for this book is available
from the British Library

ISBN 978-0-571-22583-5

Contents

7

10

11

12

13

14

15

16

17

Introduction

This anthology amassed itself like a cairn. Most of the poems lay about for the taking in places already well known to people, younger or older, who read verse; only a few came from the by-ways. They were picked up one by one and left *in situ* without much initial thought being given to the stuff already in the pile or the position that they might occupy in the final shape. Indeed, the thought of shaping did not arise until the hunt for individual poems had lost its excitement, and then we decided to arrange the material in alphabetical order according to titles or first lines rather than thematically or chronologically or according to author.

To have arranged it according to author would have robbed the order of the poems of an unexpectedness which we think it now possesses and would perhaps have encouraged readers to think of the book as an attempt to set up an exclusive list of poets suitable for younger people. To have done it thematically would have made it feel too much like a textbook. To have done it chronologically would have left whole centuries unrepresented and made the thing look a botched historical survey. We hope that our decision to impose an arbitrary alphabetical order allows the contents to discover themselves as we ourselves gradually discovered them—each poem full of its singular appeal, transmitting its own signals, taking its chances in a big, voluble world.

'Adieu, farewell earth's bliss'

Adieu, farewell earth's bliss,
This world uncertain is;
Fond are life's lustful joys,
Death proves them all but toys,
None from his darts can fly.
I am sick, I must die.
   Lord have mercy on us!

Rich men, trust not in wealth,
Gold cannot buy you health;
Physic himself must fade,
All things to end are made.
The plague full swift goes by;
I am sick, I must die.
   Lord have mercy on us!

Beauty is but a flower
Which wrinkles will devour;
Brightness falls from the air,
Queens have died young and fair,
Dust hath closed Helen's eye.
I am sick, I must die.
   Lord have mercy on us!

Strength stoops unto the grave,
Worms feed on Hector brave,
Swords may not fight with fate.
Earth still holds ope her gate;
Come! come! the bells do cry.
I am sick, I must die.
   Lord have mercy on us!

Wit with his wantonness
Tasteth death's bitterness;
Hell's executioner
Hath no ears for to hear

What vain art can reply.
I am sick, I must die.
       Lord have mercy on us!

Haste, therefore, each degree,
To welcome destiny.
Heaven is our heritage,
Earth but a player's stage;
Mount we unto the sky;
I am sick, I must die.
       Lord have mercy on us!

THOMAS NASHE
From *Summer's Last Will and Testament*

After his Death

It turned out
that the bombs he had thrown
raised buildings:

that the acid he had sprayed
had painfully opened
the eyes of the blind.

Fishermen hauled
prizewinning fish
from the water he had polluted.

We sat with astonishment
enjoying the shade
of the vicious words he had planted.

The government decreed that
on the anniversary of his birth
the people should observe
two minutes pandemonium.

NORMAN MACCAIG

After Looking into a Book Belonging to My Great-Grandfather, Eli Eliakim Plutzik

I am troubled by the blank fields, the speechless graves.
Since the names were carved upon wood, there is no word
For the thousand years that shaped this scribbling fist
And the eyes staring at strange places and times
Beyond the veldt dragging to Poland.
Lovers of words make simple peace with death,
At last demanding, to close the door to the cold,
Only *Here lies someone*.
Here lie no one and no one, your fathers and mothers.

HYAM PLUTZIK

Afterwards

When the Present has latched its postern behind my tremulous
    stay,
    And the May month flaps its glad green leaves like wings,
Delicate-filmed as new-spun silk, will the neighbours say,
    'He was a man who used to notice such things'?

If it be in the dusk when, like an eyelid's soundless blink,
    The dewfall-hawk comes crossing the shades to alight
Upon the wind-warped upland thorn, a gazer may think,
    'To him this must have been a familiar sight.'

If I pass during some nocturnal blackness, mothy and warm,
    When the hedgehog travels furtively over the lawn,
One may say, 'He strove that such innocent creatures should
        come to no harm,
    But he could do little for them; and now he is gone.'

If, when hearing that I have been stilled at last, they stand at the
        door,
    Watching the full-starred heavens that winter sees,
Will this thought rise on those who will meet my face no more,
    'He was one who had an eye for such mysteries'?

And will any say when my bell of quittance is heard in the
    gloom,
  And a crossing breeze cuts a pause in its outrollings,
Till they rise again, as they were a new bell's boom,
    'He hears it not now, but used to notice such things'?

THOMAS HARDY

Ah! Sunflower

Ah, Sunflower! weary of time,
Who countest the steps of the Sun,
Seeking after that sweet golden clime
Where the traveller's journey is done:

Where the Youth pined away with desire,
And the pale Virgin shrouded in snow
Arise from their graves, and aspire
Where my Sunflower wishes to go.

WILLIAM BLAKE

Alfred Corning Clark
(1916–1961)

You read the *New York Times*
every day at recess,
but in its dry
obituary, a list
of your wives, nothing is news,
except the ninety-five
thousand dollar engagement ring
you gave the sixth.

Poor rich boy,
you were unseasonably adult
at taking your time,
and died at forty-five.
Poor Al Clark,
behind your enlarged,
hardly recognizable photograph,
I feel the pain.
You were alive. You are dead.
You wore bow-ties and dark
blue coats, and sucked
wintergreen or cinnamon lifesavers
to sweeten your breath.
There must be something—
some one to praise
your triumphant diffidence,
your refusal of exertion,
the intelligence
that pulsed in the sensitive,
pale concavities of your forehead.
You never worked,
and were third in the form.
I owe you something—
I was befogged,
and you were too bored,
quick and cool to laugh.
You are dear to me, Alfred;
our reluctant souls united
in our unconventional
illegal games of chess
on the St Mark's quadrangle.
You usually won—
motionless
as a lizard in the sun.

ROBERT LOWELL

25

The Allansford Pursuit

Cunning and art he did not lack
But aye her whistle would fetch him back.

O, I shall go into a hare
With sorrow and sighing and mickle care,
And I shall go in the Devil's name
Aye, till I be fetchèd hame.
   —Hare, take heed of a bitch greyhound
   Will harry thee all these fells around,
   For here come I in Our Lady's name
   All but for to fetch thee hame.

Cunning and art he did not lack
But aye her whistle would fetch him back.

Yet, I shall go into a trout
With sorrow and sighing and mickle doubt,
And show thee many a crooked game
Ere that I be fetchèd hame,
   —Trout, take heed of an otter lank
   Will harry thee close from bank to bank,
   For here come I in Our Lady's name
   All but for to fetch thee hame.

Cunning and art he did not lack
But aye her whistle would fetch him back.

Yet I shall go into a bee
With mickle horror and dread of thee
And flit to hive in the Devil's name
Ere that I be fetchèd hame.
   —Bee, take heed of a swallow hen
   Will harry thee close, both butt and ben,
   For here come I in Our Lady's Name
   All but for to fetch thee hame.

Cunning and art he did not lack
But aye her whistle would fetch him back.

Yet I shall go into a mouse
And haste me unto the miller's house,
There in his corn to have good game
Ere that I be fetchèd hame.
　　—Mouse, take heed of a white tib-cat
　　That never was baulked of mouse or rat,
　　For I'll crack thy bones in Our Lady's name:
　　Thus shalt thou be fetchèd hame.

Cunning and art he did not lack
But aye her whistle would fetch him back.

ROBERT GRAVES

A restoration of the fragmentary seventeenth-century text, sung
by north-country witches at their sabbaths.

'All the world's a stage'

All the world's a stage,
And all the men and women merely players:
They have their exits and their entrances;
And one man in his time plays many parts,
His acts being seven ages. At first the infant,
Mewling and puking in the nurse's arms.
And then the whining schoolboy, with his satchel,
And shining morning face, creeping like snail
Unwillingly to school. And then the lover,
Sighing like furnace, with a woeful ballad
Made to his mistress' eyebrow. Then a soldier,
Full of strange oaths, and bearded like the pard,
Jealous in honour, sudden and quick in quarrel,
Seeking the bubble reputation
Even in the cannon's mouth. And then the justice,
In fair round belly with good capon lin'd,
With eyes severe, and beard of formal cut,

Full of wise saws and modern instances;
And so he plays his part. The sixth age shifts
Into the lean and slipper'd pantaloon,
With spectacles on nose and pouch on side,
His youthful hose well sav'd, a world too wide
For his shrunk shank; and his big manly voice,
Turning again toward childish treble, pipes
And whistles in his sound. Last scene of all,
That ends this strange eventful history,
Is second childishness and mere oblivion,
Sans teeth, sans eyes, sans taste, sans everything.

WILLIAM SHAKESPEARE
From *As You Like It*, Act 2 Scene 7

Among the Narcissi

Spry, wry, and gray as these March sticks,
Percy bows, in his blue peajacket, among the narcissi.
He is recuperating from something on the lung.

The narcissi, too, are bowing to some big thing:
It rattles their stars on the green hill where Percy
Nurses the hardship of his stitches, and walks and walks.

There is a dignity to this; there is a formality—
The flowers vivid as bandages, and the man mending.
They bow and stand: they suffer such attacks!

And the octogenarian loves the little flocks.
He is quite blue; the terrible wind tries his breathing.
The narcissi look up like children, quickly and whitely.

SYLVIA PLATH

The Ancients of the World

The salmon lying in the depths of Llyn Llifon,
    Secretly as a thought in a dark mind,
Is not so old as the owl of Cwm Cowlyd
    Who tells her sorrow nightly on the wind.

The ousel singing in the woods of Cilgwri,
    Tirelessly as a stream over the mossed stones,
    Is not so old as the toad of Cors Fochno
    Who feels the cold skin sagging round his bones.

The toad and the ousel and the stag of Rhedynfre,
    That has cropped each leaf from the tree of life,
Are not so old as the owl of Cwm Cowlyd,
    That the proud eagle would have to wife.

R. S. THOMAS

'And death shall have no dominion'

And death shall have no dominion.
Dead men naked they shall be one
With the man in the wind and the west moon;
When their bones are picked clean and the clean bones gone,
They shall have stars at elbow and foot;
Though they go mad they shall be sane,
Though they sink through the sea they shall rise again;
Though lovers be lost love shall not;
And death shall have no dominion.

And death shall have no dominion.
Under the windings of the sea
They lying long shall not die windily;
Twisting on racks when sinews give way,
Strapped to a wheel, yet they shall not break;

Faith in their hands shall snap in two,
And the unicorn evils run them through;
Split all ends up they shan't crack;
And death shall have no dominion.

And death shall have no dominion.
No more may gulls cry at their ears
Or waves break loud on the seashores;
Where blew a flower may a flower no more
Lift its head to the blows of the rain;
Though they be mad and dead as nails,
Heads of the characters hammer through daisies;
Break in the sun till the sun breaks down,
And death shall have no dominion.

DYLAN THOMAS

And in the 51st Year of that Century, while My Brother Cried in the Trench, while My Enemy Glared from the Cave

This star is only an augury of the morning,
Gift-bearer of another day.

A wind has brought the musk of thirty fields,
Each like a coin of silver under that sky.

Precious, the soundless breathing of wife and children
In a house on a field lit by the morning star.

HYAM PLUTZIK

'And the days are not full enough'

And the days are not full enough
And the nights are not full enough
And life slips by like a field mouse
             Not shaking the grass.

EZRA POUND

Angelica the Doorkeeper

The falcon soars
The town's gates are even higher

Angelica's their doorkeeper
She's wound the sun round her head
She's tied the moon round her waist

She's hung herself with stars.

ANON
From the Serbian (trans. Anne Pennington)

'The Angel that presided o'er my birth'

The Angel that presided o'er my birth
Said, 'Little creature, form'd of Joy and Mirth,
'Go love without the help of any Thing on Earth.'

WILLIAM BLAKE

31

'Anger lay by me all night long'

Anger lay by me all night long,
    His breath was hot upon my brow,
He told me of my burning wrong,
    All night he talked and would not go.

He stood by me all through the day,
    Struck from my hand the book, the pen;
He said: 'Hear first what I've to say,
    And sing, if you've the heart to, then.'

And can I cast him from my couch?
    And can I lock him from my room?
Ah no, his honest words are such
    That he's my true-lord, and my doom.

ELIZABETH DARYUSH

An Animal Alphabet

A   The Absolutely Abstemious Ass,
who resided in a Barrel, and only lived on
Soda Water and Pickled Cucumbers.

B   The Bountiful Beetle,
who always carried a Green Umbrella when it didn't rain,
and left it at home when it did.

C   The Comfortable Confidential Cow,
who sate in her Red Morocco Armchair and
toasted her own Bread at the parlour Fire.

D   The Dolomphious Duck,
who caught spotted frogs for her dinner
with a Runcible Spoon.

32

E   The Enthusiastic Elephant,
who ferried himself across the water with the
Kitchen Poker and a New pair of Ear-rings.

F   The Fizzgiggious Fish,
who always walked about upon Stilts,
because he had no legs.

G   The Good-natured Gray Gull,
who carried the Old Owl, and his Crimson Carpetbag,
across the river, because he could not swim.

H   The Hasty Higgeldipiggledy Hen,
who went to market in a Blue Bonnet and Shawl,
and bought a Fish for Supper.

I   The Inventive Indian,
who caught a Remarkable Rabbit in a
Stupendous Silver Spoon.

J   The Judicious Jubilant Jay,
who did up her Back Hair every morning with a Wreath
    of Roses,
Three feathers, and a Gold Pin.

K   The Kicking Kangaroo,
who wore a Pale Pink Muslin dress
with Blue spots.

L   The Lively Learned Lobster,
who mended his own Clothes with
a Needle and Thread.

M   The Melodious Meritorious Mouse.
who played a merry minuet on the
Pianoforte.

N   The Nutritious Newt,
who purchased a Round Plum-pudding,
for his granddaughter.

O   The Obsequious Ornamental Ostrich,
     who wore boots to keep his
     feet quite dry.

P   The Perpendicular Purple Polly,
     who read the Newspaper and ate Parsnip Pie
     with his Spectacles.

Q   The Queer Querulous Quail,
     who smoked a pipe of tobacco on the top of
     a Tin Tea-kettle.

R   The Rural Runcible Raven,
     who wore a White Wig and flew away
     with the Carpet Broom.

S   The Scroobious Snake,
     who always wore a Hat on his Head, for
     fear he should bite anybody.

T   The Tumultuous Tom-tommy Tortoise,
     who beat a Drum all day long in the
     middle of the wilderness.

U   The Umbrageous Umbrella-maker,
     whose Face nobody ever saw, because it was
     always covered by his Umbrella.

V   The Visibly Vicious Vulture,
     who wrote some verses to a Veal-cutlet in a
     Volume bound in Vellum.

W   The Worrying Whizzing Wasp,
     who stood on a Table, and played sweetly on a
     Flute with a Morning Cap.

X   The Excellent Double-extra XX
     imbibing King Xerxes, who lived a
     long while ago.

Y   The Yonghy-Bonghy-Bo,
    whose Head was ever so much bigger than his
    Body, and whose Hat was rather small.

Z   The Zigzag Zealous Zebra,
    who carried five Monkeys on his back all
    the way to Jellibolee.

EDWARD LEAR

Another Epitaph on an Army of Mercenaries

It is a God-damned lie to say that these
Saved, or knew, anything worth any man's pride.
They were professional murderers and they took
Their blood money and impious risks and died.
In spite of all their kind some elements of worth
With difficulty persist here and there on earth.

HUGH MACDIARMID

In reply to A. E. Housman (see p. 142)

'anyone lived in a pretty how town'

anyone lived in a pretty how town
(with up so floating many bells down)
spring summer autumn winter
he sang his didn't he danced his did.

Women and men(both little and small)
cared for anyone not at all
they sowed their isn't they reaped their same
sun moon stars rain

children guessed(but only a few
and down they forgot as up they grew
autumn winter spring summer)
that noone loved him more by more

35

when by now and tree by leaf
she laughed his joy she cried his grief
bird by snow and stir by still
anyone's any was all to her

someones married their everyones
laughed their cryings and did their dance
(sleep wake hope and then)they
said their nevers they slept their dream

stars rain sun moon
(and only the snow can begin to explain
how children are apt to forget to remember
with up so floating many bells down)

one day anyone died i guess
(and noone stooped to kiss his face)
busy folk buried them side by side
little by little and was by was

all by all and deep by deep
and more by more they dream their sleep
noone and anyone earth by april
wish by spirit and if by yes.

Women and men(both dong and ding)
summer autumn winter spring
reaped their sowing and went their came
sun moon stars rain

E. E. CUMMINGS

Apple Blossom

The first blossom was the best blossom
For the child who never had seen an orchard;
For the youth whom whisky had led astray
The morning after was the first day.

The first apple was the best apple
For Adam before he heard the sentence;
When the flaming sword endorsed the Fall
The trees were his to plant for all.

The first ocean was the best ocean
For the child from streets of doubt and litter;
For the youth for whom the skies unfurled
His first love was his first world.

But the first verdict seemed the worst verdict
When Adam and Eve were expelled from Eden;
Yet when the bitter gates clanged to
The sky beyond was just as blue.

For the next ocean is the first ocean
And the last ocean is the first ocean
And, however often the sun may rise,
A new thing dawns upon our eyes.

For the last blossom is the first blossom
And the first blossom is the best blossom
And when from Eden we take our way
The morning after is the first day.

LOUIS MACNEICE

The Artist

Mr T.
          bareheaded
                    in a soiled undershirt
his hair standing out
          on all sides
                    stood on his toes
heels together
          arms gracefully
                    for the moment

37

curled above his head.
        Then he whirled about
                bounded
into the air
        and with an entrechat
                perfectly achieved
completed the figure.
        My mother
                taken by surprise
where she sat
        in her invalid's chair
                was left speechless.
Bravo! she cried at last
        and clapped her hands.
                The man's wife
came from the kitchen:
        What goes on here? she said.
                But the show was over.
           WILLIAM CARLOS WILLIAMS

'As I came in by Fiddich-side'

As I came in by Fiddich-side,
    In a May morning,
I met Willie Mackintosh,
    An hour before the dawning.

'Turn again, turn again,
    Turn again, I bid ye;
If ye burn Auchindown,
    Huntly he will head ye.'

'Head me, hang me,
    That sall never fear me;
I'll burn Auchindown
    Before the life leaves me.'

38

As I came in by Auchindown,
   In a May morning,
Auchindown was in a bleeze,
   An hour before the dawning.

Crawing, crawing,
   For my crowse crawing,
I lost the best feather i my wing
   For my crowse crawing.

ANON
A Scottish ballad

'As I walked out one evening'

As I walked out one evening,
   Walking down Bristol Street,
The crowds upon the pavement
   Were fields of harvest wheat.

And down by the brimming river
   I heard a lover sing
Under an arch of the railway:
   'Love has no ending.

'I'll love you, dear, I'll love you
   Till China and Africa meet,
And the river jumps over the mountain
   And the salmon sing in the street,

'I'll love you till the ocean
   Is folded and hung up to dry
And the seven stars go squawking
   Like geese about the sky.

'The years shall run like rabbits,
    For in my arms I hold
The Flower of the Ages,
    And the first love of the world.'

But all the clocks in the city
    Began to whirr and chime:
'O let not Time deceive you,
    You cannot conquer Time.

'In the burrows of the Nightmare
    Where Justice naked is,
Time watches from the shadow
    And coughs when you would kiss.

'In headaches and in worry
    Vaguely life leaks away,
And Time will have his fancy
    Tomorrow or today.

'Into many a green valley
    Drifts the appalling snow;
Time breaks the threaded dances
    And the diver's brilliant bow.

'O plunge your hands in water,
    Plunge them in up to the wrist;
Stare, stare in the basin
    And wonder what you've missed.

'The glacier knocks in the cupboard,
    The desert sighs in the bed,
And the crack in the tea-cup opens
    A lane to the land of the dead.

'Where the beggars raffle the banknotes
    And the Giant is enchanting to Jack,
And the Lily-white Boy is a Roarer,
    And Jill goes down on her back.

'O look, look in the mirror,
    O look in your distress;
Life remains a blessing
    Although you cannot bless.

'O stand, stand at the window
    As the tears scald and start;
You shall love your crooked neighbour
    With your crooked heart.'

It was late, late in the evening,
    The lovers they were gone;
The clocks had ceased their chiming
    And the deep river ran on.

W. H. AUDEN

'As kingfishers catch fire, dragonflies draw flame'

As kingfishers catch fire, dragonflies draw flame;
    As tumbled over rim in roundy wells
    Stones ring; like each tucked string tells, each hung bell's
Bow swung finds tongue to fling out broad its name;
Each mortal thing does one thing and the same:
    Deals out that being indoors each one dwells;
    Selves—goes itself; *myself* it speaks and spells,
Crying *What I do is me: for that I came.*

I say more: the just man justices;
    Keeps grace: that keeps all his goings graces;
Acts in God's eye what in God's eye he is—
    Christ. For Christ plays in ten thousand places,
Lovely in limbs, and lovely in eyes not his
    To the Father through the features of men's faces.

GERARD MANLEY HOPKINS

As Much as You Can

Even if you can't shape your life the way you want,
at least try as much as you can
not to degrade it
by too much contact with the world,
by too much activity and talk.

Do not degrade it by dragging it along,
taking it around and exposing it so often
to the daily silliness
of social relations and parties,
until it comes to seem a boring hanger-on.

C. P. CAVAFY
From the Greek (trans. Edmund Keeley and Philip Sherrard)

'As the team's head-brass flashed out'

As the team's head-brass flashed out on the turn
The lovers disappeared into the wood.
I sat among the boughs of the fallen elm
That strewed an angle of the fallow, and
Watched the plough narrowing a yellow square
Of charlock. Every time the horses turned
Instead of treading me down, the ploughman leaned
Upon the handles to say or ask a word,
About the weather, next about the war.
Scraping the share he faced towards the wood,
And screwed along the furrow till the brass flashed
Once more.
         The blizzard felled the elm whose crest
I sat in, by a woodpecker's round hole,
The ploughman said. 'When will they take it away?'
'When the war's over.' So the talk began—
One minute and an interval of ten,
A minute more and the same interval.
'Have you been out?' 'No.' 'And don't want to, perhaps?'

42

'If I could only come back again, I should.
I could spare an arm. I shouldn't want to lose
A leg. If I should lose my head, why, so,
I should want nothing more. . . . Have many gone
From here?' 'Yes.' 'Many lost?' 'Yes, a good few.
Only two teams work on the farm this year.
One of my mates is dead. The second day
In France they killed him. It was back in March,
The very night of the blizzard, too. Now if
He had stayed here we should have moved the tree.'
'And I should not have sat here. Everything
Would have been different. For it would have been
Another world.' 'Ay, and a better, though
If we could see all all might seem good.' Then
The lovers came out of the wood again:
The horses started and for the last time
I watched the clods crumble and topple over
After the ploughshare and the stumbling team.

EDWARD THOMAS

'As you came from the holy land'

'As you came from the holy land
      Of Walsinghame,
Met you not with my true love
      By the way as you came?'

'How shall I know your true love,
      That have met many a one
As I went to the holy land,
      That have come, that have gone?'

'She is neither white nor brown,
      But as the heavens fair,
There is none hath a form so divine
      In the earth or the air.'

43

'Such an one did I meet, good Sir,
   Such an angelic face,
Who like a queen, like a nymph did appear
   By her gait, by her grace.'

'She hath left me here alone,
   All alone as unknown,
Who sometime did me lead with herself,
   And me loved as her own.'

'What's the cause that she leaves you alone
   And a new way doth take,
Who loved you once as her own
   And her joy did you make?'

'I have loved her all my youth,
   But now old as you see,
Love likes not the falling fruit
   From the withered tree.

'Know that Love is a careless child,
   And forgets promise past;
He is blind, he is deaf when he list
   And in faith never fast.

'His desire is a dureless content
   And a trustless joy;
He is won with a world of despair
   And is lost with a toy.'

'Of womenkind such indeed is the love
   Or the word love abused,
Under which many childish desires
   And conceits are excused.

'But love is a durable fire
   In the mind ever burning;
Never sick, never old, never dead,
   From itself never turning.'

44

At Grass

The eye can hardly pick them out
From the cold shade they shelter in,
Till wind distresses tail and mane;
Then one crops grass, and moves about
—The other seeming to look on—
And stands anonymous again.

Yet fifteen years ago, perhaps
Two dozen distances sufficed
To fable them: faint afternoons
Of Cups and Stakes and Handicaps,
Whereby their names were artificed
To inlay faded, classic Junes—

Silks at the start: against the sky
Numbers and parasols: outside,
Squadrons of empty cars, and heat,
And littered grass: then the long cry
Hanging unhushed till it subside
To stop-press columns on the street.

Do memories plague their ears like flies?
They shake their heads. Dusk brims the shadows.
Summer by summer all stole away,
The starting-gates, the crowds and cries—
All but the unmolesting meadows.
Almanacked, their names live; they

Have slipped their names, and stand at ease,
Or gallop for what must be joy,
And not a fieldglass sees them home,
Or curious stop-watch prophesies:
Only the groom, and the groom's boy,
With bridles in the evening come.

PHILIP LARKIN

At the Bomb Testing Site

At noon in the desert a panting lizard
waited for history, its elbows tense,
watching the curve of a particular road
as if something might happen.

It was looking at something farther off
than people could see, an important scene
acted in stone for little selves
at the flute end of consequences.

There was just a continent without much on it
under a sky that never cared less.
Ready for a change, the elbows waited.
The hands gripped hard on the desert.

WILLIAM STAFFORD

'At the grey round of the hill'

At the grey round of the hill
Music of a lost kingdom
Runs, runs and is suddenly still.
The winds out of Clare-Galway
Carry it: suddenly it is still.

I have heard in the night air
A wandering airy music;
And moidered in that snare
A man is lost of a sudden,
In that sweet wandering snare.

What finger first began
Music of a lost kingdom?
They dream that laughed in the sun.
Dry bones that dream are bitter.
They dream and darken our sun.

Those crazy fingers play
A wandering airy music;
Our luck is withered away
And wheat in the wheat-ear withered,
And the wind blows it away.

My heart ran wild when it heard
The curlew cry before dawn
And the eddying cat-headed bird;
But now the night is gone.
I have heard from far below
The strong March birds a–crow.
Stretch neck and clap the wing,
Red cocks, and crow!

W. B. YEATS

Song for the Cloth: *The Dreaming of the Bones*

Auguries of Innocence

To see a World in a Grain of Sand
And a Heaven in a Wild Flower,
Hold Infinity in the palm of your hand
And Eternity in an hour.

A Robin Redbreast in a Cage
Puts all Heaven in a Rage.
A dove house fill'd with doves and pigeons
Shudders Hell thro' all its regions.
A dog starv'd at his Master's Gate
Predicts the ruin of the State.
A Horse misus'd upon the Road
Calls to Heaven for Human blood.
Each outcry of the hunted Hare
A fibre from the Brain does tear.
A Skylark wounded in the wing,
A Cherubim does cease to sing.

The Game Cock clip'd and arm'd for fight
Does the Rising Sun affright.
Every Wolf's and Lion's howl
Raises from Hell a Human Soul.
The wild deer, wand'ring here and there,
Keeps the Human Soul from Care.
The Lamb Misus'd breeds Public strife
And yet forgives the Butcher's Knife.
The Bat that flits at close of Eve
Has left the Brain that won't Believe.
The Owl that calls upon the Night
Speaks the Unbeliever's fright.
He who shall hurt the little Wren
Shall never be belov'd by Men.
He who the Ox to wrath has mov'd
Shall never be by Woman lov'd.
The wanton Boy that kills the Fly
Shall feel the Spider's enmity.
He who torments the Chafer's sprite
Weaves a Bower in endless Night.
The Catterpiller on the Leaf
Repeats to thee thy Mother's grief.
Kill not the Moth nor Butterfly,
For the Last Judgement draweth nigh.
He who shall train the Horse to War
Shall never pass the Polar Bar.
The Beggar's Dog and Widow's Cat,
Feed them and thou wilt grow fat.
The Gnat that sings his Summer's song
Poison gets from Slander's tongue.
The poison of the Snake and Newt
Is the sweat of Envy's Foot.
The Poison of the Honey Bee
Is the Artist's Jealousy.
The Prince's Robes and Beggar's Rags
Are Toadstools on the Miser's Bags.
A truth that's told with bad intent
Beats all the Lies you can invent.
It is right it should be so;

Man was made for Joy and Woe;
And when this we rightly know
Thro' the World we safely go,
Joy and Woe are woven fine,
A Clothing for the Soul divine;
Under every grief and pine
Runs a joy with silken twine.
The Babe is more than swaddling Bands;
Throughout all these Human Lands
Tools were made, and Born were hands,
Every Farmer Understands.
Every Tear from Every Eye
Becomes a Babe in Eternity;
This is caught by Females bright
And return'd to its own delight.
The Bleat, the Bark, Bellow and Roar
Are Waves that Beat on Heaven's Shore.
The Babe that weeps the Rod beneath
Writes Revenge in realms of death.
The Beggar's Rags, fluttering in Air,
Does to Rags the Heavens tear.
The Soldier, arm'd with Sword and Gun,
Palsied strikes the Summer's Sun.
The poor Man's Farthing is worth more
Than all the Gold on Afric's Shore.
One Mite wrung from the Labrer's hands
Shall buy and sell the Miser's Lands:
Or, if protected from on high,
Does that whole Nation sell and buy.
He who mocks the Infant's Faith
Shall be mock'd in Age and Death.
He who shall teach the Child to Doubt
The rotting Grave shall ne'er get out.
He who respects the Infant's faith
Triumphs over Hell and Death.
The Child's Toys and the Old Man's Reasons
Are the Fruits of the Two seasons.
The Questioner, who sits so sly,
Shall never know how to Reply.

He who replies to words of Doubt
Doth put the Light of Knowledge out.
The Strongest Poison ever known
Came from Caesar's Laurel Crown.
Nought can deform the Human Race
Like to the Armour's iron brace.
When Gold and Gems adorn the Plow
To peaceful Arts shall Envy Bow.
A Riddle or the Cricket's Cry
Is to Doubt a fit Reply.
The Emmet's Inch and Eagle's Mile
Make Lame Philosophy to smile.
He who Doubts from what he sees
Will ne'er Believe, do what you Please.
If the Sun and Moon should doubt,
They'd immediately Go out.
To be in a Passion you Good may do,
But no Good if a Passion is in you.
The Whore and Gambler, by the State
Licenc'd, build that Nation's Fate.
The Harlot's cry from Street to Street
Shall weave Old England's winding Sheet.
The Winner's Shout, the Loser's Curse,
Dance before dead England's Hearse.
Every Night and every Morn
Some to Misery are Born.
Every Morn and every Night
Some are Born to sweet delight.
Some are Born to sweet delight,
Some are Born to Endless Night.
We are led to Believe a Lie
When we see not Thro' the Eye
Which was Born in a Night to perish in a Night
When the Soul Slept in Beams of Light.
God Appears and God is Light
To those poor Souls who dwell in Night,
But does a Human Form Display
To those who Dwell in Realms of day.

WILLIAM BLAKE

50

Aunt Julia

Aunt Julia spoke Gaelic
very loud and very fast.
I could not answer her—
I could not understand her.

She wore men's boots
when she wore any.
—I can see her strong foot,
stained with peat,
paddling the treadle of the spinning wheel
while her right hand drew yarn
marvellously out of the air.

Hers was the only house
where I lay at night
in the absolute darkness
of the box bed, listening to
crickets being friendly.

She was buckets
and water flouncing into them.
She was winds pouring wetly
round house-ends.
She was brown eggs, black skirts
and a keeper of threepennybits
in a teapot.

Aunt Julia spoke Gaelic
very loud and very fast.
By the time I had learned
a little, she lay
silenced in the absolute black
of a sandy grave
at Luskentyre.
But I hear her still, welcoming me
with a seagull's voice
across a hundred yards

of peatscapes and lazybeds
and getting angry, getting angry
with so many questions
unanswered.

NORMAN MACCAIG

Autobahnmotorwayautoroute

Around the gleaming map of Europe
A gigantic wedding ring
Slowly revolves through Londonoslowestberlin
Athensromemadridparis and home again,
Slowly revolving.

That's no ring,
It's the Great European Limousine,
The Famous Goldenwhite Circular Car

Slowly revolving

All the cars in Europe have been welded together
Into a mortal unity,
A roundaboutgrandtourroundabout
Trafficjamroundaboutagain,
All the cars melted together,
Citroenjaguarbugattivolkswagenporschedaf.

Each passenger, lugging his
Colourpiano, frozenmagazines, high-fidog,
Clambers over the seat in front of him
Towards what looks like the front of the car.
They are dragging behind them
Worksofart, lampshades made of human money,
Instant children and exploding clocks.

But the car's a circle
No front no back
No driver no steering wheel no windscreen no brakes no

Autobiography

In my childhood trees were green
And there was plenty to be seen.

Come back early or never come.

My father made the walls resound,
He wore his collar the wrong way round.

Come back early or never come.

My mother wore a yellow dress;
Gently, gently, gentleness.

Come back early or never come.

When I was five the black dreams came;
Nothing after was quite the same.

Come back early or never come.

The dark was talking to the dead;
The lamp was dark beside my bed.

Come back early or never come.

When I woke they did not care;
Nobody, nobody was there.

Come back early or never come.

When my silent terror cried,
Nobody, nobody replied.

Come back early or never come.

I got up; the chilly sun
Saw me walk away alone.

Come back early or never come.
LOUIS MACNEICE

Auto Wreck

Its quick soft silver bell beating, beating,
And down the dark one ruby flare
Pulsing out red light like an artery,
The ambulance at top speed floating down
Past beacons and illuminated clocks
Wings in a heavy curve, dips down,
And brakes speed, entering the crowd.
The doors leap open, emptying light;
Stretchers are laid out, the mangled lifted
And stowed into the little hospital.
Then the bell, breaking the hush, tolls once,
And the ambulance with its terrible cargo
Rocking, slightly rocking, moves away,
As the doors, an afterthought, are closed.

We are deranged, walking among the cops
Who sweep glass and are large and composed.
One is still making notes under the light.
One with a bucket douches ponds of blood
Into the street and gutter.
One hangs lanterns on the wrecks that cling,
Empty husks of locusts, to iron poles.

Our throats were tight as tourniquets,
Our feet were bound with splints, but now,
Like convalescents intimate and gauche,
We speak through sickly smiles and warn
With the stubborn saw of common sense,
The grim joke and the banal resolution.
The traffic moves around with care,
But we remain, touching a wound
That opens to our richest horror.
Already old, the question Who shall die?
Becomes unspoken Who is innocent?
For death in war is done by hands;
Suicide has cause and stillbirth, logic;
And cancer, simple as a flower, blooms.
But this invites the occult mind,
Cancels our physics with a sneer,
And spatters all we knew of denouement
Across the expedient and wicked stones.

KARL SHAPIRO

'Aye, but to die, and go we know not where'

Aye, but to die, and go we know not where;
To lie in cold obstruction and to rot;
This sensible warm motion to become
A kneaded clod; and the delighted spirit
To bathe in fiery floods, or to reside
In thrilling region of thick-ribbed ice;
To be imprison'd in the viewless winds,
And blown with restless violence round about
The pendant world; or to be worse than worst
Of those that lawless and incertain thoughts
Imagine howling: 'tis too horrible!
The weariest and most loathed worldly life

That age, ache, penury and imprisonment
Can lay on nature is a paradise
To what we fear of death.
WILLIAM SHAKESPEARE
From *Measure for Measure*, Act 3 Scene 1

Baby Song

From the private ease of Mother's womb
I fall into the lighted room.

Why don't they simply put me back
Where it is warm and wet and black?

But one thing follows on another.
Things were different inside Mother.

Padded and jolly I would ride
The perfect comfort of her inside.

They tuck me in a rustling bed
—I lie there, raging, small, and red.

I may sleep soon, I may forget,
But I won't forget that I regret.

A rain of blood poured round her womb,
But all time roars outside this room.
THOM GUNN

The Badger

The badger grunting on his woodland track
With shaggy hide and sharp nose scrowed with black
Roots in the bushes and the woods and makes
A great hugh burrow in the ferns and brakes
With nose on ground he runs a awkard pace
And anything will beat him in the race
The shepherds dog will run him to his den
Followed and hooted by the dogs and men
The woodman when the hunting comes about
Go round at night to stop the foxes out
And hurrying through the bushes ferns and brakes
Nor sees the many holes the badger makes
And often through the bushes to the chin
Breaks the old holes and tumbles headlong in.

When midnight comes a host of dogs and men
Go out and track the badger to his den
And put a sack within the hole and lye
Till the old grunting badger passes bye
He comes and hears they let the strongest loose
The old fox hears the noise and drops the goose
The poacher shoots and hurrys from the cry
And the old hare half wounded buzzes bye
They get a forked stick to bear him down
And clapt the dogs and bore him to the town
And bait him all the day with many dogs
And laugh and shout and fright the scampering hogs
He runs along and bites at all he meets
They shout and hollo down the noisey streets.

He turns about to face the loud uproar
And drives the rebels to their very doors
The frequent stone is hurled where ere they go
When badgers fight and every ones a foe
The dogs are clapt and urged to join the fray
The badger turns and drives them all away
Though scarcely half as big dimute and small

He fights with dogs for hours and beats them all
The heavy mastiff savage in the fray
Lies down and licks his feet and turns away
The bull dog knows his match and waxes cold
The badger grins and never leaves his hold
He drives the crowd and follows at their heels
And bites them through the drunkard swears and reels.

The frighted women takes the boys away
The blackguard laughs and hurrys on the fray
He tries to reach the woods a awkward race
But sticks and cudgels quickly stop the chace
He turns agen and drives the noisey crowd
And beats the many dogs in noises loud
He drives away and beats them every one
And then they loose them all and set them on
He falls as dead and kicked by boys and men
Then starts and grins and drives the crowd agen
Till kicked and torn and beaten out he lies
And leaves his hold and cackles groans and dies.

Some keep a baited badger tame as hog
And tame him till he follows like the dog
They urge him on like dogs and show fair play
He beats and scarcely wounded goes away
Lapt up as if asleep he scorns to fly
And siezes any dog that ventures nigh
Clapt like a dog he never bites the men
But worrys dogs and hurrys to his den
They let him out and turn a harrow down
And there he fights the host of all the town
He licks the patting hand and trys to play
And never trys to bite or run away
And runs away from noise in hollow trees
Burnt by the boys to get a swarm of bees.

JOHN CLARE

Bagpipe Music

It's no go the merrygoround, it's no go the rickshaw,
All we want is a limousine and a ticket for the peepshow.
Their knickers are made of crêpe-de-chine, their shoes are made
    of python,
Their halls are lined with tiger rugs and their walls with heads
    of bison.

John MacDonald found a corpse, put it under the sofa,
Waited till it came to life and hit it with a poker,
Sold its eyes for souvenirs, sold its blood for whisky,
Kept its bones for dumb-bells to use when he was fifty.

It's no go the Yogi-Man, it's no go Blavatsky,
All we want is a bank balance and a bit of skirt in a taxi.

Annie MacDougall went to milk, caught her foot in the heather,
Woke to hear a dance record playing of Old Vienna.
It's no go your maidenheads, it's no go your culture,
All we want is a Dunlop tyre and the devil mend the puncture.

The Laird o' Phelps spent Hogmanay declaring he was sober,
Counted his feet to prove the fact and found he had one foot
    over.
Mrs Carmichael had her fifth, looked at the job with repulsion,
Said to the midwife 'Take it away; I'm through with
    over-production'.

It's no go the gossip column, it's no go the ceilidh,
All we want is a mother's help and a sugar-stick for the baby.

Willie Murray cut his thumb, couldn't count the damage.
Took the hide of an Ayrshire cow and used it for a bandage.
His brother caught three hundred cran when the seas were
    lavish,
Threw the bleeders back in the sea and went upon the parish.

It's no go the Herring Board, it's no go the Bible,
All we want is a packet of fags when our hands are idle.

It's no go the picture palace, it's no go the stadium,
It's no go the country cot with a pot of pink geraniums,
It's no go the Government grants, it's no go the elections,
Sit on your arse for fifty years and hang your hat on a pension.

It's no go my honey love, it's no go my poppet;
Work your hands from day to day, the winds will blow the
    profit.
The glass is falling hour by hour, the glass will fall for ever,
But if you break the bloody glass you won't hold up the
    weather.

LOUIS MACNEICE

Bags of Meat

'Here's a fine bag of meat,'
Says the master-auctioneer,
As the timid, quivering steer,
Starting a couple of feet
At the prod of a drover's stick,
And trotting lightly and quick,
A ticket stuck on his rump,
Enters with a bewildered jump.

'Where he's lived lately, friends,
I'd live till lifetime ends:
They've a whole life everyday
Down there in the Vale, have they!
He'd be worth the money to kill
And give away Christmas for goodwill.'

'Now here's a heifer—worth more
Than bid, were she bone-poor;
Yet she's round as a barrel of beer';
'She's a plum,' said the second auctioneer.

'Now this young bull—for thirty pound?
    Worth that to manure your ground!'
    'Or to stand,' chimed the second one,
    'And have his picter done!'

The beast was rapped on the horns and snout
    To make him turn about.
'Well,' cried a buyer, 'another crown—
Since I've dragged here from Taunton Town!'

    'That calf, she sucked three cows,
    Which is not matched for bouse
    In the nurseries of high life
By the first-born of a nobleman's wife!'
The stick falls, meaning, 'A true tale's told,'
On the buttock of the creature sold,
    And the buyer leans over and snips
His mark on one of the animal's hips.

    Each beast, when driven in,
Looks round at the ring of bidders there
With a much-amazed reproachful stare,
    As at unnatural kin,
For bringing him to a sinister scene
So strange, unhomelike, hungry, mean;
His fate the while suspended between
    A butcher, to kill out of hand,
    And a farmer, to keep on the land;
One can fancy a tear runs down his face
When the butcher wins, and he's driven from the place.

THOMAS HARDY

The Ballad of Rudolph Reed

Rudolph Reed was oaken.
His wife was oaken too.
And his two good girls and his good little man
Oakened as they grew.

'I am not hungry for berries.
I am not hungry for bread.
But hungry hungry for a house
Where at night a man in bed

'May never hear the plaster
Stir as if in pain.
May never hear the roaches
Falling like fat rain.

'Where never wife and children need
Go blinking through the gloom.
Where every room of many rooms
Will be full of room.

'Oh my home may have its east or west
Or north or south behind it.
All I know is I shall know it,
And fight for it when I find it.'

It was in a street of bitter white
That he made his application.
For Rudolph Reed was oakener
Than others in the nation.

The agent's steep and steady stare
Corroded to a grin.
Why, you black old, tough old hell of a man,
Move your family in!

Nary a grin grinned Rudolph Reed,
Nary a curse cursed he,
But moved in his House. With his dark little wife,
And his dark little children three.

A neighbor would *look*, with a yawning eye
That squeezed into a slit.
But the Rudolph Reeds and the children three
Were too joyous to notice it.

For were they not firm in a home of their own
With windows everywhere
And a beautiful banistered stair
And a front yard for flowers and a back yard for grass?

The first night, a rock, big as two fists.
The second, a rock big as three.
But nary a curse cursed Rudolph Reed.
(Though oaken as man could be.)

The third night, a silvery ring of glass.
Patience ached to endure.
But he looked, and lo! small Mabel's blood
Was staining her gaze so pure.

Then up did rise our Rudolph Reed
And pressed the hand of his wife,
And went to the door with a thirty-four
And a beastly butcher knife.

He ran like a mad thing into the night.
And the words in his mouth were stinking.
By the time he had hurt his first white man
He was no longer thinking.

By the time he had hurt his fourth white man
Rudolph Reed was dead.
His neighbors gathered and kicked his corpse.
'Nigger—' his neighbors said.

Small Mabel whimpered all night long,
For calling herself the cause.
Her oak-eyed mother did no thing
But change the bloody gauze.

GWENDOLYN BROOKS

63

Ballad of the Bread Man

Mary stood in the kitchen
  Baking a loaf of bread.
An angel flew in through the window.
  'We've a job for you,' he said.

'God in his big gold heaven,
  Sitting in his big blue chair,
Wanted a mother for his little son.
  Suddenly saw you there.'

Mary shook and trembled,
  'It isn't true what you say.'
'Don't say that,' said the angel.
  'The baby's on its way.'

Joseph was in the workshop
  Planing a piece of wood.
'The old man's past it,' the neighbours said.
  'That girl's been up to no good.'

'And who was that elegant fellow,'
  They said, 'in the shiny gear?'
The things they said about Gabriel
  Were hardly fit to hear.

Mary never answered,
  Mary never replied.
She kept the information,
  Like the baby, safe inside.

It was election winter.
  They went to vote in town.
When Mary found her time had come
  The hotels let her down.

The baby was born in an annexe
  Next to the local pub.
At midnight, a delegation
  Turned up from the Farmers' Club.

They talked about an explosion
  That made a hole in the sky,
Said they'd been sent to the Lamb and Flag
  To see God come down from on high.

A few days later a bishop
  And a five-star general were seen
With the head of an African country
  In a bullet-proof limousine.

'We've come,' they said, 'with tokens
  For the little boy to choose.'
Told the tale about war and peace
  In the television news.

After them came the soldiers
  With rifle and bomb and gun,
Looking for enemies of the state.
  The family had packed and gone.

When they got back to the village
  The neighbours said, to a man,
'That boy will never be one of us,
  Though he does what he blessed well can.'

He went round to all the people
  A paper crown on his head.
Here is some bread from my father.
  Take, eat, he said.

Nobody seemed very hungry.
  Nobody seemed to care.
Nobody saw the god in himself
  Quietly standing there.

He finished up in the papers,
  He came to a very bad end.
He was charged with bringing the living to life.
  No man was that prisoner's friend.

There's only one kind of punishment
    To fit that kind of a crime.
They rigged a trial and shot him dead.
    They were only just in time.

They lifted the young man by the leg,
    They lifted him by the arm,
They locked him in a cathedral
    In case he came to harm.

They stored him safe as water
    Under seven rocks.
One Sunday morning he burst out
    Like a jack-in-the-box.

Through the town he went walking.
    He showed them the holes in his head.
Now do you want any loaves? he cried.
    'Not today,' they said.

CHARLES CAUSLEY

Be Merry

Whenever you see the hearse go by
And think to yourself that you're gonna die,
Be merry, my friends, be merry.

They put you in a big white shirt
And cover you over with tons of dirt,
Be merry, my friends, be merry.

They put you in a long-shaped box
And cover you over with tons of rocks,
Be merry, my friends, be merry.

The worms crawl out and the worms crawl in,
The ones that crawl in are lean and thin,
The ones that crawl out are fat and stout,
Be merry, my friends, be merry.

Your eyes fall in and your hair falls out
And your brains come tumbling down your snout,
Be merry, my friends, be merry.

ANON

Beeny Cliff

March 1870–March 1913

I

O the opal and the sapphire of that wandering western sea,
And the woman riding high above with bright hair flapping
    free—
The woman whom I loved so, and who loyally loved me.

II

The pale mews plained below us, and the waves seemed far
    away
In a nether sky, engrossed in saying their ceaseless babbling say,
As we laughed light-heartedly aloft on that clear-sunned March
    day.

III

A little cloud then cloaked us, and there flew an irised rain,
And the Atlantic dyed its levels with a dull misfeatured stain,
And then the sun burst out again, and purples prinked the main.

IV

—Still in all its chasmal beauty bulks old Beeny to the sky,
And shall she and I not go there once again now March is nigh,
And the sweet things said in that March say anew there by and
    by?

67

What if still in chasmal beauty looms that wild weird western
    shore,
The woman now is—elsewhere—whom the ambling pony
    bore,
And nor knows nor cares for Beeny, and will laugh there never
    more.

THOMAS HARDY

'Before I knocked and flesh let enter'

Before I knocked and flesh let enter,
With liquid hands tapped on the womb,
I who was shapeless as the water
That shaped the Jordan near my home
Was brother to Mnetha's daughter
And sister to the fathering worm.

I who was deaf to spring and summer,
Who knew not sun nor moon by name,
Felt thud beneath my flesh's armour,
As yet was in a molten form,
The leaden stars, the rainy hammer
Swung by my father from his dome.

I knew the message of the winter,
The darted hail, the childish snow,
And the wind was my sister suitor;
Wind in me leaped, the hellborn dew;
My veins flowed with the Eastern weather;
Ungotten I knew night and day.

As yet ungotten, I did suffer;
The rack of dreams my lily bones
Did twist into a living cipher,

And flesh was snipped to cross the lines
Of gallow crosses on the liver
And brambles in the wringing brains.

My throat knew thirst before the structure
Of skin and vein around the well
Where words and water make a mixture
Unfailing till the blood runs foul;
My heart knew love, my belly hunger;
I smelt the maggot in my stool.

And time cast forth my mortal creature
To drift or drown upon the seas
Acquainted with the salt adventure
Of tides that never touch the shores.
I who was rich was made the richer
By sipping at the vine of days.

I, born of flesh and ghost, was neither
A ghost nor man, but mortal ghost.
And I was struck down by death's feather.
I was a mortal to the last
Long breath that carried to my father
The message of his dying christ.

You who bow down at cross and altar,
Remember me and pity Him
Who took my flesh and bone for armour
And doublecrossed my mother's womb.

DYLAN THOMAS

69

Behaviour of Fish in an Egyptian
Tea Garden

As a white stone draws down the fish
she on the seafloor of the afternoon
draws down men's glances and their cruel wish
for love. Slyly red lip on the spoon

slips in a morsel of ice-cream; her hands
white as a milky stone; white submarine
fronds, sink with spread fingers, lean
along the table, carmined at the ends.

A cotton magnate, an important fish
with great eyepouches and a golden mouth
through the frail reefs of furniture swims out
and idling, suspended, stays to watch.

A crustacean old man clamped to his chair
sits coldly near her and might see
her charms through fissures where the eyes should be
or else his teeth are parted in a stare.

Captain on leave, a lean dark mackerel,
lies in the offing; turns himself and looks
through currents of sound. The flat-eyed flatfish sucks
on a straw, staring from its repose, laxly.

And gallants in shoals swim up and lag,
circling and passing near the white attraction:
sometimes pausing, opening a conversation;
fish pause so to nibble or tug.

Now the ice-cream is finished, is
paid for. The fish swim off on business
and she sits alone at the table, a white stone
useless except to a collector, a rich man.

KEITH DOUGLAS

La Belle Dame Sans Merci

O, what can ail thee, knight at arms,
    Alone and palely loitering;
The sedge has withered from the lake,
    And no birds sing.

O, what can ail thee, knight at arms,
    So haggard and so woe-begone?
The squirrel's granary is full,
    And the harvest's done.

I see a lily on thy brow
    With anguish moist and fever-dew,
And on thy cheeks a fading rose
    Fast withereth too.

I met a lady in the meads,
    Full beautiful—a faery's child,
Her hair was long, her foot was light,
    And her eyes were wild.

I made a garland for her head,
    And bracelets too, and fragrant zone,
She looked at me as she did love,
    And made sweet moan.

I set her on my pacing steed
    And nothing else saw all day long;
For sideways would she lean, and sing
    A faery's song.

She found me roots of relish sweet,
    And honey wild and manna dew;
And sure in language strange she said—
    I love thee true.

She took me to her elfin grot,
    And there she gazed and sighed full sore:
And there I shut her wild, wild eyes
    With kisses four.

71

And there she lullèd me asleep,
  And there I dreamed, ah woe betide,
The latest dream I ever dreamed
  On the cold hill side.

I saw pale kings and princes too,
  Pale warriors, death-pale were they all:
They cry'd—'La belle Dame sans Merci
  Hath thee in thrall!'

I saw their starved lips in the gloam
  With horrid warning gapèd wide,
And I awoke, and found me here
  On the cold hill side.

And this is why I sojourn here
  Alone and palely loitering,
Though the sedge is withered from the lake,
  And no birds sing.

JOHN KEATS

Bells for John Whiteside's Daughter

There was such speed in her little body,
And such lightness in her footfall,
It is no wonder her brown study
Astonishes us all.

Her wars were bruited in our high window.
We looked among orchard trees and beyond
Where she took arms against her shadow,
Or harried unto the pond

The lazy geese, like a snow cloud
Dripping their snow on the green grass,
Tricking and stopping, sleepy and proud,
Who cried in goose, Alas,

For the tireless heart within the little
Lady with rod that made them rise
From their noon apple-dreams and scuttle
Goose-fashion under the skies!

But now go the bells, and we are ready,
In one house we are sternly stopped
To say we are vexed at her brown study,
Lying so primly propped.

JOHN CROWE RANSOM

'Be not afeard: the isle is full of noises'

Be not afeard: the isle is full of noises,
Sounds and sweet airs, that give delight, and hurt not.
Sometimes a thousand twangling instruments
Will hum about mine ears; and sometimes voices,
That, if I then had wak'd after long sleep,
Will make me sleep again: and then, in dreaming,
The clouds methought would open and show riches
Ready to drop upon me; that, when I wak'd
I cried to dream again.

WILLIAM SHAKESPEARE
From The Tempest, Act 3 Scene 2

Bermudas

Where the remote Bermudas ride,
In th' ocean's bosom unespied,
From a small boat that rowed along,
The listening winds received this song:

'What should we do but sing His praise,
That led us through the watery maze
Unto an isle so long unknown,
And yet far kinder than our own?
Where He the huge sea monsters wracks,
That lift the deep upon their backs;
He lands us on a grassy stage,
Safe from the storms, and prelate's rage.
He gave us this eternal spring
Which here enamels everything,
And sends the fowls to us in care,
On daily visits through the air;
He hangs in shades the orange bright,
Like golden lamps in a green night,
And does in the pomegranates close
Jewels more rich than Ormus shows;
He makes the figs our mouths to meet,
And throws the melons at our feet;
But apples plants of such a price,
No tree could ever bear them twice;
With cedars, chosen by His hand,
From Lebanon, He stores the land;
And makes the hollow seas, that roar,
Proclaim the ambergris on shore;
He cast (of which we rather boast)
The Gospel's pearl upon our coast,
And in these rocks for us did frame
A temple, where to sound His name.
O! let our voice His praise exalt,
Till it arrive at heaven's vault,
Which, thence (perhaps) rebounding, may
Echo beyond the Mexique Bay.'

   Thus sung they in the English boat,
An holy and a cheerful note;
And all the way, to guide their chime,
With falling oars they kept the time.

ANDREW MARVELL

Bethsabe's Song

Hot sun, cool fire, tempered with sweet air,
Black shade, fair nurse, shadow my white hair;
Shine, sun; burn, fire; breathe, air, and ease me;
Black shade, fair nurse, shroud me and please me:
Shadow, my sweet nurse, keep me from burning,
Make not my glad cause cause of mourning.
      Let not my beauty's fire
      Inflame unstaid desire,
      Nor pierce any bright eye
      That wandereth lightly.

GEORGE PEELE

Bifocal

Sometimes up out of this land
a legend begins to move.
Is it a coming near
of something under love?

Love is of the earth only,
the surface, a map of roads
leading wherever go miles
or little bushes nod.

Not so the legend under,
fixed, inexorable,
deep as the darkest mine
the thick rocks won't tell.

As fire burns the leaf
and out of the green appears
the vein in the centre line
and the legend veins under there,

75

So, the world happens twice—
once what we see it as;
second it legends itself
deep, the way it is.

WILLIAM STAFFORD

The Bight

On my birthday

At low tide like this how sheer the water is.
White, crumbling ribs of marl protrude and glare
and the boats are dry, the pilings dry as matches.
Absorbing, rather than being absorbed,
the water in the bight doesn't wet anything,
the color of the gas flame turned as low as possible.
One can smell it turning to gas; if one were Baudelaire
one could probably hear it turning to marimba music.
The little ocher dredge at work off the end of the dock
already plays the dry perfectly off-beat claves.
The birds are outsize. Pelicans crash
into this peculiar gas unnecessarily hard,
it seems to me, like pickaxes,
rarely coming up with anything to show for it,
and going off with humorous elbowings.
Black-and-white man-of-war birds soar
on impalpable drafts
and open their tails like scissors on the curves
or tense them like wishbones, till they tremble.
The frowsy sponge boats keep coming in
with the obliging air of retrievers,
bristling with jackstraw gaffs and hooks
and decorated with bobbles of sponges.
There is a fence of chicken wire along the dock
where, glinting like little plowshares,
the blue-gray shark tails are hung up to dry
for the Chinese-restaurant trade.
Some of the little white boats are still piled up
against each other, or lie on their sides, stove in,

76

and not yet salvaged, if they ever will be, from the last bad
    storm,
like torn-open, unanswered letters.
The bight is littered with old correspondences.
Click. Click. Goes the dredge,
and brings up a dripping jawful of marl.
All the untidy activity continues,
awful but cheerful.   ELIZABETH BISHOP

Binsey Poplars

Felled 1879

My aspens dear, whose airy cages quelled,
Quelled or quenched in leaves the leaping sun,
All felled, felled, are all felled;
    Of a fresh and following folded rank
                Not spared, not one
                That dandled a sandalled
        Shadow that swam or sank
On meadow and river and wind-wandering weed-winding
    bank.

O if we but knew what we do
        When we delve or hew—
    Hack and rack the growing green!
        Since country is so tender
    To touch, her being so slender,
    That, like this sleek and seeing ball
    But a prick will make no eye at all,
        Where we, even where we mean
                To mend her we end her,
                When we hew or delve:
After-comers cannot guess the beauty been.
    Ten or twelve, only ten or twelve
        Strokes of havoc unselve
            The sweet especial scene,
        Rural scene, a rural scene,
        Sweet especial rural scene.
                                GERARD MANLEY HOPKINS

77

Birches

When I see birches bend to left and right
Across the lines of straighter darker trees,
I like to think some boy's been swinging them.
But swinging doesn't bend them down to stay
As ice-storms do. Often you must have seen them
Loaded with ice a sunny winter morning
After a rain. They click upon themselves
As the breeze rises, and turn many-colored
As the stir cracks and crazes their enamel.
Soon the sun's warmth makes them shed crystal shells
Shattering and avalanching on the snow-crust—
Such heaps of broken glass to sweep away
You'd think the inner dome of heaven had fallen.
They are dragged to the withered bracken by the load,
And they seem not to break; though once they are bowed
So low for long, they never right themselves:
You may see their trunks arching in the woods
Years afterwards, trailing their leaves on the ground
Like girls on hands and knees that throw their hair
Before them over their heads to dry in the sun.
But I was going to say when Truth broke in
With all her matter-of-fact about the ice-storm
I should prefer to have some boy bend them
As he went out and in to fetch the cows—
Some boy too far from town to learn baseball,
Whose only play was what he found himself,
Summer or winter, and could play alone.
One by one he subdued his father's trees
By riding them down over and over again
Until he took the stiffness out of them,
And not one but hung limp, not one was left
For him to conquer. He learned all there was
To learn about not launching out too soon
And so not carrying the tree away
Clear to the ground. He always kept his poise
To the top branches, climbing carefully
With the same pains you use to fill a cup

Up to the brim, and even above the brim.
Then he flung outward, feet first, with a swish,
Kicking his way down through the air to the ground.
So was I once myself a swinger of birches.
And so I dream of going back to be.
It's when I'm weary of considerations,
And life is too much like a pathless wood
Where your face burns and tickles with the cobwebs
Broken across it, and one eye is weeping
From a twig's having lashed across it open.
I'd like to get away from earth awhile
And then come back to it and begin over.
May no fate willfully misunderstand me
And half grant what I wish and snatch me away
Not to return. Earth's the right place for love:
I don't know where it's likely to go better.
I'd like to go by climbing a birch tree,
And climb black branches up a snow-white trunk
Toward heaven, till the tree could bear no more,
But dipped its top and set me down again.
That would be good both going and coming back.
One could do worse than be a swinger of birches.

ROBERT FROST

Birth of the Foal

As May was opening the rosebuds,
elder and lilac beginning to bloom,
it was time for the mare to foal.
She'd rest herself, or hobble lazily

after the boy who sang as he led her
to pasture, wading through the meadowflowers.
They wandered back at dusk, bone-tired,
the moon perched on a blue shoulder of sky.

Then the mare lay down,
sweating and trembling, on her straw in the stable.
The drowsy, heavy-bellied cows
surrounded her, waiting, watching, snuffing.

Later, when even the hay slept
and the shaft of the Plough pointed south,
the foal was born. Hours the mare
spent licking the foal with its glue-blind eyes.

And the foal slept at her side,
a heap of feathers ripped from a bed.
Straw never spread as soft as this.
Milk or snow never slept like a foal.

Dawn bounced up in a bright red hat,
waved at the world and skipped away.
Up staggered the foal,
its hooves were jelly-knots of foam.

Then day sniffed with its blue nose
through the open stable window, and found them—
the foal nuzzling its mother,
velvet fumbling for her milk.

Then all the trees were talking at once,
chickens scrabbled in the yard,
like golden flowers
envy withered the last stars.

FERENC JUHÁSZ
From the Hungarian (trans. David Wevill)

The Black Cloud

Little flocks of peaceful clouds,
   Lying in your fields so blue,
While my eyes look up they see
   A black Ram coming close to you.

He will scatter you poor flocks,
   He will tear up north and south;
Lightning will come from his eye,
   And fierce thunder from his mouth.

Little flocks of peaceful clouds,
   Soon there'll be a dreadful rout;
That Ram's horns can toss big ships,
   Tear an oak tree's bowels out.

W. H. DAVIES

Black Rock of Kiltearn

They named it Aultgraat—Ugly Burn,
This water through the crevice hurled
Scouring the entrails of the world—
Not ugly in the rising smoke
That clothes it with a rainbowed cloak.
But slip a foot on frost-spiked stone
Above this rock-lipped Phlegethon
And you shall have
The Black Rock of Kiltearn
For tombstone, grave
And trumpet of your resurrection.

ANDREW YOUNG

The Blacksmiths

Swart swarthy smiths besmattered with smoke
Drive me to death with din of their dints.
Such noise on nights heard no one never;
What knavish cry and clattering of knocks!
The snub-nosed changelings cry after 'col, col!'
And blow their bellows till all their brains burst:
'Huf, puf!' saith one; 'Haf, paf!' another.
They spit and sprawl and spell many spells;
They grind their teeth and gnash them, and groan together,
And hold them hot in their hard hammers.
Of bulls hide are their leather aprons.
Their shanks are shielded from the fierce sparks:
Heavy hammers they have; that are hard handled,
Stark strokes they strike on an anvil of steel
Lus, bus! Las, das! they strike in rotation
The Devil destroy such an doleful noise.
The master lengthens a little piece, belabours a smaller,
Twines the two together, strikes a treble note
Tik, tak! Hic, hac! Ticket, taket! Tyk, tak!
Lus, bus! Las das! such lives they lead
All horseshoers: Christ give them sorrow
For none for these waterburners at night may rest.

ANON

Blue Girls

Twirling your blue skirts, travelling the sward
Under the towers of your seminary,
Go listen to your teachers old and contrary
Without believing a word.

Tie the white fillets then about your hair
And think no more of what will come to pass
Than bluebirds that go walking on the grass
And chattering on the air.

Practise your beauty, blue girls, before it fail;
And I will cry with my loud lips and publish
Beauty which all our power shall never establish,
It is so frail.

For I could tell you a story which is true;
I know a woman with a terrible tongue,
Blear eyes fallen from blue,
All her perfections tarnished—yet it is not long
Since she was lovelier than any of you.

JOHN CROWE RANSOM

Boat Stealing

One evening (surely I was led by her)
I went alone into a shepherd's boat,
A skiff that to a willow tree was tied
Within a rocky cave, its usual home.
'Twas by the shores of Patterdale, a vale
Wherein I was a stranger, thither come
A schoolboy traveller, at the holidays.
Forth rambled from the village inn alone,
No sooner had I sight of this small skiff,
Discovered thus by unexpected chance,
Than I unloosed her tether and embarked.
The moon was up, the lake was shining clear
Among the hoary mountains; from the shore
I pushed, and struck the oars and struck again
In cadence, and my little boat moved on,
Even like a man who walks with stately step
Though bent on speed. It was an act of stealth
And troubled pleasure, nor without the voice
Of mountain-echoes did my boat move on;
Leaving behind her still, on either side,
Small circles glittering idly in the moon,

Until they melted all into one track
Of sparkling light. A rocky steep uprose
Above the cavern of the willow tree,
And now, as suited one who proudly rowed
With his best skill, I fixed a steady view
Upon the top of that same craggy ridge,
The bound of the horizon, for behind
Was nothing but the stars and the grey sky.
She was an elfin pinnace; lustily
I dipped my oars into the silent lake,
And, as I rose upon the stroke, my boat
Went heaving through the water like a swan;
When, from behind that craggy steep till then
The bound of the horizon, a huge cliff,
As if with voluntary power instinct,
Upreared its head. I struck and struck again,
And growing still in stature the huge cliff
Rose up between me and the stars, and still,
With measured motion, like a living thing,
Strode after me. With trembling hands I turned,
And through the silent water stole my way
Back to the cavern of the willow tree;
There in her mooring-place I left my bark,—
And through the meadows homeward went, with grave
And serious thoughts; and after I had seen
That spectacle, for many days, my brain
Worked with a dim and undetermined sense
Of unknown modes of being; in my thoughts
There was a darkness, call it solitude
Or blank desertion. No familiar shapes
Of hourly objects, images of trees,
Of sea or sky, no colours of green fields;
But huge and mighty forms, that do not live
Like living men, moved slowly through my mind
By day, and were the trouble of my dreams.

WILLIAM WORDSWORTH
From *The Prelude*, Book I

Bog-Face

Dear little Bog-Face,
Why are you so cold?
And why do you lie with your eyes shut?—
You are not very old.

I am a Child of this World,
And a Child of Grace,
And Mother, I shall be glad when it is over,
I am Bog-Face.

STEVIE SMITH

'Break, break, break'

Break, break, break,
   On thy cold gray stones, O Sea!
And I would that my tongue could utter
   The thoughts that arise in me.

O well for the fisherman's boy,
   That he shouts with his sister at play!
O well for the sailor lad,
   That he sings in his boat on the bay!

And the stately ships go on
   To their haven under the hill;
But O for the touch of a vanish'd hand,
   And the sound of a voice that is still!

Break, break, break
   At the foot of thy crags, O Sea!
But the tender grace of a day that is dead
   Will never come back to me.

ALFRED LORD TENNYSON

Breathing Space July

The man who lies on his back under huge trees
is also up in them. He branches out into thousands of tiny
   branches.
He sways back and forth,
he sits in a catapult chair that hurtles forward in slow motion.

The man who stands down at the dock screws up his eyes
   against the water.
Ocean docks get older faster than men.
They have silver grey posts and boulders in their gut.
The dazzling light drives straight in.

The man who spends the whole day in an open boat
moving over the luminous bays
will fall asleep at last inside the shade of his blue lamp
as the islands crawl like huge moths over the globe.

TOMAS TRANSTROMER
From the Swedish (trans. Robert Bly)

Brian O'Linn

Brian O'Linn was a gentleman born,
He lived at a time when no clothes they were worn.
As fashions were out of course Brian walked in—
'I'll soon head the fashions,' says Brian O'Linn.

Brian O'Linn had no breeches to wear,
He got an old sheepskin to make him a pair,
With the fleshy side out and the woolly side in,
'They'll be pleasant and cool,' says Brian O'Linn.

Brian O'Linn had no shirt to his back,
He went to a neighbour's, and borrowed a sack,
Then he puckered the meal bag in under his chin,
'Sure they'll take them for ruffles,' says Brian O'Linn.

Brian O'Linn was hard up for a coat,
So he borrowed the skin of a neighbouring goat,
With the horns sticking out from his oxsters, and then,
'Sure they'll take them for pistols,' says Brian O'Linn.

Brian O'Linn had no hat to put on,
So he got an old beaver to make him a one,
There was none of the crown left and less of the brim,
'Sure there's fine ventilation,' says Brian O'Linn.

Brian O'Linn had no brogues for his toes,
He hopped in two crab-shells to serve him for those.
Then he split up two oysters that match'd like a twin,
'Sure they'll shine out like buckles,' says Brian O'Linn.

Brian O'Linn had no watch to put on,
So he scooped out a turnip to make him a one.
Then he placed a young cricket in under the skin,
'Sure they'll think it is ticking,' says Brian O'Linn.

Brian O'Linn to his house had no door,
He'd the sky for a roof, and the bog for a floor;
He'd a way to jump out, and a way to swim in,
''Tis a fine habitation,' says Brian O'Linn.

Brian O'Linn went a–courting one night,
He set both the mother and daughter to fight;
To fight for his hand they both stripped to the skin,
'Sure! I'll marry you both,' says Brian O'Linn.

Brian O'Linn, his wife and wife's mother,
They all lay down in the bed together,
The sheets they were old and the blankets were thin,
'Lie close to the wall,' says Brian O'Linn.

Brian O'Linn, his wife and wife's mother,
Were all going home o'er the bridge together,
The bridge it broke down, and they all tumbled in,
'We'll go home by the water,' says Brian O'Linn.

ANON

'Buffalo Bill's'

Buffalo Bill's
defunct
           who used to
           ride a watersmooth-silver
                                    stallion
and break onetwothreefourfive pigeonsjustlikethat
                                                Jesus
he was a handsome man
                        and what i want to know is
how do you like your blueeyed boy
Mister Death

E. E. CUMMINGS

The Buffalo Skinners

Come all you jolly cowboys and listen to my song,
There are not many verses, it will not detain you long;
It's concerning some young fellows who did agree to go
And spend one summer pleasantly on the range of the buffalo.

It happened in Jacksboro in the spring of seventy-three,
A man by the name of Crego came stepping up to me,
Saying, 'How do you do, young fellow, and how would you
    like to go
And spend one summer pleasantly on the range of the buffalo?

'I will pay good wages, give transportation too,
Provided you will go with me and stay the summer through;
But if you should grow homesick, come back to Jacksboro,
I won't pay transportation from the range of the buffalo.'

It's now our outfit was complete—seven able-bodied men,
With navy six and needle gun—our troubles did begin;
Our way it was a pleasant one, the route we had to go,
Until we crossed Pease River on the range of the buffalo.

It's now we've crossed Pease River, our troubles have begun.
The first damned tail I went to rip, Christ! how I cut my thumb!
While skinning the damned old stinkers our lives wasn't a
    show,
For the Indians watched to pick us off while skinning the
    buffalo.

He fed us on such sorry chuck I wished myself most dead,
It was old jerked beef, croton coffee, and sour bread.
Pease River's as salty as hell fire, the water I could never go—
Oh, God! I wished I had never come to the range of the buffalo.

Our meat it was buffalo rump and iron wedge bread,
And all we had to sleep on was a buffalo robe for a bed;
The fleas and graybacks worked on us, O boys, it was not slow,
I'll tell you there's no worse hell on earth than the range of the
    buffalo.

Our hearts were cased with buffalo hocks, our souls were cased
    with steel,
And the hardships of that summer would nearly makes us reel.
While skinning the damned old stinkers our lives they had no
    show,
For the Indians waited to pick us off on the hills of Mexico.

The season being near over, old Crego he did say
The crowd had been extravagant, was in debt to him that day,
We coaxed him and we begged him and still it was no go—
We left old Crego's bones to bleach on the range of the buffalo.

Oh, it's now we've crossed Pease River and homeward we are
    bound,
No more in that hell-fired country shall ever we be found.
Go home to our wives and sweethearts, tell others not to go,
For God's forsaken the buffalo range and the damned old
    buffalo.

ANON

Bullfight

Someone runs about,
someone scents the wind,
someone stomps the ground, but it's hard.

Red flags flutter
and on his old upholstered jade the picador
with infirm lance
scores the first wound.

Red blood spurts between the shoulder-blades.

Chest about to split,
tongue stuck out to the roots.
Hooves stamp of their own accord.

Three pairs of the bandoleros in the back.
And a matador is drawing his sword
over the railing.

And then someone (blood-spattered, all in)
stops and shouts:
Let's go, quit it,
let's go, quit it,
let's go over across the river and into the trees,
let's go across the river and into the trees,
let's leave the red rags behind,
let's go some other place,

thus he shouts,
or wheezes,
or whispers,

and the barriers roar and
no one understands because
everyone feels the same about it,

the black-and-red bull is going to fall
and be dragged away,
and be dragged away,
and be dragged away,

without grasping the way of the world,
without having grasped the way of the world,
before he has grasped the way of the world.

MIROSLAV HOLUB
From the Czech (trans. Ian and Jarmila Milner)

The Burglar of Babylon

On the fair green hills of Rio
  There grows a fearful stain:
The poor who come to Rio
  And can't go home again.

On the hills a million people,
  A million sparrows, nest,
Like a confused migration
  That's had to light and rest,

Building its nests, or houses,
  Out of nothing at all, or air.
You'd think a breath would end them,
  They perch so lightly there.

But they cling and spread like lichen,
  And the people come and come.
There's one hill called the Chicken,
  And one called Catacomb;

There's the hill of Kerosene,
  And the hill of the Skeleton,
The hill of Astonishment,
  And the hill of Babylon.

Micuçú was a burglar and killer,
  An enemy of society.
He had escaped three times
  From the worst penitentiary.

They don't know how many he murdered
  (Though they say he never raped),
And he wounded two policemen
  This last time he escaped.

They said, 'He'll go to his auntie,
  Who raised him like a son.
She has a little drink shop
  On the hill of Babylon.'

He did go straight to his auntie,
  And he drank a final beer.
He told her, 'The soldiers are coming,
  And I've got to disappear.

'Ninety years they gave me.
  Who wants to live that long?
I'll settle for ninety hours,
  On the hill of Babylon.

'Don't tell anyone you saw me.
  I'll run as long as I can.
You were good to me, and I love you,
  But I'm a doomed man.'

Going out, he met a *mulata*
  Carrying water on her head.
'If you say you saw me, daughter,
  You're just as good as dead.'

There are caves up there, and hideouts,
  And an old fort, falling down.
They used to watch for Frenchmen
  From the hill of Babylon.

Below him was the ocean.
  It reached far up the sky,
Flat as a wall, and on it
  Were freighters passing by,

Or climbing the wall, and climbing
  Till each looked like a fly,
And then fell over and vanished;
  And he knew he was going to die.

He could hear the goats *baa-baa*-ing,
  He could hear the babies cry;
Fluttering kites strained upward;
  And he knew he was going to die.

A buzzard flapped so near him
  He could see its naked neck.
He waved his arms and shouted,
  'Not yet, my son, not yet!'

An Army helicopter
  Came nosing around and in.
He could see two men inside it,
  But they never spotted him.

The soldiers were all over,
  On all sides of the hill,
And right against the skyline
  A row of them, small and still.

Children peeked out of windows,
  And men in the drink shop swore,
And spat a little *cachaça*
  At the light cracks in the floor.

But the soldiers were nervous, even
  With tommy guns in hand,
And one of them, in a panic,
  Shot the officer in command.

He hit him in three places;
  The other shots went wild.
The soldier had hysterics
  And sobbed like a little child.

The dying man said, 'Finish
  The job we came here for.'
He committed his soul to God
  And his sons to the Governor.

They ran and got a priest,
  And he died in hope of Heaven
—A man from Pernambuco,
  The youngest of eleven.

They wanted to stop the search,
    But the Army said, 'No, go on,'
So the soldiers swarmed again
    Up the hill of Babylon.

Rich people in apartments
    Watched through binoculars
As long as the daylight lasted.
    And all night, under the stars,

Micuçú hid in the grasses
    Or sat in a little tree,
Listening for sounds, and staring
    At the lighthouse out at sea.

And the lighthouse stared back at him,
    Till finally it was dawn.
He was soaked with dew, and hungry,
    On the hill of Babylon.

The yellow sun was ugly,
    Like a raw egg on a plate—
Slick from the sea. He cursed it,
    For he knew it sealed his fate.

He saw the long white beaches
    And people going to swim,
With towels and beach umbrellas,
    But the soldiers were after him.

Far, far below, the people
    Were little colored spots,
And the heads of those in swimming
    Were floating coconuts.

He heard the peanut vendor
    Go *peep-peep* on his whistle,
And the man that sells umbrellas
    Swinging his watchman's rattle.

Women with market baskets
    Stood on the corners and talked,
Then went on their way to market,
    Gazing up as they walked.

The rich with their binoculars
    Were back again, and many
Were standing on the rooftops,
    Among TV antennae.

It was early, eight or eight-thirty.
    He saw a soldier climb,
Looking right at him. He fired,
    And missed for the last time.

He could hear the soldier panting,
    Though he never got very near.
Micuçú dashed for shelter.
    But he got it, behind the ear.

He heard the babies crying
    Far, far away in his head,
And the mongrels barking and barking.
    Then Micuçú was dead.

He had a Taurus revolver,
    And just the clothes he had on,
With two contos in the pockets,
    On the hill of Babylon.

The police and the populace
    Heaved a sigh of relief,
But behind the counter his auntie
    Wiped her eyes in grief.

'We have always been respected.
    My shop is honest and clean.
I loved him, but from a baby
    Micuçú was always mean.

'We have always been respected.
    His sister has a job.
Both of us gave him money.
    Why did he have to rob?

'I raised him to be honest,
    Even here, in Babylon slum.'
The customers had another,
    Looking serious and glum.

But one of them said to another,
    When he got outside the door,
'He wasn't much of a burglar,
    He got caught six times—or more.'

This morning the little soldiers
    Are on Babylon hill again;
Their gun barrels and helmets
    Shine in a gentle rain.

Micuçú is buried already.
    They're after another two,
But they say they aren't as dangerous
    As the poor Micuçú.

On the fair green hills of Rio
    There grows a fearful stain:
The poor who come to Rio
    And can't go home again.

There's the hill of Kerosene,
    And the hill of the Skeleton,
The hill of Astonishment,
    And the hill of Babylon.

ELIZABETH BISHOP

The Burning Babe

As I in hoary winter's night stood shivering in the snow,
Surprised I was with sudden heat which made my heart to
    glow;
And lifting up a fearful eye to view what fire was near,
A pretty babe all burning bright did in the air appear;
Who, scorchèd with excessive heat, such floods of tears did shed
As though his floods should quench his flames which with his
    tears were fed.
'Alas,' quoth he, 'but newly born in fiery heats I fry,
Yet none approach to warm their hearts or feel my fire but I!
My faultless breast the furnace is, the fuel wounding thorns,
Love is the fire, and sighs the smoke, and mercy blows the
    coals,
The metal in this furnace wrought are men's defilèd souls,
For which, as now on fire I am to work them to their good,
So will I melt into a bath to wash them in my blood.'
With this he vanished out of sight and swiftly shrunk away,
And straight I callèd unto mind that it was Christmas day.

ROBERT SOUTHWELL

The Cable Ship

We fished up the Atlantic Cable one day between the Barbadoes
    and the Tortugas,
held up our lanterns
and put some rubber over the wound in its back,
latitude 15 degrees north, longitude 61 degrees west.
When we laid our ear down to the gnawed place
we could hear something humming inside the cable.

'It's some millionaires in Montreal and St John
talking over the price of Cuban sugar, and ways to
reduce our wages,' one of us said.

98

For a long time we stood there thinking, in a circle of lanterns,
we're all patient cable fishermen,
then we let the coated cable fall back
to its place in the sea.

HARRY EDMUND MARTINSON
From the Swedish (trans. Robert Bly)

'Call for the Robin Redbreast and the Wren'

Call for the Robin Redbreast and the Wren,
Since o'er shadie groves they hover,
And with leaves and flowres doe cover
The friendlesse bodies of unburied men.
Call unto his funerall Dole
The Ante, the field-mouse, and the mole
To reare him hillockes, that shall keepe him warme,
And (when gay tombes are robb'd) sustaine no harme,
But keepe the wolfe far thence, that's foe to men,
For with his nailes he'll dig them up agen.

JOHN WEBSTER

The Cap and Bells

The jester walked in the garden:
The garden had fallen still;
He bade his soul rise upward
And stand on her windowsill.

It rose in a straight blue garment,
When owls began to call:
It had grown wise-tongued by thinking
Of a quiet and light footfall;

99

But the young queen would not listen;
She rose in her pale nightgown;
She drew in the heavy casement
And pushed the latches down.

He bade his heart go to her,
When the owls called out no more;
In a red and quivering garment
It sang to her through the door.

It had grown sweet-tongued by dreaming
Of a flutter of flower-like hair;
But she took up her fan from the table
And waved it off on the air.

'I have cap and bells,' he pondered,
'I will send them to her and die';
And when the morning whitened
He left them where she went by.

She laid them upon her bosom,
Under a cloud of her hair,
And her red lips sang them a love-song
Till stars grew out of the air.

She opened her door and her window,
And the heart and the soul came through,
To her right hand came the red one,
To her left hand came the blue.

They set up a noise like crickets,
A chattering wise and sweet,
And her hair was a folded flower
And the quiet of love in her feet.

W. B. YEATS

Carentan O Carentan

Trees in the old days used to stand
And shape a shady lane
Where lovers wandered hand in hand
Who came from Carentan.

This was the shining green canal
Where we came two by two
Walking at combat-interval.
Such trees we never knew.

The day was early June, the ground
Was soft and bright with dew.
Far away the guns did sound,
But here the sky was blue.

The sky was blue, but there a smoke
Hung still above the sea
Where the ships together spoke
To towns we could not see.

Could you have seen us through a glass
You would have said a walk
Of farmers out to turn the grass,
Each with his own hay-fork.

The watchers in their leopard suits
Waited till it was time,
And aimed between the belt and boot
And let the barrel climb.

I must lie down at once, there is
A hammer at my knee.
And call it death or cowardice,
Don't count again on me.

Everything's alright, Mother,
Everyone gets the same
At one time or another.
It's all in the game.

I never strolled, nor ever shall,
Down such a leafy lane.
I never drank in a canal,
Nor ever shall again.

There is a whistling in the leaves
And it is not the wind,
The twigs are falling from the knives
That cut men to the ground.

Tell me, Master-Sergeant,
The way to turn and shoot.
But the Sergeant's silent
That taught me how to do it.

O Captain, show us quickly
Our place upon the map.
But the Captain's sickly
And taking a long nap.

Lieutenant, what's my duty,
My place in the platoon?
He too's a sleeping beauty,
Charmed by that strange tune.

Carentan O Carentan
Before we met with you
We never yet had lost a man
Or known what death could do.

LOUIS SIMPSON

'Carry her over the water'

Carry her over the water,
    And set her down under the tree,
Where the culvers white all day and all night,
    And the winds from every quarter,
Sing agreeably, agreeably, agreeably of love.

Put a gold ring on her finger,
    And press her close to your heart,
While the fish in the lake their snapshots take,
    And the frog, that sanguine singer,
Sings agreeably, agreeably, agreeably of love.

The streets shall all flock to your marriage,
    The houses turn round to look,
The tables and chairs say suitable prayers,
    And the horses drawing your carriage
Sing agreeably, agreeably, agreeably of love.

W. H. AUDEN

Channel Firing

That night your great guns, unawares,
Shook all our coffins as we lay,
And broke the chancel window-squares,
We thought it was the Judgement-day

And sat upright. While drearisome
Arose the howl of wakened hounds:
The mouse let fall the altar-crumb,
The worms drew back into the mounds,

The glebe cow drooled. Till God called, 'No;
It's gunnery practice out at sea
Just as before you went below;
The world is as it used to be:

103

'All nations striving strong to make
Red war yet redder. Mad as hatters
They do no more for Christés sake
Than you who are helpless in such matters.

'That this is not the judgement-hour
For some of them's a blessed thing,
For if it were they'd have to scour
Hell's floor for so much threatening . . .

'Ha, ha. It will be warmer when
I blow the trumpet (if indeed
I ever do; for you are men,
And rest eternal sorely need).'

So down we lay again. 'I wonder,
Will the world ever saner be,'
Said one, 'than when He sent us under
In our indifferent century!'

And many a skeleton shook his head.
'Instead of preaching forty year,'
My neighbour Parson Thirdly said,
'I wish I had stuck to pipes and beer.'

Again the guns disturbed the hour,
Roaring their readiness to avenge,
As far inland as Stourton Tower,
And Camelot, and starlit Stonehenge.

THOMAS HARDY

A Charm

O wen, wen, O little wennikins,
Here shall you build not, here have no abode,
But you must northwards to the nearby hill,
For there, O wretched one, you have a brother,
And he shall lay a leaf upon your head.
Under wolf's foot and under eagle's wing,
'Neath claw of eagle ever may you fade.
May you decrease like coal upon the hearth,
Shrivel away like dirt upon the wall,
Evaporate like water in a pail,
Become as little as a linseed-grain,
Much smaller than a hand-worm's hip-bone is,
And so diminish that you come to nothing.

ANON

From the Anglo-Saxon (trans. Richard Hamer)

The Child Dying

Unfriendly friendly universe,
I pack your stars into my purse,
And bid you, bid you so farewell.
That I can leave you, quite go out,
Go out, go out beyond all doubt,
My father says, is the miracle.

You are so great, and I so small:
I am nothing, you are all:
Being nothing, I can take this way.
Oh I need neither rise nor fall,
For when I do not move at all
I shall be out of all your day.

It's said some memory will remain
In the other place, grass in the rain,
Light on the land, sun on the sea,
A flitting grace, a phantom face,
But the world is out. There is no place
Where it and its ghost can ever be.

Father, father, I dread this air
Blown from the far side of despair,
The cold cold corner. What house, what hold,
What hand is there? I look and see
Nothing-filled eternity,
And the great round world grows weak and old.

Hold my hand, oh hold it fast—
I am changing!—until at last
My hand in yours no more will change,
Though yours change on. You here, I there,
So hand in hand, twin-leafed despair—
I did not know death was so strange.

EDWIN MUIR

A Child's Pet

When I sailed out of Baltimore,
    With twice a thousand head of sheep,
They would not eat, they would not drink,
    But bleated o'er the deep.

Inside the pens we crawled each day,
    To sort the living from the dead;
And when we reached the Mersey's mouth,
    Had lost five hundred head.

Yet every night and day one sheep,
    That had no fear of man or sea,
Stuck through the bars its pleading face,
    And it was stroked by me.

And to the sheep-men standing near,
  'You see,' I said, 'this one tame sheep?
It seems a child has lost her pet,
  And cried herself to sleep.'

So every time we passed it by,
  Sailing to England's slaughter-house,
Eight ragged sheep-men—tramps and thieves—
  Would stroke that sheep's black nose.

W. H. DAVIES

Child's Song

My cheap toy lamp
gives little light
all night, all night,
when my muscles cramp.

Sometimes I touch your hand
across my cot,
and our fingers knot,
but there's no hand

to take me home—
no Caribbean
island, where even
the shark is at home.

It must be heaven.
There on that island
the white sand shines
like a birchwood fire.

Help, saw me in two,
put me on the shelf!
Sometimes the little muddler
can't stand itself!

ROBERT LOWELL

107

The Chimney Sweeper

A little black thing among the snow,
Crying 'weep! weep!' in notes of woe!
'Where are thy father and mother? say?'
'They are both gone up to the church to pray.

'Because I was happy upon the heath,
'And smil'd among the winter's snow,
'They clothed me in the clothes of death,
'And taught me to sing the notes of woe.

'And because I am happy and dance and sing,
'They think they have done me no injury,
'And are gone to praise God and his Priest and King,
'Who make up a heaven of our misery.'

WILLIAM BLAKE
From *Songs of Experience*

The Clod and the Pebble

'Love seeketh not Itself to please,
'Nor for itself hath any care,
'But for another gives its ease,
'And builds a Heaven in Hell's despair.'

So sung a little Clod of Clay
Trodden with the cattle's feet,
But a Pebble of the brook
Warbled out these metres meet:

'Love seeketh only Self to please,
'To bind another to Its delight,
'Joys in another's loss of ease,
'And builds a Hell in Heaven's despite.'

WILLIAM BLAKE
From *Songs of Experience*

Cocaine Lil and Morphine Sue

Did you ever hear about Cocaine Lil?
She lived in Cocaine town on Cocaine hill,
She had a cocaine dog and a cocaine cat,
They fought all night with a cocaine rat.

She had cocaine hair on her cocaine head.
She had a cocaine dress that was poppy red:
She wore a snowbird hat and sleigh-riding clothes,
On her coat she wore a crimson, cocaine rose.

Big gold chariots on the Milky Way,
Snakes and elephants silver and gray.
Oh the cocaine blues they make me sad,
Oh the cocaine blues make me feel bad.

Lil went to a snow party one cold night,
And the way she sniffed was sure a fright.
There was Hophead Mag with Dopey Slim,
Kankakee Liz and Yen Shee Jim.

There was Morphine Sue and the Poppy Face Kid,
Climbed up snow ladders and down they skid;
There was the Stepladder Kit, a good six feet,
And the Sleigh-riding Sister who were hard to beat.

Along in the morning about half past three
They were all lit up like a Christmas tree;
Lil got home and started for bed,
Took another sniff and it knocked her dead.

They laid her out in her cocaine clothes:
She wore a snowbird hat with a crimson rose;
On her headstone you'll find this refrain:
'She died as she lived, sniffing cocaine.'

ANON

Cock-Crow

Out of the wood of thoughts that grows by night
To be cut down by the sharp axe of light,—
Out of the night, two cocks together crow,
Cleaving the darkness with a silver blow:
And bright before my eyes twin trumpeters stand,
Heralds of splendour, one at either hand,
Each facing each as in a coat of arms:
The milkers lace their boots up at the farms.

EDWARD THOMAS

The Cold Heaven

Suddenly I saw the cold and rook-delighting heaven
That seemed as though ice burned and was but the more ice,
And thereupon imagination and heart were driven
So wild that every casual thought of that and this
Vanished, and left but memories, that should be out of season
With the hot blood of youth, of love crossed long ago;
And I took all the blame out of all sense and reason,
Until I cried and trembled and rocked to and fro,
Riddled with light. Ah! when the ghost begins to quicken,
Confusion of the death-bed over, is it sent
Out naked on the roads, as the books say, and stricken
By the injustice of the skies for punishment?

W. B. YEATS

The Collarbone of a Hare

Would I could cast a sail on the water
Where many a king has gone
And many a king's daughter,
And alight at the comely trees and the lawn,
The playing upon pipes and the dancing,
And learn that the best thing is
To change my loves while dancing
And pay but a kiss for a kiss.

I would find by the edge of that water
The collarbone of a hare
Worn thin by the lapping of water,
And pierce it through with a gimlet, and stare
At the old bitter world where they marry in churches,
And laugh over the untroubled water
At all who marry in churches,
Through the white thin bone of a hare.

W. B. YEATS

The Combe

The Combe was ever dark, ancient and dark.
Its mouth is stopped with bramble, thorn, and briar;
And no one scrambles over the sliding chalk
By beech and yew and perishing juniper
Down the half precipices of its sides, with roots
And rabbit holes for steps. The sun of Winter,
The moon of Summer, and all the singing birds
Except the missel-thrush that loves juniper,
Are quite shut out. But far more ancient and dark
The Combe looks since they killed the badger there,
Dug him out and gave him to the hounds,
That most ancient Briton of English beasts.

EDWARD THOMAS

111

The Compassionate Fool

My enemy had bidden me as guest.
His table all set out with wine and cake,
His ordered chairs, he to beguile me dressed
So neatly, moved my pity for his sake.

I knew it was an ambush, but could not
Leave him to eat his cake up by himself
And put his unused glasses on the shelf.
I made pretence of falling in his plot,

And trembled when in his anxiety
He bared it too absurdly to my view.
And even as he stabbed me through and through
I pitied him for his small strategy.

NORMAN CAMERON

Cotton

The day they strung the cable from America to Europe
they did a lot of singing.
The cable, the huge singing cable was put in use
and Europe said to America:
Give me three million tons of cotton!
And three million tons of cotton wandered over the ocean
and turned to cloth:
cloth with which one fascinated the savages of Senegambia,
and cotton wads, with which one killed them.
Raise your voice in song, sing
on all the Senegambic trading routes!
sing cotton!
cotton!

Yes, cotton, your descent on the earth like snow!
Your white peace for our dead bodies!
Your white anklelength gowns when we wander into heaven
saved in all the world's harbors by Booth's Jesus-like face.
Cotton, cotton, your snowfall:
wrapping the world in the fur of new necessities,
you shut us in, you blinded our eyes with your cloud.
At the mouth of the Trade River,
and on the wide oceans of markets and fairs,
cotton, we have met there
the laws of your flood,
the threat of your flood.

HARRY EDMUND MARTINSON
From the Swedish (trans. Robert Bly)

'Could mortal lip divine'

Could mortal lip divine
The undeveloped Freight
Of a delivered syllable
'Twould crumble with the weight.

EMILY DICKINSON

The Cow

The cow is of the bovine ilk;
One end is moo, the other, milk.

OGDEN NASH

Cowper's Tame Hare

She came to him in dreams—her ears
Diddering like antennae, and her eyes
Wide as dark flowers where the dew
Holds and dissolves a purple hoard of shadow.
The thunder clouds crouched back, and the world opened
Tiny and bright as a celandine after rain.
A gentle light was on her, so that he
Who saw the talons in the vetch
Remembered now how buttercup and daisy
Would bounce like springs when a child's foot stepped off
    them.
Oh, but never dared he touch—
Her fur was still electric to the fingers.

Yet of all the beasts blazoned in gilt and blood
In the black-bound scriptures of his mind,
Pentecostal dove and paschal lamb,
Eagle, lion, serpent, she alone
Lived also in the noon of ducks and sparrows;
And the cleft-mouthed kiss which plugged the night with
    fever
Was sweetened by a lunch of docks and lettuce.

NORMAN NICHOLSON

A Crocodile

Hard by the lilied Nile I saw
A duskish river dragon stretched along.
The brown habergeon of his limbs enamelled
With sanguine alamandines and rainy pearl:
And on his back there lay a young one sleeping,
No bigger than a mouse; with eyes like beads,
And a small fragment of its speckled egg
Remaining on its harmless, pulpy snout;

114

A thing to laugh at, as it gaped to catch
The baulking merry flies. In the iron jaws
Of the great devil-beast, like a pale soul
Fluttering in rocky hell, lightsomely flew
A snowy trochilus, with roseate beak
Tearing the hairy leeches from his throat.

THOMAS LOVELL BEDDOES

Crossing the Alps

Far different dejection once was mine,
A deep and genuine sadness then I felt;
The circumstances here I will relate
Even as they were. Upturning with a band
Of travellers, from the Vallais we had clomb
Along the road that leads to Italy;
A length of hours, making of these our guides
Did we advance, and having reached an inn
Among the mountains, we together ate
Our noon's repast, from which the travellers rose,
Leaving us at the board. Ere long we followed,
Descending by the beaten road that led
Right to a rivulet's edge, and there broke off.
The only track now visible was one
Upon the further side, right opposite,
And up a lofty mountain. This we took
After a little scruple, and short pause,
And climbed with eagerness, though not at length
Without surprise, and some anxiety
In finding that we did not overtake
Our comrades gone before. By fortunate chance,
While every moment now encreased our doubts,
A peasant met us, and from him we learned
That to the place which had perplexed us first
We must descend, and there should find the road,

115

Which in the stony channel of the stream,
Lay a few steps, and then along its banks;
And further, that thenceforward all our course
Was downwards, with the current of that stream.
Hard of belief, we questioned him again,
And all the answers which the man returned
To our inquiries, in their sense and substance,
Translated by the feelings which we had,
Ended in this, that we had crossed the Alps.

  Imagination! lifting up itself
Before the eye and progress of my song
Like an unfathered vapour—here that Power,
In all the might of its endowments, came
Athwart me; I was lost as in a cloud,
Halted without a struggle to break through;
And now recovering, to my soul I say—
'I recognize thy glory': in such strength
Of usurpation, in such visitings
Of awful promise, when the light of sense
Goes out in flashes that have shown to us
The invisible world, doth greatness make abode,
There harbours, whether we be young or old.
Our destiny, our nature, and our home
Is with infinitude, and only there;
With hope it is, hope that can never die,
Effort, and expectation, and desire,
And something evermore about to be.
The mind beneath such banners militant
Thinks not of spoils or trophies, nor of aught
That may attest its prowess, blest in thoughts
That are their own perfection and reward,
Strong in itself, and in the access of joy
Which hides it like the overflowing Nile.

  The dull and heavy slackening that ensued
Upon those tidings by the peasant given
Was soon dislodged. Downwards we hurried fast,
And entered with the road which we had missed

Into a narrow chasm. The brook and road
Were fellow-travellers in this gloomy pass,
And with them did we journey several hours
At a slow step. The immeasurable height
Of woods decaying, never to be decayed,
The stationary blasts of waterfalls,
And everywhere along the hollow rent
Winds thwarting winds, bewildered and forlorn,
The torrents shooting from the clear blue sky,
The rocks that muttered close upon our ears,
Black drizzling crags that spake by the wayside
As if a voice were in them, the sick sight
And giddy prospect of the raving stream,
The unfettered clouds and region of the Heavens,
Tumult and peace, the darkness and the light—
Were all like workings of one mind, the features
Of the same face, blossoms upon one tree;
Characters of the great Apocalypse,
The types and symbols of Eternity,
Of first, and last, and midst, and without end.

WILLIAM WORDSWORTH
From The Prelude, Book VI

Crossing the Water

Black lake, black boat, two black, cut-paper people.
Where do the black trees go that drink here?
Their shadows must cover Canada.

A little light is filtering from the water flowers.
Their leaves do not wish us to hurry:
They are round and flat and full of dark advice.

Cold worlds shake from the oar.
The spirit of blackness is in us, it is in the fishes.
A snag is lifting a valedictory, pale hand;

Stars open among the lilies.
Are you not blinded by such expressionless sirens?
This is the silence of astounded souls.

SYLVIA PLATH

Crystals Like Blood

I remember how, long ago, I found
Crystals like blood in a broken stone.

I picked up a broken chunk of bed-rock
And turned it this way and that,
It was heavier than one would have expected
From its size. One face was caked
With brown limestone. But the rest
Was a hard greenish-grey quartz-like stone
Faintly dappled with darker shadows,
And in this quartz ran veins and beads
Of bright magenta.

And I remember how later on I saw
How mercury is extracted from cinnebar
—The double ring of iron piledrivers
Like the multiple legs of a fantastically symmetrical spider
Rising and falling with monotonous precision,
Marching round in an endless circle
And pounding up and down with a tireless, thunderous force,
While, beyond, another conveyor drew the crumbled ore
From the bottom and raised it to an opening high
In the side of a gigantic grey-white kiln.

So I remember how mercury is got
When I contrast my living memory of you
And your dear body rotting here in the clay
—And feel once again released in me
The bright torrents of felicity, naturalness, and faith
My treadmill memory draws from you yet.

HUGH MACDIARMID

The Cuckoo

O the cuckoo she's a pretty bird,
   She singeth as she flies,
She bringeth good tidings,
   She telleth no lies.

She sucketh white flowers
   For to keep her voice clear,
And the more she singeth cuckoo
   The summer draweth near.

ANON

Cut Grass

Cut grass lies frail:
Brief is the breath
Mown stalks exhale.
Long, long the death

It dies in the white hours
Of young-leafed June
With chestnut flowers,
With hedges snowlike strewn,

White lilac bowed,
Lost lanes of Queen Anne's lace,
And that high-builded cloud
Moving at summer's pace.

PHILIP LARKIN

Dahn the Plug'ole

A muvver was barfin' 'er biby one night,
The youngest of ten and a tiny young mite,
The muvver was pore and the biby was thin,
Only a skelington covered in skin;
The muvver turned rahnd for the soap orf the rack,
She was but a moment, but when she turned back,
The biby was gorn; and in anguish she cried,
'Oh, where is my biby?'—the Angels replied:
'Your biby 'as fell dahn the plug'ole,
Your biby 'as gorn dahn the plug;
The poor little thing was so skinny and thin
'E oughter been barfed in a jug;
Your biby is perfectly 'appy,
'E won't need a barf any more,
Your biby 'as fell dahn the plug'ole,
Not lorst, but gorn before!'

ANON

The Darkling Thrush

I leant upon a coppice gate
    When Frost was spectre-gray,
And Winter's dregs made desolate
    The weakening eye of day.
The tangled bine-stems scored the sky
    Like strings of broken lyres,
And all mankind that haunted nigh
    Had sought their household fires.

The land's sharp features seemed to be
    The Century's corpse outleant,
His crypt the cloudy canopy,
    The wind his death-lament.

120

The ancient pulse of germ and birth
    Was shrunken hard and dry,
And every spirit upon earth
    Seemed fervourless as I.

At once a voice arose among
    The bleak twigs overhead
In a full-hearted evensong
    Of joy illimited;
An aged thrush, frail, gaunt, and small,
    In blast-beruffled plume,
Had chosen thus to fling his soul
    Upon the growing gloom.

So little cause for carolings
    Of such ecstatic sound
Was written on terrestrial things
    Afar or nigh around,
That I could think there trembled through
    His happy goodnight air
Some blessed Hope, whereof he knew
    And I was unaware.

THOMAS HARDY

Days

What are days for?
Days are where we live.
They come, they wake us
Time and time over.
They are to be happy in:
Where can we live but days?

121

Ah, solving that question
Brings the priest and the doctor
In their long coats
Running over the fields.

PHILIP LARKIN

The Dead Crab

A rosy shield upon its back,
That not the hardest storm could crack,
From whose sharp edge projected out
Black pinpoint eyes staring about;
Beneath, the well-knit cote-armure
That gave to its weak belly power;
The clustered legs with plated joints
That ended in stiletto points;
The claws like mouths it held outside:
I cannot think this creature died
By storm or fish or sea-fowl harmed
Walking the sea so heavily armed;
Or does it make for death to be
Oneself a living armoury?

ANDREW YOUNG

Death

One night as I lay on my bed,
And sleep on fleeting foot had fled,
Because, no doubt, my mind was heavy
With concern for my last journey:

I got me up and called for water,
That I might wash, and so feel better;
But before I wet my eyes so dim,
There was Death on the bowl's rim.

I went to church that I might pray,
Thinking sure he'd keep away;
But before I got on to my feet,
There sat Death upon my seat.

To my chamber then I hied,
Thinking sure he'd keep outside;
But though I firmly locked the door,
Death came from underneath the floor.

Then to sea I rowed a boat,
Thinking surely Death can't float;
But before I reached the deep,
Death was captain of the ship.

ANON

From the Welsh (trans. Aneirin Talfan Davies)

Death in Leamington

She died in the upstairs bedroom
   By the light of the ev'ning star
That shone through the plate glass window
   From over Leamington Spa.

Beside her the lonely crochet
   Lay patiently and unstirred,
But the fingers that would have work'd it
   Were dead as the spoken word.

And Nurse came in with the tea-things
  Breast high 'mid the stands and chairs—
But Nurse was alone with her own little soul,
  And the things were alone with theirs.

She bolted the big round window,
  She let the blinds unroll,
She set a match to the mantle,
  She covered the fire with coal.

And 'Tea!' she said in a tiny voice
  'Wake up! It's nearly *five.*'
Oh! Chintzy, chintzy cheeriness,
  Half dead and half alive!

Do you know that the stucco is peeling?
  Do you know that the heart will stop?
From those yellow Italianate arches
  Do you hear the plaster drop?

Nurse looked at the silent bedstead,
  At the gray, decaying face,
As the calm of a Leamington ev'ning
  Drifted into the place.

She moved the table of bottles
  Away from the bed to the wall;
And tiptoeing gently over the stairs
  Turned down the gas in the hall.

SIR JOHN BETJEMAN

The Death of the Ball Turret Gunner

From my mother's sleep I fell into the State,
And I hunched in its belly till my wet fur froze.
Six miles from earth, loosed from its dream of life,
I woke to black flak and the nightmare fighters.
When I died they washed me out of the turret with a hose.

RANDALL JARRELL

Delayed Action

Korf invents some jokes of a new sort
That only many hours later work.
Everybody listens to them, bored.

Yet, like some still fuse glowing in the dark,
You wake up suddenly that night in bed
Beaming like a baby newly fed.

CHRISTIAN MORGENSTERN

from the German (trans. W. D. Snodgrass and Lore Segal)

Desert Places

Snow falling and night falling fast, oh, fast
In a field I looked into going past,
And the ground almost covered smooth in snow,
But a few weeds and stubble showing last.

The woods around it have it—it is theirs.
All animals are smothered in their lairs.
I am too absent-spirited to count;
The loneliness includes me unawares.

125

And lonely as it is that loneliness
Will be more lonely ere it will be less—
A blanker whiteness of benighted snow
With no expression, nothing to express.

They cannot scare me with their empty spaces
Between stars—on stars where no human race is.
I have it in me so much nearer home
To scare myself with my own desert places.

ROBERT FROST

The Destruction of Sennacherib

The Assyrian came down like the wolf on the fold,
And his cohorts were gleaming in purple and gold;
And the sheen of their spears was like stars on the sea,
When the blue wave rolls nightly on deep Galilee.

Like the leaves of the forest when Summer is green,
That host with their banners at sunset were seen:
Like the leaves of the forest when Autumn hath blown,
That host on the morrow lay withered and strown.

For the Angel of Death spread his wings on the blast,
And breathed in the face of the foe as he passed;
And the eyes of the sleepers waxed deadly and chill,
And their hearts but once heaved, and for ever grew still.

And there lay the steed with his nostril all wide,
But through it there rolled not the breath of his pride:
And the foam of his gasping lay white on the turf,
And cold as the spray of the rock-beating surf.

And there lay the rider distorted and pale,
With the dew on his brow and the rust on his mail;
And the tents were all silent, the banners alone,
The lances unlifted, the trumpet unblown.

And the widows of Ashur are loud in their wail,
And the idols are broke in the temple of Baal;
And the might of the Gentile, unsmote by the sword,
Hath melted like snow in the glance of the Lord!

LORD BYRON

A Devil

He is an utter failure as a devil. Even his tail. Not long and fleshy
with a black brush of hair at the end, but short, fluffy and sticking
out comically like a rabbit's. His skin is pink, only under his left
shoulder-blade a mark the size of a gold ducat. But his horns are
the worst. They don't grow outward like other devils' but
inward, into the brain. That's why he suffers so often from
headaches.

He is sad. He sleeps for days on end. Neither good nor evil
attract him. When he walks down the street, you see distinctly
the motion of his rosy wings of lungs.

ZBIGNIEW HERBERT
From the Polish (trans. Czeslaw Milosz)

The Devil in Texas

He scattered tarantulas over the roads,
Put thorns on the cactus and horns on the toads,
He sprinkled the sands with millions of ants
So the man who sits down must wear soles on his pants.
He lengthened the horns of the Texas steer,
And added an inch to the jack rabbit's ear;
He put mouths full of teeth in all of the lakes,
And under the rocks he put rattlesnakes.

127

He hung thorns and brambles on all of the trees,
He mixed up the dust with jiggers and fleas;
The rattlesnake bites you, the scorpion stings,
The mosquito delights you by buzzing his wings.
The heat in the summer's a hundred and ten,
Too hot for the Devil and too hot for men;
And all who remain in that climate soon bear
Cuts, bites, and stings, from their feet to their hair.

He quickened the buck of the bronco steed,
And poisoned the feet of the centipede;
The wild boar roams in the black chaparral;
It's a hell of a place that we've got for a hell.
He planted red pepper beside every brook;
The Mexicans use them in all that they cook.
Just dine with a Mexican, then you will shout,
'I've hell on the inside as well as the out!'

ANON

Dinogad's Petticoat

Dinogad's speckled petticoat
was made of skins of speckled stoat:
whip whip whipalong
eight times we'll sing the song.
When your father hunted the land
spear on shoulder club in hand
thus his speedy dogs he'd teach
Giff Gaff catch her catch her fetch!
In his coracle he'd slay
fish as a lion does its prey.
When your father went to the moor
he'd bring back heads of stag fawn boar
the speckled grouse's head from the mountain
fishes' heads from the falls of Oak Fountain.

128

Whatever your father struck with his spear
wild pig wild cat fox from his lair
unless it had wings it would never get clear.

ANON
From the Welsh (trans. Gwyn Williams)

Dirge

1–2–3 was the number he played but today the number came
    3–2–1;
Bought his Carbide at 30 and it went to 29; had the favourite at
    Bowie but the track was slow—

O executive type, would you like to drive a floating-power,
    knee-action silk-upholstered six? Wed a Hollywood star?
    Shoot the course in 58? Draw to the ace, king, jack?
O fellow with a will who won't take no, watch out for three
    cigarettes on the same single match; O democratic voter born
    in August under Mars, beware of liquidated rails—

Denouement to denouement, he took a personal pride in the
    certain, certain way he lived his own, private life,
But nevertheless, they shut off his gas; nevertheless, the bank
    foreclosed; nevertheless, the landlord called; nevertheless, the
    radio broke,

And twelve o'clock arrived just once too often,
Just the same he wore one gray tweed suit, bought one straw
    hat, drank one straight Scotch, walked one short step, took
    one long look, drew one deep breath,
Just one too many,

And wow he died as wow he lived,
Going whop to the office and blooie home to sleep and biff got
    married and bam had children and oof got fired,
Zowie did he live and zowie did he die,

With who the hell are you at the corner of his casket, and where
the hell're we going on the right-hand silver knob, and who
the hell cares walking second from the end with an American
Beauty wreath from why the hell not,

Very much missed by the circulation staff of the *New York
Evening Post*; deeply, deeply mourned by the B. M. T.

Wham, Mr Roosevelt; pow, Sears Roebuck; awk, big dipper;
bop, summer rain;
Bong, Mr, bong, Mr, bong, Mr, bong.

KENNETH FEARING

Disillusionment of Ten O'Clock

The houses are haunted
By white night-gowns.
None are green,
Or purple with green rings,
Or green with yellow rings,
Or yellow with blue rings.
None of them are strange,
With socks of lace
And beaded ceintures.
People are not going
To dream of baboons and periwinkles.
Only, here and there, an old sailor,
Drunk and asleep in his boots,
Catches tigers
In red weather.

WALLACE STEVENS

A Divine Image

Cruelty has a Human Heart,
And Jealousy a Human Face;
Terror the Human Form Divine,
And Secrecy the Human Dress.

The Human Dress is forged Iron,
The Human Form a fiery Forge,
The Human Face a Furnace seal'd,
The Human Heart its hungry Gorge.

WILLIAM BLAKE
From *Songs of Experience*

'Do not go gentle into that good night'

Do not go gentle into that good night,
Old age should burn and rave at close of day;
Rage, rage against the dying of the light.

Though wise men at their end know dark is right,
Because their words had forked no lightning they
Do not go gentle into that good night.

Good men, the last wave by, crying how bright
Their frail deeds might have danced in a green bay,
Rage, rage against the dying of the light.

Wild men who caught and sang the sun in flight,
And learn, too late, they grieved it on its way,
Do not go gentle into that good night.

Grave men, near death, who see with blinding sight
Blind eyes could blaze like meteors and be gay,
Rage, rage against the dying of the light.

And you, my father, there on the sad height,
Curse, bless, me now with your fierce tears, I pray.
Do not go gentle into that good night.
Rage, rage against the dying of the light.

DYLAN THOMAS

Donal Og

It is late last night the dog was speaking of you;
the snipe was speaking of you in her deep marsh.
It is you are the lonely bird through the woods;
and that you may be without a mate until you find me.

You promised me, and you said a lie to me,
that you would be before me where the sheep are flocked;
I gave a whistle and three hundred cries to you,
and I found nothing there but a bleating lamb.

You promised me a thing that was hard for you,
a ship of gold under a silver mast;
twelve towns with a market in all of them,
and a fine white court by the side of the sea.

You promised me a thing that is not possible,
that you would give me gloves of the skin of a fish;
that you would give me shoes of the skin of a bird;
and a suit of the dearest silk in Ireland.

When I go by myself to the Well of Loneliness,
I sit down and I go through my trouble;
when I see the world and do not see my boy,
he that has an amber shade in his hair.

It was on that Sunday I gave my love to you;
the Sunday that is last before Easter Sunday.
And myself on my knees reading the Passion;
and my two eyes giving love to you for ever.

My mother said to me not to be talking with you today,
or tomorrow, or on the Sunday;
it was a bad time she took for telling me that;
it was shutting the door after the house was robbed.

My heart is as black as the blackness of the sloe,
or as the black coal that is on the smith's forge;
or as the sole of a shoe left in white halls;
it was you put that darkness over my life.

You have taken the east from me; you have taken the west from
    me;
you have taken what is before me and what is behind me;
you have taken the moon, you have taken the sun from me;
and my fear is great that you have taken God from me!

ANON

From the Irish (trans. Lady Augusta Gregory)

The Donkey

When fishes flew and forests walked
    And figs grew upon thorn,
Some moment when the moon was blood
    Then surely I was born.

With monstrous head and sickening cry
    And ears like errant wings,
The devil's walking parody
    On all four-footed things.

The tattered outlaw of the earth,
    Of ancient crooked will;
Starve, scourge, deride me: I am dumb,
    I keep my secret still.

Fools! For I also had my hour;
One far fierce hour and sweet:
There was a shout about my ears,
And palms before my feet.

Don't Let that Horse

Don't let that horse
                    eat that violin

    cried Chagall's mother

                        But he
            kept right on
                        painting

And became famous

And kept on painting
                    The Horse With Violin In Mouth
And when he finally finished it
he jumped up upon the horse
                        and rode away
            waving the violin

And then with a low bow gave it
to the first naked nude he ran across

And there were no strings
                    attached
                        LAWRENCE FERLINGHETTI

The Dream About Our Master, William Shakespeare

This midnight dream whispered to me:
Be swift as a runner, take the lane
Into the green mystery
Beyond the farm and haystack at Stone.
You leave tomorrow, not to return.

Hands that were fastened in a vise,
A useless body, rooted feet,
While time like a bell thundered the loss,
Witnessed the closing of the gate.
Thus sleep and waking both betrayed.

I had one glimpse: In a close of shadow
There rose the form of a manor-house,
And in a corner a curtained window.
All was lost in a well of trees,
Yet I knew for certain this was the place.

If the hound of air, the ropes of shade,
And the gate between that is no gate,
Had not so held me and delayed
These cowardly limbs of bone and blood,
I would have met him as he lived!

HYAM PLUTZIK

A Drover

To Meath of the pastures,
From wet hills by the sea,
Through Leitrim and Longford,
Go my cattle and me.

I hear in the darkness
Their slipping and breathing—
I name them the by-ways
They're to pass without heeding;

Then the wet, winding roads,
Brown bogs with black water,
And my thoughts on white ships
And the King o' Spain's daughter.

O farmer, strong farmer!
You can spend at the fair,
But your face you must turn
To your crops and your care;

And soldiers, red soldiers!
You've seen many lands,
But you walk two by two,
And by captain's commands!

O the smell of the beasts,
The wet wind in the morn,
And the proud and hard earth
Never broken for corn!

And the crowds at the fair,
The herds loosened and blind,
Loud words and dark faces,
And the wild blood behind!

(O strong men with your best
I would strive breast to breast,
I could quiet your herds
With my words, with my words!)

I will bring you, my kine,
Where there's grass to the knee,
But you'll think of scant croppings
Harsh with salt of the sea.

PADRAIC COLUM

The Duck

Behold the duck.
It does not cluck.
A cluck it lacks.
It quacks.
It is specially fond
Of a puddle or pond.
When it dines or sups,
It bottoms ups.

OGDEN NASH

Dusk in the Country

The riddle silently sees its image. It spins evening
among the motionless reeds.
There is a frailty no one notices
there, in the web of grass.

Silent cattle stare with green eyes.
They mosey in evening calm down to the water.
And the lake holds its immense spoon
up to all the mouths.

HARRY EDMUND MARTINSON
From the Swedish (trans. Robert Bly)

The Dying Airman

A handsome young airman lay dying,
And as on the tarmac he lay,
To the mechanics who round him came sighing,
These last dying words he did say:

137

'Take the cylinders out of my kidneys,
Take the connecting-rod out of my brains,
Take the cam-shaft from out of my backbone,
And assemble the engine again.'

ANON

Eagle in New Mexico
(An extract)

Towards the sun, towards the south-west
A scorched breast.
A scorched breast, breasting the sun like an answer,
Like a retort.

An eagle at the top of a low cedar-bush
On the sage-ash desert
Reflecting the scorch of the sun from his breast;
Eagle, with the sickle dripping darkly above.

Erect, scorched-pallid out of the hair of the cedar,
Erect, with the god-thrust entering him from below,
Eagle gloved in feathers
In scorched white feathers
In burnt dark feathers
In feathers still fire-rusted;
Sickle-overswept, sickle dripping over and above.

Sun-breaster,
Staring two ways at once, to right and left;
Masked-one
Dark-visaged
Sickle-masked
With iron between your two eyes;
You feather-gloved
To the feet;
Foot-fierce;
Erect one;
The god-thrust entering you steadily from below.

You never look at the sun with your two eyes.
Only the inner eye of your scorched broad breast
Looks straight at the sun.

You are dark
Except scorch-pale-breasted;
And dark cleaves down and weapon-hard downward curving
At your scorched breast,
Like a sword of Damocles,
Beaked eagle.

You've dipped it in blood so many times
That dark face-weapon, to temper it well,
Blood-thirsty bird....

D. H. LAWRENCE

The Earthworm

Who really respects the earthworm,
the farmworker far under the grass in the soil.
He keeps the earth always changing.
He works entirely full of soil,
speechless with soil, and blind.

He is the underneath farmer, the underground one,
where the fields are getting on their harvest clothes.
Who really respects him,
this deep and calm earth-worker,
this deathless, gray, tiny farmer in the planet's soil.

HARRY EDMUND MARTINSON
From the Swedish (trans. Robert Bly)

Earthy Anecdote

Every time the bucks went clattering
Over Oklahoma
A firecat bristled in the way.

Wherever they went,
They went clattering,
Until they swerved
In a swift, circular line
To the right,
Because of the firecat.

Or until they swerved
In a swift, circular line
To the left,
Because of the firecat.

The bucks clattered.
The firecat went leaping,
To the right, to the left,
And
Bristled in the way.

Later, the firecat closed his bright eyes
And slept.

WALLACE STEVENS

Elegy for Himself

Written in the Tower before his execution, 1586

My prime of youth is but a frost of cares;
    My feast of joy is but a dish of pain;
My crop of corn is but a field of tares;
    And all my good is but vain hope of gain:
The day is past, and yet I saw no sun;
And now I live, and now my life is done.

My tale was heard, and yet it was not told;
    My fruit is fall'n, and yet my leaves are green;
My youth is spent, and yet I am not old;
    I saw the world, and yet I was not seen:
My thread is cut, and yet it is not spun;
And now I live, and now my life is done.

I sought my death, and found it in my womb;
    I looked for life, and saw it was a shade;
I trod the earth, and knew it was my tomb;
    And now I die, and now I was but made;
My glass is full, and now my glass is run;
And now I live, and now my life is done.

CHIDIOCK TICHBORNE

Epigrams

Within this mindless vault
Lie Tristan and Isolt
Tranced in each other's beauties.
They had no other duties.

This Humanist whom no beliefs constrained
Grew so broad-minded he was scatter-brained.

My name is Ebenezer Brown.
I carted all the trash of town
For sixty years. On the last day
I trust my Lord will cart me away.

I married in my youth a wife.
She was my own, my very first.
She gave the best years of her life.
I hope nobody gets the worst.

J. V. CUNNINGHAM

141

An Epitaph

Here lies a most beautiful lady:
Light of step and heart was she;
I think she was the most beautiful lady
That ever was in the West Country.
But beauty vanishes; beauty passes;
However rare—rare it be;
And when I crumble, who will remember
This lady of the West Country?

WALTER DE LA MARE

Epitaph on an Army of Mercenaries

These, in the day when heaven was falling,
    The hour when earth's foundations fled,
Followed their mercenary calling
    And took their wages and are dead.

Their shoulders held the sky suspended;
    They stood, and earth's foundations stay;
What God abandoned, these defended,
    And saved the sum of things for pay.

A. E. HOUSMAN

Epitaph on a Tyrant

Perfection, of a kind, was what he was after,
And the poetry he invented was easy to understand;
He knew human folly like the back of his hand,
And was greatly interested in armies and fleets;
When he laughed, respectable senators burst with laughter,
And when he cried the little children died in the streets.

W. H. AUDEN

Epitaph on the Earl of Leicester

Here lies the noble Warrior that never blunted sword;
Here lies the noble Courtier that never kept his word;
Here lies his Excellency that governed all the state;
Here lies the Lord of Leicester that all the world did hate.

SIR WALTER RALEGH

Eternity

He who binds to himself a joy
Does the winged life destroy;
But he who kisses the joy as it flies
Lives in eternity's sun rise.

WILLIAM BLAKE

Even Such is Time

Even such is time, which takes in trust
Our youth, our joys, and all we have,
And pays us but with age and dust;
Who, in the dark and silent grave,
When we have wandered all our ways,
Shuts up the story of our days,
And from which earth and grave and dust,
The Lord shall raise me up, I trust.

SIR WALTER RALEGH

The Explosion

On the day of the explosion
Shadows pointed towards the pithead:
In the sun the slagheap slept.

Down the lane came men in pitboots
Coughing oath-edged talk and pipe-smoke,
Shouldering off the freshened silence.

One chased after rabbits; lost them;
Came back with a nest of lark's eggs;
Showed them; lodged them in the grasses.

So they passed in beards and moleskins,
Fathers, brothers, nicknames, laughter,
Through the tall gates standing open.

At noon, there came a tremor; cows
Stopped chewing for a second; sun,
Scarfed as in a heat-haze, dimmed.

The dead go on before us, they
Are sitting in God's house in comfort,
We shall see them face to face—

Plain as lettering in the chapels
It was said, and for a second
Wives saw men of the explosion

Larger than in life they managed—
Gold as on a coin, or walking
Somehow from the sun towards them,

One showing the eggs unbroken.

PHILIP LARKIN

Exposure

Our brains ache, in the merciless iced east winds that knive
    us . . .
Wearied we keep awake because the night is silent . . .
Low, drooping flares confuse our memory of the salient . . .
Worried by silence, sentries whisper, curious, nervous,
       But nothing happens.

Watching, we hear the mad gusts tugging on the wire,
Like twitching agonies of men among its brambles.
Northward, incessantly, the flickering gunnery rumbles,
Far off, like a dull rumour of some other war.
       What are we doing here?

The poignant misery of dawn begins to grow . . .
We only know war lasts, rain soaks, and clouds sag stormy.
Dawn massing in the east her melancholy army
Attacks once more in ranks on shivering ranks of gray,
       But nothing happens.

Sudden successive flights of bullets streak the silence.
Less deadly than the air that shudders black with snow,
With sidelong flowing flakes that flock, pause, and renew,
We watch them wandering up and down the wind's
    nonchalance,
       But nothing happens.

Pale flakes with fingering stealth come feeling for our faces—
We cringe in holes, back on forgotten dreams, and stare,
    snow-dazed,
Deep into grassier ditches. So we drowse, sun-dozed,
Littered with blossoms trickling where the blackbird fusses.
       Is it that we are dying?

Slowly our ghosts drag home: glimpsing the sunk fires, glozed
With crusted dark-red jewels; crickets jingle there;
For hours the innocent mice rejoice: the house is theirs;
Shutters and doors, all closed: on us the doors are closed,—
       We turn back to our dying.

Since we believe not otherwise can kind fires burn;
Nor ever suns smile true on child, or field, or fruit.
For God's invincible spring our love is made afraid;
Therefore, not loath, we lie out here; therefore were born,
        For love of God seems dying.

Tonight, His frost will fasten on this mud and us,
Shrivelling many hands, puckering foreheads crisp.
The burying-party, picks and shovels in their shaking grasp,
Pause over half-known faces. All their eyes are ice,
        But nothing happens.

                                    WILFRED OWEN

Fable

            Once upon a time
            there was a lonely wolf
            lonelier than the angels.

            He happened to come to a village.
            He fell in love with the first house he saw.

            Already he loved its walls
            the caresses of its bricklayers.
            But the windows stopped him.

            In the room sat people.
            Apart from God nobody ever
            found them so beautiful
            as this child-like beast.

            So at night he went into the house.
            He stopped in the middle of the room
            and never moved from there any more.

146

He stood all through the night, with wide eyes
and on into the morning when he was beaten to death.

JANOS PILINSZKY
Detail from the KZ-Oratorio, *Dark Heaven*
From the Hungarian (trans. Ted Hughes)

The Face of the Horse

Animals do not sleep. At night
They stand over the world like a stone wall.

The cow's retreating head
Rustles the straw with its smooth horns,
The rocky brow a wedge
Between age-old cheek bones,
And the mute eyes
Turning sluggishly.

There's more intelligence and beauty in the horse's face.
He hears the talk of leaves and stones.
Intent, he knows the animal's cry
And the nightingale's murmur in the copse.

And knowing all, to whom may he recount
His wonderful visions?
The night is hushed. In the dark sky
Constellations rise.
The horse stands like a knight keeping watch,
The wind plays in his light hair,
His eyes burn like two huge worlds,
And his mane lifts like the imperial purple.

And if a man should see
The horse's magical face,
He would tear out his own impotent tongue
And give it to the horse. For
This magical creature is surely worthy of it.

147

Then we should hear words.
Words large as apples. Thick
As honey or buttermilk.
Words which penetrate like flame
And, once within the soul, like fire in some
    hut,
Illuminate its wretched trappings.
Words which do not die
And which we celebrate in song.

But now the stable is empty,
The trees have dispersed,
Pinch-faced morning has swaddled the
    hills,
Unlocked the fields for work.
And the horse, caged within its shafts,
Dragging a covered wagon,
Gazes out of its meek eyes,
Upon the enigmatic, stationary world.

NIKOLAI ALEKSEEVICH ZABOLOTSKY
From the Russian (trans. Daniel Weissbort)

The Fair Maid of Amsterdam

In Amsterdam there dwelt a maid,
    Mark well what I do say;
In Amsterdam there dwelt a maid,
And she was mistress of her trade.
    And I'll go no more a-roving
    With you, fair maid.
    A-roving, a-roving,
    Since roving's been my ru-i-n,
    I'll go no more a-roving
    With you, fair maid.

Her cheeks was red, her eyes was brown,
Mark well what I do say;
Her cheeks was red, her eyes was brown,
Her hair like glow-worms hanging down,
And I'll go no more a-roving
With you, fair maid.
A-roving, a-roving,
Since roving's been my ru-i-n,
I'll go no more a-roving
With you, fair maid.

ANON

Fairy Tale

He built himself a house,
  his foundations,
  his stones,
  his walls,
  his roof overhead,
  his chimney and smoke,
  his view from the window.

He made himself a garden,
  his fence,
  his thyme,
  his earthworm,
  his evening dew.

He cut out his bit of sky above.

And he wrapped the garden in the sky
and the house in the garden
and packed the lot in a handkerchief

149

and went off
lone as an arctic fox
through the cold
unending
rain
into the world.

MIROSLAV HOLUB

From the Czech (trans George Theiner)

The Faking Boy

The faking boy to the trap is gone,
At the nubbing chit you'll find him;
The hempen cord they have girded on,
And his elbows pinned behind him.
'Smash my glim!' cries the reg'lar card,
'Though the girl you love betrays you,
Don't split, but die both game and hard,
And grateful pals shall praise you!'

The bolt it fell—a jerk, a strain!
The sheriffs fled asunder;
The faking boy ne'er spoke again,
For they pulled his legs from under.
And there he dangles on the tree,
That soul of love and bravery.
Oh, that such men should victims be
Of law, and law's vile knavery!

ANON

The Fallow Deer at the Lonely House

One without looks in tonight
    Through the curtain–chink
From the sheet of glistening white;
One without looks in tonight
    As we sit and think
    By the fender–brink.

We do not discern those eyes
    Watching in the snow;
Lit by lamps of rosy dyes
We do not discern those eyes
    Wondering, aglow,
    Fourfooted, tiptoe.

THOMAS HARDY

'Fear no more the heat o' the sun'

Fear no more the heat o' the sun,
    Nor the furious winter's rages;
Thou thy worldly task hast done,
    Home art gone, and ta'en thy wages;
Golden lads and girls all must
As chimney-sweepers, come to dust.

Fear no more the frown o' the great,
    Thou art past the tyrant's stroke:
Care no more to clothe and eat;
    To thee the reed is as the oak;
The sceptre, learning, physic, must
    All follow this, and come to dust.

Fear no more the lightning-flash,
    Nor the all-dreaded thunder-stone;
Fear not slander, censure rash;
    Thou hast finish'd joy and moan:
All lovers young, all lovers must
    Consign to thee, and come to dust.

No exorcizer harm thee!
    Nor no witchcraft charm thee!
Ghost unlaid forbear thee!
    Nothing ill come near thee!
Quiet consummation have;
    And renowned be thy grave!

WILLIAM SHAKESPEARE

From *Cymbeline*, Act 4 Scene 2

Field-Glasses

Though buds still speak in hints
And frozen ground has set the flints
As fast as precious stones
And birds perch on the boughs, silent as cones,

Suddenly waked from sloth
Young trees put on a ten years' growth
And stones double their size,
Drawn nearer through field-glasses' greater eyes.

Why I borrow their sight
Is not to give small birds a fright
Creeping up close by inches;
I make the trees come, bringing tits and finches.

I lift a field itself
As lightly as I might a shelf,
And the rooks do not rage
Caught for a moment in my crystal cage.

And while I stand and look,
Their private lives an open book,
I feel so privileged
My shoulders prick, as though they were half-fledged.

The Fish

I caught a tremendous fish
and held him beside the boat
half out of water, with my hook
fast in a corner of his mouth.
He didn't fight.
He hadn't fought at all.
He hung a grunting weight,
battered and venerable
and homely. Here and there
his brown skin hung in strips
like ancient wallpaper,
and its pattern of darker brown
was like wallpaper:
shapes like full-blown roses
stained and lost through age.
He was speckled with barnacles,
fine rosettes of lime,
and infested
with tiny white sea-lice,
and underneath two or three
rags of green weed hung down.
While his gills were breathing in
the terrible oxygen
—the frightening gills,
fresh and crisp with blood,
that can cut so badly—
I thought of the coarse white flesh

153

packed in like feathers,
the big bones and the little bones,
the dramatic reds and blacks
of his shiny entrails,
and the pink swim-bladder
like a big peony.
I looked into his eyes
which were far larger than mine
but shallower, and yellowed,
the irises backed and packed
with tarnished tinfoil
seen through the lenses
of old scratched isinglass.
They shifted a little, but not
to return my stare.
—It was more like the tipping
of an object toward the light.
I admired his sullen face,
the mechanism of his jaw,
and then I saw
that from his lower lip
—if you could call it a lip—
grim, wet, and weaponlike,
hung five old pieces of fish-line,
or four and a wire leader
with the swivel still attached,
with all their five big hooks
grown firmly in his mouth.
A green line, frayed at the end
where he broke it, two heavier lines,
and a fine black thread
still crimped from the strain and snap
when it broke and he got away.
Like medals with their ribbons
frayed and wavering,
a five-haired beard of wisdom
trailing from his aching jaw.
I stared and stared
and victory filled up

the little rented boat,
from the pool of bilge
where oil had spread a rainbow
around the rusted engine
to the bailer rusted orange,
the sun-cracked thwarts,
the oarlocks on their strings,
the gunnels—until everything
was rainbow, rainbow, rainbow!
And I let the fish go.

ELIZABETH BISHOP

The Flight

At Woodlawn I heard the dead cry:
I was lulled by the slamming of iron,
A slow drip over stones,
Toads brooding wells.
All the leaves stuck out their tongues;
I shook the softening chalk of my bones,
Saying,
Snail, snail, glister me forward,
Bird, soft-sigh me home,
Worm, be with me.
This is my hard time.

Fished in an old wound,
The soft pond of repose;
Nothing nibbled my line,
Not even the minnows came.

Sat in an empty house
Watching shadows crawl,
Scratching.
There was one fly.

155

Voice, come out of the silence.
Say something.
Appear in the form of a spider
Or a moth beating the curtain.

Tell me:
Which is the way I take;
Out of what door do I go,
Where and to whom?

THEODORE ROETHKE
From 'The Lost Son'

The Flood

On Lolham Brigs in wild and lonely mood
I've seen the winter floods their gambols play
Through each old arch that trembled while I stood
Bent o'er its wall to watch the dashing spray
As their old stations would be washed away
Crash came the ice against the jambs and then
A shudder jarred the arches—yet once more
It breasted raving waves and stood agen
To wait the shock as stubborn as before
—White foam brown crested with the russet soil
As washed from new ploughd lands would dart beneath
Then round and round a thousand eddies boil
On tother side—then pause as if for breath
One minute—and engulphed—like life in death

Whose wrecky stains dart on the floods away
More swift than shadows in a stormy day
Straws trail and turn and steady—all in vain
The engulphing arches shoot them quickly through
The feather dances flutters and again
Darts through the deepest dangers still afloat

156

Seeming as faireys whisked it from the view
And danced it o'er the waves as pleasures boat
Light hearted as a thought in May—
Trays—uptorn bushes—fence demolished rails
Loaded with weeds in sluggish motions stray
Like water monsters lost each winds and trails
Till near the arches—then as in affright
It plunges—reels—and shudders out of sight

Waves trough—rebound—and fury boil again
Like plunging monsters rising underneath
Who at the top curl up a shaggy main
A moment catching at a surer breath
Then plunging headlong down and down—and on
Each following boil the shadow of the last
And other monsters rise when those are gone
Crest their fringed waves—plunge onward and are past
—The chill air comes around me ocean blea
From bank to bank the waterstrife is spread
Strange birds like snow spots o'er the huzzing sea
Hang where the wild duck hurried past and fled
On roars the flood—all restless to be free
Like trouble wandering to eternity

JOHN CLARE

A Flower Given to My Daughter

Frail the white rose and frail are
Her hands that gave
Whose soul is sere and paler
Than time's wan wave.

Rosefrail and fair—yet frailest
A wonder wild
In gentle eyes thou veilest,
My blueveined child.

JAMES JOYCE

The Flower-Fed Buffaloes

The flower-fed buffaloes of the spring
In the days of long ago,
Ranged where the locomotives sing
And the prairie flowers lie low:—
The tossing, blooming, perfumed grass
Is swept away by the wheat,
Wheels and wheels and wheels spin by
In the spring that still is sweet.
But the flower-fed buffaloes of the spring
Left us, long ago.
They gore no more, they bellow no more,
They trundle around the hills no more:—
With the Blackfeet, lying low,
With the Pawnees, lying low,
Lying low.

VACHEL LINDSAY

Flowers by the Sea

When over the flowery, sharp pasture's
edge, unseen, the salt ocean

lifts its form—chicory and daisies
tied, released, seem hardly flowers alone

but color and the movement—or the shape
perhaps—of restlessness, whereas

the sea is circled and sways
peacefully upon its plantlike stem

WILLIAM CARLOS WILLIAMS

158

The Fly

She sat on a willow-trunk
watching
part of the battle of Crécy,
the shouts,
the gasps,
the groans,
the tramping and the tumbling.

During the fourteenth charge
of the French cavalry
she mated
with a brown-eyed male fly
from Vadincourt.

She rubbed her legs together
as she sat on a disembowelled horse
meditating
on the immortality of flies.

With relief she alighted
on the blue tongue
of the Duke of Clervaux.

When silence settled
and only the whisper of decay
softly circled the bodies

and only
a few arms and legs
still twitched jerkily under the trees,

she began to lay her eggs
on the single eye
of Johann Uhr,
the Royal Armourer.

And thus it was
that she was eaten by a swift
fleeing
from the fires of Estrées.

MIROSLAV HOLUB
From the Czech (trans. George Theiner)

Flying Crooked

The butterfly, a cabbage-white,
(His honest idiocy of flight)
Will never now, it is too late,
Master the art of flying straight,
Yet has—who knows so well as I?—
A just sense of how not to fly:
He lurches here and here by guess
And God and hope and hopelessness.
Even the aerobatic swift
Has not his flying-crooked gift.

ROBERT GRAVES

For a Lamb

I saw on the slant hill a putrid lamb,
Propped with daisies. The sleep looked deep,
The face nudged in the green pillow
But the guts were out for crows to eat.

Where's the lamb? whose tender plaint
Said all for the mute breezes.
Say he's in the wind somewhere,
Say, there's a lamb in the daisies.

RICHARD EBERHART

'The force that through the green fuse drives the flower'

The force that through the green fuse drives the flower
Drives my green age; that blasts the roots of trees
Is my destroyer.
And I am dumb to tell the crooked rose
My youth is bent by the same wintry fever.

The force that drives the water through the rocks
Drives my red blood; that dries the mouthing streams
Turns mine to wax.
And I am dumb to mouth unto my veins
How at the mountain spring the same mouth sucks.

The hand that whirls the water in the pool
Stirs the quicksand; that ropes the blowing wind
Hauls my shroud sail.
And I am dumb to tell the hanging man
How of my clay is made the hangman's lime.

The lips of time leech to the fountain head;
Love drips and gathers, but the fallen blood
Shall calm her sores.
And I am dumb to tell a weather's wind
How time has ticked a heaven round the stars.

And I am dumb to tell the lover's tomb
How at my sheet goes the same crooked worm.

DYLAN THOMAS

Forgotten Girlhood

Into Laddery Street

The stove was grey, the coal was gone.
In and out of the same room
One went, one came.
One turned into nothing.
One turned into whatever
Turns into children.

But remember the coal was gone.
Old Trouble carried her down
To her cellar where the rags were warm.

And turned her sooner
Than had her mother
Into one of the Laddery children,
And called her Lida
For short and for long,
For long, for long.

In Laddery Street Herself

I am hands
And face
And feet
And things inside of me
That I can't see.

What knows in me?
Is it only something inside
That I can't see?

Children

Children sleep at night.
Children never wake up
When morning comes.
Only the old ones wake up.
Old Trouble is always awake.

Children can't see over their eyes.
Children can't hear beyond their ears.
Children can't know outside of their heads.

The old ones see.
The old ones hear.
The old ones know.
The old ones are old.

Around the Corner

But don't call Mother Damnable names.
The names will come back
At the end of a nine-tailed Damnable Strap.
Mother Damnable, Mother Damnable,
Good Mother Damnable.

Home, thieves, home.
Mother Damnable waits at her counting-table.
Thieves do the thieving,
But she does the counting.
Home, thieves, home.

Home Sparkey, home Dodo, home Henry, home Gring.
With Dodo I kiss,
With Henry and Gring
I go walking and talking,
With Sparkey I sing.

Then along comes Mother Damnable.
Off, thieves, off.
'Such nonsense is disgraceful among thieves.
Off, wench, off.'

All the Way Back

Bill Bubble in a bowler hat
Walking by picked Lida up.
Lida said 'I feel like dead.'
Bubble said
'Not dead but wed.'
No more trouble, no more trouble,
Safe in the arms of Husband Bubble.

A rocking-chair, a velvet hat,
Greengrocer, dinner, a five-room flat,
Come in, come in,
Same old pot and wooden spoon,
But it's only soup staring up at the moon.

Have you heard about Bubble?
He was called away
To fight for his country
And got stuck in the chimney.
Then hey, Lida, away
On a hobby left over from Yesterday.

One, two, three,
Mother and Moon and Old Trouble and me.
How happy we'll be
Together and all raggedy.
I'm not a full yard,
Old Trouble's not a full inch,
The moon's a hole
And mother's a pinch.
The rest is tatters,

But to rag-pickers
Faults are perfection's faults,
And only perfection matters.

Fox Dancing

Tall as a foxglove spire, on tiptoe
The fox in the wilderness dances;
His pelt and burnished claws reflect
The sun's and the moon's glances.

From blackberry nose to pride of tail
He is elegant, he is gay;
With his pawsteps as a pattern of joy
He transfigures the day.

For a hat he wears a rhubarb leaf
To keep his thinking cool,
Through which his fur-lined ears prick up.
This fox, he is no fool

And does not give a good-morning
For the condition of his soul:
With the fox dancing in the desert
Study to be whole.

SUZANNE KNOWLES

Francis Jammes: A Prayer to Go to Paradise with the Donkeys

to Máire and Jack

When I must come to you, O my God, I pray
It be some dusty-roaded holiday,
And even as in my travels here below,
I beg to choose by what road I shall go
To Paradise, where the clear stars shine by day.
I'll take my walking-stick and go my way,
And to my friends the donkeys I shall say,
'I am Francis Jammes, and I'm going to Paradise,
For there is no hell in the land of the loving God.'
And I'll say to them: 'Come, sweet friends of the blue skies,
Poor creatures who with a flap of the ears or a nod
Of the head shake off the buffets, the bees, the flies...'

Let me come with these donkeys, Lord, into your land,
These beasts who bow their heads so gently, and stand
With their small feet joined together in a fashion
Utterly gentle, asking your compassion.
I shall arrive, followed by their thousands of ears,
Followed by those with baskets at their flanks,
By those who lug the carts of mountebanks
Or loads of feather-dusters and kitchen-wares,
By those with humps of battered water-cans,
By bottle-shaped she-asses who halt and stumble,
By those tricked out in little pantaloons
To cover their wet, blue galls where flies assemble
In whirling swarms, making a drunken hum.
Dear God, let it be with these donkeys that I come,
And let it be that angels lead us in peace
To leafy streams where cherries tremble in air,
Sleek as the laughing flesh of girls; and there
In that haven of souls let it be that, leaning above
Your divine waters, I shall resemble these donkeys,
Whose humble and sweet poverty will appear
Clear in the clearness of your eternal love.

RICHARD WILBUR

166

Frankie and Johnny

Frankie and Johnny were lovers.
O my Gawd how they did love!
They swore to be true to each other,
As true as the stars above.
He was her man but he done her wrong.

Frankie went down to the hock-shop,
Went for a bucket of beer,
Said: 'O Mr Bartender
Has my loving Johnny been here?
He is my man but he's doing me wrong.'

'I don't want to make you no trouble,
I don't want to tell you no lie,
But I saw Johnny an hour ago
With a girl named Nelly Bly,
He is your man but he's doing you wrong.'

Frankie went down to the hotel,
She didn't go there for fun,
'Cause underneath her kimona
She toted a 44 Gun.
He was her man but he done her wrong.

Frankie went down to the hotel.
She rang the front-door bell,
Said: 'Stand back all you chippies
Or I'll blow you all to hell.
I want my man for he's doing me wrong.'

Frankie looked in through the key-hole
And there before her eye
She saw her Johnny on the sofa
A-loving up Nelly Bly.
He was her man; he was doing her wrong.

Frankie threw back her kimona,
Took out a big 44,
Root-a-toot-toot, three times she shot
Right through that hardware door.
He was her man but he was doing her wrong.

Johnny grabbed up his Stetson,
Said: 'O my Gawd Frankie don't shoot!'
But Frankie pulled hard on the trigger
And the gun went root-a-toot-toot.
She shot her man who was doing her wrong.

'Roll me over easy,
Roll me over slow,
Roll me over on my right side
Cause my left side hurts me so.
I was her man but I done her wrong.'

'Bring out your rubber-tired buggy,
Bring out your rubber-tired hack;
I'll take my Johnny to the graveyard
But I won't bring him back.
He was my man but he done me wrong.

'Lock me in that dungeon,
Lock me in that cell,
Lock me where the north-east wind
Blows from the corner of Hell.
I shot my man 'cause he done me wrong.'

It was not murder in the first degree,
It was not murder in the third.
A woman simply shot her man
As a hunter drops a bird.
She shot her man 'cause he done her wrong.

Frankie said to the Sheriff,
'What do you think they'll do?'
The Sheriff said to Frankie,
'It's the electric-chair for you.
You shot your man 'cause he done you wrong.'

Frankie sat in the jail-house,
Had no electric fan,
Told her sweet little sister:
'There ain't no good in a man.
I had a man but he done me wrong.'

Once more I saw Frankie,
She was sitting in the Chair
Waiting for to go and meet her God
With the sweat dripping out of her hair.
He was a man but he done her wrong.

This story has no moral,
This story has no end,
This story only goes to show
That there ain't no good in men.
He was her man but he done her wrong.

ANON

The Frog

What a wonderful bird the frog are—
When he sit, he stand almost;
When he hop, he fly almost.
He ain't got no sense hardly;
He ain't got no tail hardly either.
When he sit, he sit on what he ain't got—almost.

ANON

The Fury of Aerial Bombardment

You would think the fury of aerial bombardment
Would rouse God to relent; the infinite spaces
Are still silent. He looks on shock-pried faces.
History, even, does not know what is meant.

You would feel that after so many centuries
God would give man to repent; yet he can kill
As Cain could, but with multitudinous will,
No farther advanced than in his ancient furies.

Was man made stupid to see his own stupidity?
Is God by definition indifferent, beyond us all?
Is the eternal truth man's fighting soul
Wherein the Beast ravens in its own avidity?

Of Van Wettering I speak, and Averill,
Names on a list, whose faces I do not recall
But they are gone to early death, who late in school
Distinguished the belt feed lever from the belt holding pawl.

RICHARD EBERHART

Futility

Move him into the sun—
Gently its touch awoke him once,
At home, whispering of fields unsown.
Always it woke him, even in France,
Until this morning and this snow.
If anything might rouse him now
The kind old sun will know.

Think how it wakes the seeds,—
Woke, once, the clays of a cold star.
Are limbs, so dear-achieved, are sides,

170

Full-nerved—still warm—too hard to stir?
Was it for this the clay grew tall?
—O what made fatuous sunbeams toil
To break earth's sleep at all?

WILFRED OWEN

Games

Before Play

For Zoran Mishitch

One shuts one eye
Peers into oneself into every corner
Looks at oneself to see there are no spikes no thieves
No cuckoos' eggs

One shuts the other eye too
Crouches then jumps
Jumps high high high
To the top of oneself

Thence one drops by one's own weight
For days one drops deep deep deep
To the bottom of one's abyss

He who is not smashed to smithereens
He who remains whole and gets up whole
He plays

The Nail

One be the nail another the pincers
The others are workmen

The pincers grip the nail by the head
Grip him with their teeth with their hands
And tug him tug

To get him out of the floor
Usually they only pull his head off
It's hard to get a nail out of a floor

Then the workmen say
The pincers are no good
They smash their jaws and break their arms
And throw them out of the window

After that someone else be the pincers
Someone else the nail
The others are workmen

Hide-and-Seek

Someone hides from someone
Hides under his tongue
He looks for him under the earth

He hides in his forehead
He looks for him in the sky

He hides in his forgetting
He looks for him in the grass

Looks for him looks
Where doesn't he look for him
And looking for him loses himself

The Rose Thieves

Someone be a rose tree
Some be the wind's daughters
Some the rose thieves

172

The rose thieves creep up on the rose tree
One of them steals a rose
Hides it in his heart

The wind's daughters appear
See the tree stripped of its beauty
And give chase to the rose thieves

Open up their breasts one by one
In some they find a heart
In some so help me none

They go on opening up their breasts
Until they uncover one heart
And in that heart the stolen rose

He

Some bite off the others'
Arm or leg or whatever

Take it between their teeth
Run off as quick as they can
Bury it in the earth

The others run in all directions
Sniff search sniff search
Turn up all the earth

If any are lucky enough to find their arm
Or leg or whatever
It's their turn to bite

The game goes on briskly

As long as there are arms
As long as there are legs
As long as there is anything whatever

173

The Seed

Someone sows someone
Sows him in his head
Stamps the earth down well

Waits for the seed to sprout

The seed hollows out his head
Turns it into a mouse hole
The mice eat the seed

They drop dead

The wind comes to live in the empty head
And gives birth to chequered breezes

Ashes

Some are nights others stars

Each night lights up its star
And dances a black dance round it
Until the star burns out

Then the nights split up
Some become stars
The others remain nights

Again each night lights up its star
And dances a black dance round it
Until the star burns out

The last night becomes both star and night
It lights itself
Dances the black dance round itself

VASCO POPA
From the Serbo–Croat (trans. Anne Pennington)

The Garden of Love

I went to the Garden of Love,
And saw what I never had seen:
A Chapel was built in the midst,
Where I used to play on the green.

And the gates of this Chapel were shut,
And 'Thou shalt not' writ over the door;
So I turn'd to the Garden of Love
That so many sweet flowers bore;

And I saw it was filled with graves,
And tomb-stones where flowers should be;
And Priests in black gowns were walking their rounds,
And binding with briars my joys and desires.

WILLIAM BLAKE
From *Songs of Experience*

The Garden Seat

Its former green is blue and thin,
And its once firm legs sink in and in;
Soon it will break down unaware,
Soon it will break down unaware.

At night when reddest flowers are black
Those who once sat thereon come back;
Quite a row of them sitting there,
Quite a row of them sitting there.

With them the seat does not break down,
Nor winter freeze them, nor floods drown,
For they are as light as upper air,
They are as light as upper air!

THOMAS HARDY

175

Gathering Leaves

Spades take up leaves
No better than spoons,
And bags full of leaves
Are light as balloons.

I make a great noise
Of rustling all day
Like rabbit and deer
Running away.

But the mountains I raise
Elude my embrace,
Flowing over my arms
And into my face.

I may load and unload
Again and again
Till I fill the whole shed,
And what have I then?

Next to nothing for weight,
And since they grew duller
From contact with earth,
Next to nothing for colour.

Next to nothing for use.
But a crop is a crop,
And who's to say where
The harvest shall stop?

ROBERT FROST

The Gazelle Calf

The gazelle calf, O my children,
goes behind its mother across the desert,
goes behind its mother on blithe bare foot
requiring no shoes, O my children!

D. H. LAWRENCE

The Germ

A mighty creature is the germ,
Though smaller than the pachyderm.
His customary dwelling place
Is deep within the human race.
His childish pride he often pleases
By giving people strange diseases.
Do you, my poppet, feel infirm?
You probably contain a germ.

OGDEN NASH

Girl

How are you so smooth-faced
So slender-waisted?
Have you braided the sun's hair
Swept the moon's courtyards clean?

I haven't braided the sun's hair
Or swept the moon's courtyards
I stood outside and watched
Lightning dancing with thunder
Lightning outdanced thunder
By two or three apples
Four oranges

ANON
From the Serbian (trans. Anne Pennington)

Giving Potatoes

STRONG MAN:	Mashed potatoes cannot hurt you, darling Mashed potatoes mean no harm I have brought you mashed potatoes From my mashed potato farm.
LADY:	Take away your mashed potatoes Leave them in the desert to dry Take away your mashed potatoes— You look like shepherd's pie.
BRASH MAN:	A packet of chips, a packet of chips, Wrapped in the *Daily Mail*, Golden juicy and fried for a week In the blubber of the Great White Whale.
LADY:	Take away your fried potatoes Use them to clean your ears You can eat your fried potatoes With birds–eye frozen tears.
OLD MAN:	I have borne this baked potato O'er the Generation Gap, Pray accept this baked potato Let me lay it in your heated lap.
LADY:	Take away your baked potato In your fusty musty van Take away your baked potato You potato–skinned old man.
FRENCHMAN:	She rejected all potatoes For a thousand nights and days Till a Frenchman wooed and won her With pommes de terre Lyonnaise.
LADY:	Oh my corrugated lover So creamy and so brown Let us fly across to Lyons And lay our tubers down.

ADRIAN MITCHELL

178

A Glass of Beer

The lanky hank of a she in the inn over there,
Nearly killed me for asking the loan of a glass of beer;
May the devil grip the whey-faced slut by the hair
And beat bad manners out of her skin for a year.

That parboiled ape, with the toughest jaw you will see
On virtue's path, and a voice that would rasp the dead,
Came roaring and raging the minute she looked at me,
And threw me out of the house on the back of my head!

If I asked her master he'd give me a cask a day;
But she, with the beer at hand, not a gill would arrange!
May she marry a ghost and bear him a kitten, and may
The High King of Glory permit her to get the mange.

JAMES STEPHENS

The Goose and the Gander

O the goose and the gander walk'd over the green,
O the goose she went barefoot for fear of being seen,
For fear of being seen, boys, for fear of being seen,
And the goose she went barefoot for fear of being seen.

I had a black hen and she had a white foot,
And she laid an egg in a willow tree root,
In a willow tree root, in a willow tree root,
And she laid a white egg in a willow tree root.

ANON

Great and Strong

A little blood, more or less, he said,
He was great and strong, so strong
   it must have been from weakness.
A little blood, he said, and went to wash his hands,
Of course there are things you can't wash off.
But that he didn't know, for he was strong,
He was smart with his elbows, then used his fists,
When he spoke he guzzled the words of others,
The seeing air was stunned and the ant-swarm
   of the transistors crawled through his ears,
A little blood, this man said and
   instantly his words were the thoughts of all,
It was he who conquered at Carthage,
Clean as the map of an unnecessary battle,
Clean as the anatomy of a hyena,
Clean as the conscience of a gun,
Clean as the hands that run a slaughter-house,
Clean as the king of the ants,
Pure as the sperm of Genghis Khan,
Clean as the spore of anthrax,
Clean as the bare behind of death,
All bent their heads,
The tampons bowed to him
And only a little blood
   wept
   on the ground.

MIROSLAV HOLUB
From the Czech (trans. George Theiner)

The Habit of Perfection

Elected Silence, sing to me
And beat upon my whorlèd ear,
Pipe me to pastures still and be
The music that I care to hear.

Shape nothing, lips; be lovely-dumb:
It is the shut, the curfew sent
From there where all surrenders come
Which only makes you eloquent.

Be shellèd, eyes, with double dark
And find the uncreated light:
This ruck and reel which you remark
Coils, keeps, and teases simple sight.

Palate, the hutch of tasty lust,
Desire not to be rinsed with wine:
The can must be so sweet, the crust
So fresh that come in fasts divine!

Nostrils, your careless breath that spend
Upon the stir and keep of pride,
What relish shall the censers send
Along the sanctuary side!

O feel-of-primrose hands, O feet
That want the yield of plushy sward,
But you shall walk the golden street
And you unhouse and house the Lord.

And, Poverty, be thou the bride
And now the marriage feast begun.
And lily-coloured clothes provide
Your spouse not laboured-at nor spun.

GERARD MANLEY HOPKINS

181

Ha'nacker Mill

Sally is gone that was so kindly
Sally is gone from Ha'nacker Hill.
And the Briar grows ever since then so blindly
    And ever since then the clapper is still,
    And the sweeps have fallen from Ha'nacker Mill.

Ha'nacker Hill is in Desolation:
    Ruin a–top and a field unploughed.
And Spirits that call on a fallen nation
    Spirits that loved her calling aloud:
    Spirits abroad in a windy cloud.

Spirits that call and no one answers;
    Ha'nacker's down and England's done.
Wind and Thistle for pipe and dancers
    And never a ploughman under the Sun.
    Never a ploughman. Never a one.

HILAIRE BELLOC

'The hand that signed the paper felled a city'

The hand that signed the paper felled a city;
Five sovereign fingers taxed the breath,
Doubled the globe of dead and halved a country;
These five kings did a king to death.

The mighty hand leads to a sloping shoulder,
The finger joints are cramped with chalk;
A goose's quill has put an end to murder
That put an end to talk.

The hand that signed the treaty bred a fever,
And famine grew, and locusts came;
Great is the hand that holds dominion over
Man by a scribbled name.

The five kings count the dead but do not soften
The crusted wound nor stroke the brow;
A hand rules pity as a hand rules heaven;
Hands have no tears to flow.

DYLAN THOMAS

The Happy Heart

Art thou poor, yet hast thou golden slumbers?
 Oh sweet content!
Art thou rich, yet is thy mind perplexed?
 Oh punishment!
Dost thou laugh to see how fools are vexed
To add to golden numbers, golden numbers?
Oh sweet content! Oh sweet content!
 Work apace, apace, apace, apace;
 Honest labour bears a lovely face;
Then hey nonny nonny, hey nonny nonny!

Canst drink the waters of the crispèd spring?
 Oh sweet content!
Swim'st thou in wealth, yet sink'st in thine own tears?
 Oh punishment!
Then he that patiently want's burden bears
No burden bears, but is a king, a king!
Oh sweet content! Oh sweet content!
 Work apace, apace, apace, apace;
 Honest labour bears a lovely face;
Then hey nonny nonny, hey nonny nonny!

THOMAS DEKKER

Hares at Play

The birds are gone to bed the cows are still
And sheep lie panting on each old mole hill
And underneath the willows grey-green bough
Like toil a resting—lies the fallow plough
The timid hares throw daylights fears away
On the lanes road to dust and dance and play
Then dabble in the grain by nought deterred
To lick the dewfall from the barleys beard
Then out they sturt again and round the hill
Like happy thoughts dance squat and loiter still
Till milking maidens in the early morn
Gingle their yokes and start them in the corn
Through well known beaten paths each nimbling hare
Sturts quick as fear—and seeks its hidden lair

JOHN CLARE

'The Hart loves the high wood'

The Hart loves the high wood,
   the Hare loves the hill,
The Knight loves his bright sword,
   the Churl loves his bill.

ANON

The Hawk

On Sunday the hawk fell on Bigging
   And a chicken screamed
   Lost in its own little snowstorm.
And on Monday he fell on the moor
   And the Field Club
   Raised a hundred silent prisms.

184

And on Tuesday he fell on the hill
   And the happy lamb
   Never knew why the loud collie straddled him.
And on Wednesday he fell on a bush
   And the blackbird
   Laid by his little flute for the last time.
And on Thursday he fell on Cleat
   And peerie Tom's rabbit
   Swung in a single arc from shore to hill.
And on Friday he fell on a ditch
   But the rampant rat,
   That eye and that tooth, quenched his flame.
And on Saturday he fell on Bigging
   And Jock lowered his gun
   And nailed a small wing over the corn.

GEORGE MACKAY BROWN

He Hears the Cry of the Sedge

I wander by the edge
Of this desolate lake
Where wind cries in the sedge:
Until the axle break
That keeps the stars in their round,
And hands hurl in the deep
The banners of East and West,
And the girdle of light is unbound,
Your breast will not lie by the breast
Of your beloved in sleep.

W. B. YEATS

'Hear the voice of the Bard!'

Hear the voice of the Bard!
Who Present, Past and Future, sees;
Whose ears have heard
The Holy Word
That walk'd among the ancient trees,

Calling the lapsed Soul,
And weeping in the evening dew;
That might controll
The starry pole,
And fallen, fallen light renew!

'O Earth, O Earth, return!
'Arise from out the dewy grass;
'Night is worn,
'And the morn
'Rises from the slumberous mass.

'Turn away no more;
'Why wilt thou turn away?
'The starry floor,
'The wat'ry shore,
'Is giv'n thee till the break of day.'

WILLIAM BLAKE
From *Songs of Experience*

The Hearse Song

The old Grey Hearse goes rolling by,
You don't know whether to laugh or cry;
For you know some day it'll get you too,
And the hearse's next load may consist of you.

They'll take you out, and they'll lower you down,
While men with shovels stand all around;
They'll throw in dirt, and they'll throw in rocks,
And they won't give a damn if they break the box.

And your eyes drop out and your teeth fall in,
And the worms crawl over your mouth and chin;
They invite their friends and their friends' friends too
And you look like hell when they're through with you.

ANON

Heaven-Haven

A nun takes the veil

I have desired to go
    Where springs not fail,
To fields where flies no sharp and sided hail
    And a few lilies blow.

And I have asked to be
    Where no storms come,
Where the green swell is in the havens dumb,
    And out of the swing of the sea.

GERARD MANLEY HOPKINS

The Hen

In the waiting room of the railway,
Not built for it,
A hen
Walks up and down.
Where, where has the stationmaster gone?
Surely no one

Will harm this hen?
Let us hope not! Then,
Out loud, let us say:
Our sympathy goes out to it
Even here, where it's in the way!

CHRISTIAN MORGENSTERN

From the German (trans. W. D. Snodgrass and Lore Segal)

Here

I am a man now.
Pass your hand over my brow,
You can feel the place where the brains grow.

I am like a tree,
From my top boughs I can see
The footprints that led up to me.

There is blood in my veins
That has run clear of the stain
Contracted in so many loins.

Why, then, are my hands red
With the blood of so many dead?
Is this where I was misled?

Why are my hands this way
That they will not do as I say?
Does no God hear when I pray?

I have nowhere to go.
The swift satellites show
The clock of my whole being is slow.

It is too late to start
For destinations not of the heart.
I must stay here with my hurt.

R. S. THOMAS

Here Lies a Lady

Here lies a lady of beauty and high degree.
Of chills and fever she died, of fever and chills,
The delight of her husband, her aunt, an infant of three,
And of medicos marveling sweetly on her ills.

For either she burned, and her confident eyes would
    blaze,
And her fingers fly in a manner to puzzle their heads—
What was she making? Why, nothing; she sat in a maze
Of old scraps of laces, snipped into curious shreds—

Or this would pass, and the light of her fire decline
Till she lay discouraged and cold, like a thin stalk white and
    blown,
And would not open her eyes, to kisses, to wine;
The sixth of these states was her last; the cold settled
    down.

Sweet ladies, long may ye bloom, and toughly I hope ye may
    thole,
But was she not lucky? In flowers and lace and mourning,
In love and great honor we bade God rest her soul
After six little spaces of chill, and six of burning.

                                        JOHN CROWE RANSOM

Heredity

I am the family face;
Flesh perishes, I live on,
Projecting trait and trace
Through time to times anon,
And leaping from place to place
Over oblivion.

The years-heired feature that can
In curve and voice and eye
Despise the human span
Of durance—that is I;
The eternal thing in man,
That heeds no call to die.

THOMAS HARDY

A History Lesson

Kings
like golden gleams
made with a mirror on the wall.

A non-alcoholic pope,
knights without arms,
arms without knights.

The dead like so many strained noodles,
a pound of those fallen in battle,
two ounces of those who were executed,

several heads
like so many potatoes
shaken into a cap—

Geniuses conceived
by the mating of dates
are soaked up by the ceiling into infinity

to the sound of tinny thunder,
the rumble of bellies,
shouts of hurrah,

empires rise and fall
at a wave of the pointer,
the blood is blotted out—

190

And only one small boy,
who was not paying the least attention,
will ask
between two victorious wars:

And did it hurt in those days too?
MIROSLAV HOLUB
From the Czech (trans. George Theiner)

The Horses

Barely a twelvemonth after
The seven days war that put the world to sleep,
Late in the evening the strange horses came.
By then we had made our covenant with silence,
But in the first few days it was so still
We listened to our breathing and were afraid.
On the second day
The radios failed; we turned the knobs; no answer.
On the third day a warship passed us, heading north,
Dead bodies piled on the deck. On the sixth day
A plane plunged over us into the sea. Thereafter
Nothing. The radios dumb;
And still they stand in corners of our kitchens,
And stand, perhaps, turned on, in a million rooms
All over the world. But now if they should speak,
If on a sudden they should speak again,
If on the stroke of noon a voice should speak,
We would not listen, we would not let it bring
That old bad world that swallowed its children quick
At one great gulp. We would not have it again.
Sometimes we think of the nations lying asleep,
Curled blindly in impenetrable sorrow,
And then the thought confounds us with its strangeness.
The tractors lie about our fields; at evening

They look like dank sea-monsters couched and waiting.
We leave them where they are and let them rust:
'They'll moulder away and be like other loam'.
We make our oxen drag our rusty ploughs,
Long laid aside. We have gone back
Far past our fathers' land.
                            And then, that evening
Late in the summer the strange horses came.
We heard a distant tapping on the road,
A deepening drumming; it stopped, went on again
And at the corner changed to hollow thunder.
We saw the heads
Like a wild wave charging and were afraid.
We had sold our horses in our fathers' time
To buy new tractors. Now they were strange to us
As fabulous steeds set on an ancient shield
Or illustrations in a book of knights.
We did not dare go near them. Yet they waited,
Stubborn and shy, as if they had been sent
By an old command to find our whereabouts
And that long-lost archaic companionship.
In the first moment we had never a thought
That they were creatures to be owned and used.
Among them were some half a dozen colts
Dropped in some wilderness of the broken world,
Yet new as if they had come from their own Eden.
Since then they have pulled our ploughs and borne our loads
But that free servitude still can pierce our hearts.
Our life is changed; their coming our beginning.

EDWIN MUIR

Hospital Barge at Cérisy

Budging the sluggard ripples of the Somme,
A barge round old Cérisy slowly slewed.
Softly her engines down the current screwed
And chuckled in her, with contented hum.

Till fairy tinklings struck their croonings dumb.
The waters rumpling at the stern subdued.
The lock-gate took her bulging amplitude.
Gently from out the gurgling lock she swum.

One reading by that sunset raised his eyes
To watch her lessening westward quietly,
Till, as she neared the bend, her funnel screamed.

And that long lamentation made him wise
How unto Avalon, in agony,
Kings passed in the dark barge, which Merlin dreamed.

WILFRED OWEN

The House of Hospitalities

Here we broached the Christmas barrel,
    Pushed up the charred log-ends;
Here we sang the Christmas carol,
    And called in friends.

Time has tired me since we met here
    When the folk now dead were young,
Since the viands were outset here
    And quaint songs sung.

And the worm has bored the viol
    That used to lead the tune,
Rust eaten out the dial
    That struck night's noon.

193

Now no Christmas brings in neighbours,
　　And the New Year comes unlit;
Where we sang the mole now labours,
　　And spiders knit.

Yet at midnight if here walking,
　　When the moon sheets wall and tree,
I see forms of old time talking,
　　Who smile on me.

THOMAS HARDY

'How doth the little crocodile'

How doth the little crocodile
　　Improve his shining tail,
And pour the waters of the Nile
　　On every golden scale!

How cheerfully he seems to grin,
　　How neatly spreads his claws,
And welcomes little fishes in
　　With gently smiling jaws!

LEWIS CARROLL

'How happy is the little Stone'

How happy is the little Stone
That rambles in the Road alone,
And doesn't care about Careers
And Exigencies never fears—
Whose Coat of elemental Brown
A passing Universe put on,

194

And independent as the Sun
Associates or glows alone,
Fulfilling absolute Decree
In casual simplicity—

EMILY DICKINSON

'How the old Mountains drip with Sunset'

How the old Mountains drip with Sunset
How the Hemlocks burn—
How the Dun Brake is draped in Cinder
By the Wizard Sun—

How the old Steeples hand the Scarlet
Till the Ball is full—
Have I the lip of the Flamingo
That I dare to tell?

Then, how the Fire ebbs like Billows—
Touching all the Grass
With a departing—Sapphire—feature—
As a Duchess passed—

How a small Dusk crawls on the Village
Till the Houses blot
And the odd Flambeau, no men carry
Glimmer on the Street—

How it is Night—in Nest and Kennel—
And where was the Wood—
Just a Dome of Abyss is Bowing
Into Solitude—

These are the Visions flitted Guido—
Titian—never told—
Domenichino dropped his pencil—
Paralyzed, with Gold—

EMILY DICKINSON

How to Kill

Under the parabola of a ball,
a child turning into a man,
I looked into the air too long.
The ball fell in my hand, it sang
in the closed fist: *Open Open*
Behold a gift designed to kill.

Now in my dial of glass appears
the soldier who is going to die.
He smiles, and moves about in ways
his mother knows, habits of his.
The wires touch his face: I cry
NOW. Death, like a familiar, hears

and look, has made a man of dust
of a man of flesh. This sorcery
I do. Being damned, I am amused
to see the centre of love diffused
and the waves of love travel into vacancy.
How easy it is to make a ghost.

The weightless mosquito touches
her tiny shadow on the stone,
and with how like, how infinite
a lightness, man and shadow meet.
They fuse. A shadow is a man
when the mosquito death approaches.

KEITH DOUGLAS

Humming-Bird

I can imagine, in some otherworld
Primeval-dumb, far back
In that most awful stillness, that only gasped and hummed,
Humming-birds raced down the avenues.

Before anything had a soul,
While life was a heave of Matter, half inanimate,
This little bit chipped off in brilliance
And went whizzing through the slow, vast, succulent stems.

I believe there were no flowers, then,
In the world where the humming-bird flashed ahead of
    creation.
I believe he pierced the slow vegetable veins with his long beak.

Probably he was big
As mosses, and little lizards, they say were once big.
Probably he was a jabbing, terrifying monster.
We look at him through the wrong end of the long telescope of
    Time,
Luckily for us.

D. H. LAWRENCE

Hunter Poems of the Yoruba

Baboon

So proud in his furry robe
he thinks he can seduce
the hunter's wife.
He rolls his eyes
his fingernails are golden
he has carved himself
a fine long mouth.

197

Sitting on top of the tree
he teaches the dog to hunt.
He pelts the farmer
with his own fruit.
He collects creepers
to pay his bride price.
Father of many children
whose wife's breasts
are never at rest.
Destroyer of our farms,
you pile the corn into the sack
of your mouth.
Four hundred when coming
one thousand two hundred on your return.
You say:
I am restraining myself today.
If this were not my in-laws' farm
then trees would fall on trees
and palm trees would fall on palm trees.

ANON
From the Yoruba (trans. Ulli Beier)

Blue Cuckoo

The blue cuckoo
lays white eggs in the bush.
When war captures the town
the blue cuckoo cries:
'Kill twenty, kill twenty!'
The red–bellied coucal cries:
'Kill thirty, kill thirty.'
Then death will not fail to come,
then death will not fail to come.
When men begin war,
the blue cuckoo cries:

198

'Fools, fools!'
The red-bellied coucal cries:
'The world is spoiled,
the world is spoiled!'
Then death cannot fail to come,
then death cannot fail to come.

ANON
From the Yoruba (trans. Ulli Beier)

Buffalo

The buffalo is the death
that makes a child climb a thorn tree.
When the buffalo dies in the forest
the head of the household is hiding in the roof.
When the hunter meets the buffalo
he promises never to hunt again.
He will cry out: 'I only borrowed the gun!
I only look after it for my friend!'
Little he cares about your hunting medicines:
he carries two knives on his head,
little he cares about your danegun,
he wears the thickest skin.
He is the butterfly of the savannah:
he flies along without touching the grass.
When you hear thunder without rain—
it is the buffalo approaching.

ANON
From the Yoruba (trans. Ulli Beier)

Chicken

One who sees corn and is glad.
Happily eating the worm
unaware of her fate.
Every fool will be buried in the cheek.
The foolish chicken has many relatives:
oil is her uncle on the mother's side
pepper and onion are her aunts on the father's side
pounded yam is her in-law.
If she does not see her friend salt for a day
she does not sleep peacefully.

ANON
From the Yoruba (trans. Ulli Beier)

Colobus Monkey

We invite him to die
he smiles.
He dies at last
his cheeks full of laughter.
Two rows of bared white teeth.

At daybreak
the housewife sweeps the floor
the eagle sweeps the sky
and colobus
sweeps the top of his tree.

Abuse him
and he will follow you home.
Praise him
and he leaves you alone.
The ragged man
and the man in the embroidered gown
both covet his skin.

200

Lice killer
with black nails
deep-set eyes
sweeping tail.
Too beautiful to live.
Death always follows greed.
Too beautiful to survive
death always follows war.

ANON

From the Yoruba (trans. Ulli Beier)

Elephant

Elephant, a spirit in the bush,
Elephant who brings death.
He swallows a whole palmfruit
thorns and all.
He tramples down the grass
with his mortar legs.
Wherever he walks
the grass is forbidden to stand up again.
He tears a man like an old rag
and hangs him up in the tree.
With his single hand
he pulls two palm trees to the ground.
If he had two hands
he would tear the heaven to shreds.
An elephant is not a load for an old man—
nor for a young man either.

ANON

From the Yoruba (trans. Ulli Beier)

Hyena

The scruffy one
who eats the meat
together with the bag
in which it is kept.
The greedy one
who eats the mother
and does not spare the child.
God's bandy-legged creature.
Killer in the night.

ANON
From the Yoruba (trans. Ulli Beier)

Kob Antelope

A creature to pet and spoil
like a child.
Smooth-skinned
stepping cautiously
in the lemon grass.
Round and plump
like a newly married wife.
The neck
heavy with brass rings.
The eyes
gentle like a bird's.
The head
beautiful like carved wood.
When you suddenly escape
you spread fine dust
like a butterfly
shaking its wings.
Your neck seems long,
so very long
to the greedy hunter.

ANON
From the Yoruba (trans. Ulli Beier)

Leopard

Gentle hunter
his tail plays on the ground
while he crushes the skull.

Beautiful death
who puts on a spotted robe
when he goes to his victim.

Playful killer
whose loving embrace
splits the antelope's heart.

ANON
From the Yoruba (trans. Ulli Beier)

Red Monkey

Child of maize!
Owner of the farm!
You have never borne a black child.
Your child is the colour of the farm.
Wise old man
possessor of charms!
You continue to steal
though you are old enough not to steal.
O no!
Since he was born
the red monkey never stole anything:
he merely picks what he wants
in the presence of the farmer!
He does not fight the farmer:
he only stares at him.

ANON
From the Yoruba (trans. Ulli Beier)

Hurt Hawks

I

The broken pillar of the wing jags from the clotted shoulder,
The wing trails like a banner in defeat,
No more to use the sky forever but live with famine
And pain a few days: cat nor coyote
Will shorten the week of waiting for death, there is game
    without talons.
He stands under the oak-bush and waits
The lame feet of salvation; at night he remembers freedom
And flies in a dream, the dawns ruin it.
He is strong and pain is worse to the strong, incapacity is worse.
The curs of the day come and torment him
At distance, no one but death the redeemer will humble that head,
The intrepid readiness, the terrible eyes.
The wild God of the world is sometimes merciful to those
That ask mercy, not often to the arrogant.
You do not know him, you communal people, or you have
    forgotten him;
Intemperate and savage, the hawk remembers him;
Beautiful and wild, the hawks, and men that are dying,
    remember him.

II

I'd sooner, except the penalties, kill a man than a hawk; but the
    great redtail
Had nothing left but unable misery
From the bone too shattered for mending, the wing that trailed
    under his talons when he moved.
We had fed him six weeks, I gave him freedom,
He wandered over the foreland hill and returned in the evening,
    asking for death,
Not like a beggar, still eyed with the old
Implacable arrogance. I gave him the lead gift in the twilight.
    What fell was relaxed,
Owl-downy, soft feminine feathers; but what
Soared: the fierce rush: the night-herons by the flooded river
    cried fear at its rising
Before it was quite unsheathed from reality. ROBINSON JEFFERS

204

'I cannot grow'

I cannot grow;
I have no shadow
To run away from,
I only play.

I cannot err;
There is no creature
Whom I belong to,
Whom I could wrong.

I am defeat
When it knows it
Can now do nothing
By suffering.

All you lived through,
Dancing because you
No longer need it
For any deed.

I shall never be
Different. Love me.

W. H. AUDEN

'I saw a Peacock with a fiery tail'

I saw a Peacock with a fiery tail,
I saw a blazing Comet drop down hail,
I saw a Cloud with ivy circled round,
I saw a sturdy Oak creep on the ground,
I saw a Pismire swallow up a whale,
I saw a raging Sea brim full of ale,

205

I saw a Venice Glass sixteen foot deep,
I saw a Well full of men's tears that weep,
I saw their Eyes all in a flame of fire,
I saw a House as big as the moon and higher,
I saw the Sun even in the midst of night,
I saw the Man that saw this wondrous sight.

ANON

'I think that the Root of the Wind is Water'

I think that the Root of the Wind is Water—
It would not sound so deep
Were it a Firmamental Product—
Airs no Oceans keep—
Mediterranean intonations—
To a Current's Ear—
There is a maritime conviction
In the Atmosphere—

EMILY DICKINSON

'I will give my love an apple without e'er a core'

I will give my love an apple without e'er a core,
I will give my love a house without e'er a door,
I will give my love a palace wherein she may be
And she may unlock it without e'er a key.

My head is the apple without e'er a core,
My mind is the house without e'er a door,
My heart is the palace wherein she may be
And she may unlock it without e'er a key.

I will give my love a cherry without e'er a stone,
I will give my love a chick without e'er a bone,
I will give my love a ring, not a rent to be seen,
I will get my love children without any crying.

When the cherry's in blossom there's never no stone,
When the chick's in the womb there's never no bone,
And when they're rinning running not a rent to be seen,
And when they're child-making they're seldom crying.

ANON

'If I might be an ox'

If I might be an ox,
An ox, a beautiful ox,
Beautiful but stubborn:
The merchant would buy me,
Would buy me and slaughter me,
Would spread my skin,
Would bring me to the market,
The coarse woman would bargain for me,
The beautiful girl would buy me.
She would crush perfumes for me,
I would spend the night rolled up round her,
I would spend the afternoon rolled up round her.
Her husband would say: 'It is a dead skin.'
But I would have her love.

ANON

A song of the Galla tribe in Ethiopia (trans. unknown)

207

'In beauty may I walk'

In beauty	may I walk
All day long	may I walk
Through the returning seasons	may I walk

Beautifully will I possess again
Beautifully birds
Beautifully joyful birds

On the trail marked with pollen	may I walk
With grasshoppers about my feet	may I walk
With dew about my feet	may I walk
With beauty	may I walk
With beauty before me	may I walk
With beauty behind me	may I walk
With beauty above me	may I walk
With beauty all around me	may I walk
In old age, wandering on a trail of beauty, lively,	may I walk
In old age, wandering on a trail of beauty, living again,	may I walk

It is finished in beauty
It is finished in beauty

ANO
From the Navajo (trans. Jerome K. Rothenberg

'In Golden Gate Park that day'

In Golden Gate Park that day
          a man and his wife were coming along
     thru the enormous meadow
               which was the meadow of the world
He was wearing green suspenders
               and carrying an old beat–up flute
                              in one hand
     while his wife had a bunch of grapes
               which she kept handing out
                              individually

                    to various squirrels
                                        as if each
                    were a little joke

And then the two of them came on
                            thru the enormous meadow
which was the meadow of the world
                            and then
    at a very still spot where the trees dreamed
        and seemed to have been waiting thru all time
                                        for them
        they sat down together on the grass
                            without looking at each other
        and ate oranges
                    without looking at each other
                                    and put the peels
        in a basket which they seemed
                        to have brought for that purpose
        without looking at each other

And then
            he took his shirt and undershirt off
        but kept his hat on
                        sideways
                            and without saying anything
        fell asleep under it
                        And his wife just sat there looking
at the birds which flew about
    calling to each other
                    in the stilly air
    as if they were questioning existence
                        or trying to recall something forgotten

But then finally
            she too lay down flat
                        and just lay there looking up
                                            at nothing
        yet fingering the old flute
                        which nobody played

            and finally looking over
                              at him
          without any particular expression
                              except a certain awful look
            of terrible depression
                                   LAWRENCE FERLINGHETTI

In the Deep Channel

Setting a trotline after sundown
if we went far enough away in the night
sometimes up out of deep water
would come a secret-headed channel cat,

Eyes that were still eyes in the rush of darkness,
flowing feelers noncommittal and black,
and hidden in the fins those rasping bone daggers,
with one spiking upward on its back.

We would come at daylight and find the line sag,
the fishbelly gleam and the rush on the tether:
to feel the swerve and the deep current
which tugged at the tree roots below the river.

                                   WILLIAM STAFFORD

'In the touch of this bosom there worketh a spell'

'In the touch of this bosom there worketh a spell
Which is lord of thy utterance, Christabel!
Thou knowest to-night, and wilt know to-morrow,
This mark of my shame, this seal of my sorrow;
        But vainly thou warrest,
          For this is alone in

Thy power to declare,
     That in the dim forest
Thou heard'st a low moaning,
And found'st a bright lady, surpassingly fair;
And didst bring her home with thee in love and in charity,
To shield her and shelter her from the damp air.'

SAMUEL TAYLOR COLERIDGE
From Christabel, Part I

In Time of 'The Breaking of Nations'

I

Only a man harrowing clods
     In a slow silent walk
With an old horse that stumbles and nods
     Half asleep as they stalk.

II

Only thin smoke without flame
     From the heaps of couch-grass;
Yet this will go onward the same
     Though Dynasties pass.

III

Yonder a maid and her wight
     Come whispering by:
War's annals will cloud into night
     Ere their story die.

THOMAS HARDY

Infant Sorrow

My mother groan'd! my father wept.
Into the dangerous world I leapt:
Helpless, naked, piping loud:
Like a fiend hid in a cloud.

Struggling in my father's hands,
Striving against my swadling bands,
Bound and weary I thought best
To sulk upon my mother's breast.

WILLIAM BLAKE
From *Songs of Experience*

Innocence

They laughed at one I loved—
The triangular hill that hung
Under the Big Forth. They said
That I was bounded by the whitethorn hedges
Of the little farm and did not know the world.
But I knew that love's doorway to life
Is the same doorway everywhere.

Ashamed of what I loved
I flung her from me and called her a ditch
Although she was smiling at me with violets.

But now I am back in her briary arms
The dew of an Indian Summer morning lies
On bleached potato-stalks—
What age am I?

I do not know what age I am,
I am no mortal age;
I know nothing of women,

Nothing of cities,
I cannot die
Unless I walk outside these whitethorn hedges.
                              PATRICK KAVANAGH

The Inquest

I took my oath I would inquire,
    Without affection, hate, or wrath,
Into the death of Ada Wright—
    So help me God! I took that oath.

When I went out to see the corpse,
    The four months' babe that died so young,
I judged it was seven pounds in weight,
    And little more than one foot long.

One eye, that had a yellow lid,
    Was shut—so was the mouth, that smiled;
The left eye open, shining bright—
    It seemed a knowing little child.

For as I looked at that one eye,
    It seemed to laugh, and say with glee:
'What caused my death you'll never know—
    Perhaps my mother murdered me.'

When I went into court again,
    To hear the mother's evidence—
It was a love-child, she explained.
    And smiled, for our intelligence.

'Now, Gentlemen of the Jury,' said
    The coroner—'this woman's child
By misadventure met its death.'
    'Aye, aye,' said we. The mother smiled.

And I could see that child's one eye
    Which seemed to laugh, and say with glee:
'What caused my death you'll never know—
    Perhaps my mother murdered me.'

Interruption to a Journey

The hare we had run over
Bounced about the road
On the springing curve
Of its spine.

Cornfields breathed in the darkness,
We were going through the darkness and
The breathing cornfields from one
Important place to another.

We broke the hare's neck
And made that place, for a moment,
The most important place there was,
Where a bowstring was cut
And a bow broken forever
That had shot itself through so many
Darknesses and cornfields.

It was left in that landscape.
It left us in another.

NORMAN MACCAIG

Inversnaid

This darksome burn, horseback brown,
His rollrock highroad roaring down,
In coop and in comb the fleece of his foam
Flutes and low to the lake falls home.

A windpuff-bonnet of fáwn-fróth
Turns and twindles over the broth
Of a pool so pitchblack, féll frówning,
It rounds and rounds Despair to drowning.

Degged with dew, dappled with dew
Are the groins of the braes that the brook treads through,
Wiry heathpacks, flitches of fern,
And the beadbonny ash that sits over the burn.

What would the world be, once bereft
Of wet and of wildness? Let them be left,
O let them be left, wildness and wet;
Long live the weeds and the wilderness yet.

GERARD MANLEY HOPKINS

Invictus

Out of the night that covers me,
   Black as the pit from pole to pole,
I thank whatever gods may be
   For my unconquerable soul.

In the fell clutch of circumstance
   I have not winced nor cried aloud.
Under the bludgeonings of chance
   My head is bloody, but unbowed.

215

Beyond this place of wrath and tears
   Looms but the Horror of the shade,
And yet the menace of the years
   Finds, and shall find, me unafraid.

It matters not how strait the gate,
   How charged with punishments the scroll,
I am the master of my fate:
   I am the captain of my soul.

W. E. HENLEY

'It is not growing like a tree'

It is not growing like a tree
In bulk, doth make Man better be;
Or standing long an oak, three hundred year,
To fall a log at last, dry, bald, and sere:
   A lily of a day
   Is fairer far in May,
Although it fall and die that night;
It was the plant and flower of Light.
In small proportions we just beauties see;
And in short measures life may perfect be.

BEN JONSON

'It's such a little thing to weep'

It's such a little thing to weep—
So short a thing to sigh—
And yet—by Trades—the size of *these*
We men and women die!

EMILY DICKINSON

It Was All Very Tidy

When I reached his place,
The grass was smooth,
The wind was delicate,
The wit well timed,
The limbs well formed,
The pictures straight on the wall:
It was all very tidy.

He was cancelling out
The last row of figures,
He had his beard tied up in ribbons,
There was no dust on his shoe,
Everyone nodded:
It was all very tidy.

Music was not playing,
There were no sudden noises,
The sun shone blandly,
The clock ticked:
It was all very tidy.

'Apart from and above all this,'
I reassured myself,
'There is now myself.'
It was all very tidy.

Death did not address me,
He had nearly done:
It was all very tidy.
They asked, did I not think
It was all very tidy?

I could not bring myself
To laugh, or untie
His beard's neat ribbons,
Or jog his elbow,
Or whistle, or sing,

Or make disturbance.
I consented, frozenly,
He was unexceptionable:
It was all very tidy.

ROBERT GRAVES

'It was a lover and his lass'

It was a lover and his lass,
   With a hey, and a ho, and a hey nonino,
That o'er the green cornfield did pass,
   In the spring time, the only pretty ring time,
When birds do sing, hey ding a ding, ding;
Sweet lovers love the spring.

Between the acres of the rye,
   With a hey, and a ho, and a hey nonino,
These pretty country folks would lie,
   In the spring time, etc.

This carol they began that hour,
   With a hey, and a ho, and a hey nonino,
How that a life was but a flower
   In the spring time, etc.

And therefore take the present time,
   With a hey, and a ho, and a hey nonino;
For love is crowned with the prime
   In the spring time, etc.

WILLIAM SHAKESPEARE
From As You Like It, Act 5, Scene 3

Jabberwocky

'Twas brillig, and the slithy toves
  Did gyre and gimble in the wabe;
All mimsy were the borogoves,
    And the mome raths outgrabe.

'Beware the Jabberwock, my son!
  The jaws that bite, the claws that catch!
Beware the Jubjub bird, and shun
    The frumious Bandersnatch!'

He took his vorpal sword in hand:
  Long time the manxome foe he sought—
So rested he by the Tumtum tree,
    And stood awhile in thought.

And as in uffish thought he stood,
  The Jabberwock, with eyes of flame,
Came whiffling through the tulgey wood,
    And burbled as it came!

One, two! One, two! And through and through
  The vorpal blade went snicker-snack!
He left it dead, and with its head
    He went galumphing back.

'And hast thou slain the Jabberwock?
  Come to my arms, my beamish boy!
O frabjous day! Callooh! Callay!'
    He chortled in his joy.

'Twas brillig, and the slithy toves
  Did gyre and gimble in the wabe;
All mimsy were the borogoves,
    And the mome raths outgrabe.

LEWIS CARROLL

Janet Waking

Beautifully Janet slept
Till it was deeply morning. She woke then
And thought about her dainty-feathered hen,
To see how it had kept.

One kiss she gave her mother.
Only a small one gave she to her daddy
Who would have kissed each curl of his shining baby;
No kiss at all for her brother.

'Old Chucky, old Chucky!' she cried,
Running across the world upon the grass
To Chucky's house, and listening. But alas,
Her Chucky had died.

It was a transmogrifying bee
Came droning down on Chucky's old bald head
And sat and put the poison. It scarcely bled,
But how exceedingly

And purply did the knot
Swell with the venom and communicate
Its rigor! Now the poor comb stood up straight
But Chucky did not.

So there was Janet
Kneeling on the wet grass, crying her brown hen
(Translated far beyond the daughters of men)
To rise and walk upon it.

And weeping fast as she had breath
Janet implored us, 'Wake her from her sleep!'
And would not be instructed in how deep
Was the forgetful kingdom of death.

JOHN CROWE RANSOM

Jerusalem

And did those feet in ancient time
Walk upon England's mountains green?
And was the holy Lamb of God
On England's pleasant pastures seen?

And did the Countenance Divine
Shine forth upon our clouded hills?
And was Jerusalem builded here
Among these dark Satanic Mills?

Bring me my Bow of burning gold:
Bring me my Arrows of desire:
Bring me my Spear: O clouds unfold!
Bring me my Chariot of fire.

I will not cease from Mental Fight,
Nor shall my Sword sleep in my hand
Till we have built Jerusalem
In England's green and pleasant Land.

WILLIAM BLAKE
From *Milton*, Preface

Jim Desterland

As I was fishing off Pondy Point
Between the tides, the sea so still—
Only a whisper against the boat—
No other sound but the scream of a gull,
I heard the voice you will never hear
Filling the crannies of the air.

The doors swung open, the little doors,
The door, the hatch within the brain,
And like the bellowing of ruin

221

The surf upon the thousand shores
Swept through me, and the thunder-noise
Of all the waves of all the seas.

The doors swung shut, the little doors,
The door, the hatch within the ear,
And I was fishing off Pondy Pier,
And all was as it was before,
With only the whisper of the swell
Against the boat, and the cry of a gull.

I draw a sight from tree to tree
Crossing this other from knoll to rock,
To mark the place. Into the sea _
My line falls with an empty hook,
Yet fools the world. So day and night
I crouch upon the thwarts and wait.

There is a roaring in the skies
The great globes make, and there is the sound
Of all the atoms whirling round
That one can hear if one is wise—
Wiser than most—if one has heard
The doors, the little doors, swing wide.

HYAM PLUTZIK

John Barleycorn

There was three Kings into the east,
  Three Kings both great and high,
And they hae sworn a solemn oath
  John Barleycorn should die.

They took a plough and plough'd him down,
  Put clods upon his head,
And they hae sworn a solemn oath
  John Barleycorn was dead.

But the cheerfu' Spring came kindly on,
  And show'rs began to fall;
John Barleycorn got up again,
  And sore surpris'd them all.

The sultry suns of Summer came,
  And he grew thick and strong,
His head weel arm'd wi' pointed spears,
  That no one should him wrong.

The sober Autumn enter'd mild,
  When he grew wan and pale;
His bending joints and drooping head
  Show'd he began to fail.

His colour sicken'd more and more,
  He faded into age;
And then his enemies began
  To shew their deadly rage.

They've ta'en a weapon, long and sharp,
  And cut him by the knee;
Then tied him fast upon a cart,
  Like a rogue for forgerie.

They laid him down upon his back,
  And cudgell'd him full sore;
They hung him up before the storm,
  And turn'd him o'er and o'er.

They fillèd up a darksome pit
  With water to the brim,
They heavèd in John Barleycorn,
  There let him sink or swim.

They laid him out upon the floor,
  To work him farther woe,
And still, as signs of life appear'd,
  They toss'd him to and fro.

They wasted, o'er a scorching flame,
  The marrow of his bones;
But a miller us'd him worst of all,
  For he crush'd him between two stones.

And they hae ta'en his very heart's blood,
  And drank it round and round;
And still the more and more they drank,
  Their joy did more abound.

John Barleycorn was a hero bold,
  Of noble enterprise,
For if you do but taste his blood,
  'Twill make your courage rise;

'Twill make a man forget his woe;
  'Twill heighten all his joy:
'Twill make the widow's heart to sing,
  Tho' the tear were in her eye.

Then let us toast John Barleycorn,
  Each man a glass in hand;
And may his great posterity
  Ne'er fail in old Scotland!

                          ROBERT BURNS

John Kinsella's Lament for Mrs Mary Moore

A bloody and a sudden end,
  Gunshot or a noose,
For Death who takes what man would keep,
  Leaves what man would lose.
He might have had my sister,
  My cousins by the score,
But nothing satisfied the fool
  But my dear Mary Moore,

None other knows what pleasures man
    At table or in bed.
What shall I do for pretty girls
    Now my old bawd is dead?

Though stiff to strike a bargain,
    Like an old Jew man,
Her bargain struck we laughed and talked
    And emptied many a can;
And O! but she had stories,
    Though not for the priest's ear,
To keep the soul of man alive,
    Banish age and care,
And being old she put a skin
    On everything she said.
What shall I do for pretty girls
    Now my old bawd is dead?

The priests have got a book that says
    But for Adam's sin
Eden's Garden would be there
    And I there within.
No expectation fails there,
    No pleasing habit ends,
No man grows old, no girl grows cold,
    But friends walk by friends.
Who quarrels over halfpennies
    That plucks the trees for bread?
What shall I do for pretty girls
    Now my old bawd is dead?

W. B. YEATS

John Mouldy

I spied John Mouldy in his cellar,
Deep down twenty steps of stone;
In the dusk he sat a-smiling,
    Smiling there alone.

He read no book, he snuffed no candle;
The rats ran in, the rats ran out;
And far and near, the drip of water
    Went whisp'ring about.

The dusk was still, with dew a-falling,
I saw the Dog-star bleak and grim,
I saw a slim brown rat of Norway
    Creep over him.

I spied John Mouldy in his cellar,
Deep down twenty steps of stone;
In the dusk he sat a-smiling,
    Smiling there alone.

WALTER DE LA MARE

The Jungle Husband

Dearest Evelyn, I often think of you
Out with the guns in the jungle stew
Yesterday I hittapotamus
I put the measurements down for you but they got lost in the
    fuss.
It's not a good thing to drink out here
You know, I've practically given it up dear.
Tomorrow I am going alone a long way
Into the jungle. It is all gray
But green on top

226

Only sometimes when a tree has fallen
The sun comes down plop, it is quite appalling.
You never want to go in a jungle pool
In the hot sun, it would be the act of a fool
Because it's always full of anacondas, Evelyn, not looking
  ill-fed
I'll say. So no more now, from your loving husband, Wilfred.

STEVIE SMITH

Kerr's Ass

We borrowed the loan of Kerr's big ass
To go to Dundalk with butter,
Brought him home the evening before the market
An exile that night in Mucker.

We heeled up the cart before the door,
We took the harness inside—
The straw-stuffed straddle, the broken breeching
With bits of bull-wire tied;

The winkers that had no choke-band,
The collar and the reins...
In Ealing Broadway, London Town
I name their several names

Until a world comes to life—
Morning, the silent bog,
And the God of imagination waking
In a Mucker fog.

PATRICK KAVANAGH

The Knee

There wanders through the world, a knee
It's just a knee, no more.
It's not a tent; it's not a tree;
Only a knee, no more.

There was a man once in a war
Overkilled, killed fatally.
Alone, unhurt, remained the knee
Like a saint's relics, pure.

Since then it roams the whole world, lonely.
It is a knee, now, only.
It's not a tent; it's not a tree;
Only a knee, no more.

CHRISTIAN MORGENSTERN

From the German (trans. W. D. Snodgrass and Lore Segal)

The Knight's Tomb

Where is the grave of Sir Arthur O'Kellyn?
Where may the grave of that good man be?—
By the side of a spring, on the breast of Helvellyn,
Under the twigs of a young birch tree!
The oak that in summer was sweet to hear,
And rustled its leaves in the fall of the year,
And whistled and roared in the winter alone,
Is gone,—and the birch in its stead is grown.—
The Knight's bones are dust,
And his good sword rust;—
His soul is with the saints, I trust.

SAMUEL TAYLOR COLERIDGE

Lament for Tadhg Cronin's Children

based on a poem by Aodhagán O Rathaille

That day the sails of the ship were torn
and a fog obscured the lawns.
In the whitewashed house the music stopped.
A spark jumped up at the gables
and the silk quilts on the bed caught fire.
They cry without tears—
their hearts cry—
for the three dead children.

Christ God neglect them not
nor leave them in the ground!

They were ears of corn!
They were apples!
They were three harpstrings!
And now their limbs lie underground
and the black beetle walks across their faces.
I, too, cry without tears—
my heart cries—
for the three dead children.

MICHAEL HARTNETT

Landscapes

I New Hampshire

Children's voices in the orchard
Between the blossom- and the fruit-time:
Golden head, crimson head,
Between the green tip and the root.
Black wing, brown wing, hover over;
Twenty years and the spring is over;
To-day grieves, to-morrow grieves,
Cover me over, light-in-leaves;

229

Golden head, black wing,
Cling, swing,
Spring, sing,
Swing up into the apple-tree.

II Virginia

Red river, red river,
Slow flow heat is silence
No will is still as a river
Still. Will heat move
Only through the mocking-bird
Heard once? Still hills
Wait. Gates wait. Purple trees,
White trees, wait, wait,
Delay, decay. Living, living,
Never moving. Ever moving
Iron thoughts came with me
And go with me:
Red river, river, river.

III Usk

Do not suddenly break the branch, or
Hope to find
The white hart behind the white well.
Glance aside, not for lance, do not spell
Old enchantments. Let them sleep.
'Gently dip, but not too deep',
Lift your eyes
Where the roads dip and where the roads rise
Seek only there
Where the grey light meets the green air
The hermit's chapel, the pilgrim's prayer.

IV Rannoch, by Glencoe

Here the crow starves, here the patient stag
Breeds for the rifle. Between the soft moor
And the soft sky, scarcely room
To leap or soar. Substance crumbles, in the thin air
Moon cold or moon hot. The road winds in
Listlessness of ancient war,
Languor of broken steel,
Clamour of confused wrong, apt
In silence. Memory is strong
Beyond the bone. Pride snapped,
Shadow of pride is long, in the long pass
No concurrence of bone.

V Cape Ann

O quick quick quick, quick hear the song-sparrow,
Swamp-sparrow, fox-sparrow, vesper-sparrow
At dawn and dusk. Follow the dance
Of the goldfinch at noon. Leave to chance
The Blackburnian warbler, the shy one. Hail
With shrill whistle the note of the quail, the bob-white
Dodging by bay-bush. Follow the feet
Of the walker, the water-thrush. Follow the flight
Of the dancing arrow, the purple martin. Greet
In silence the bullbat. All are delectable. Sweet sweet sweet
But resign this land at the end, resign it
To its true owner, the tough one, the sea-gull.

The palaver is finished.

T. S. ELIOT

The Last Words of My English Grandmother

There were some dirty plates
and a glass of milk
beside her on a small table
near the rank, disheveled bed—

Wrinkled and nearly blind
she lay and snored
rousing with anger in her tones
to cry for food,

Gimme something to eat—
They're starving me—
I'm all right I won't go
to the hospital. No, no, no

Give me something to eat
Let me take you
to the hospital, I said
and after you are well

you can do as you please.
She smiled, Yes
you do what you please first
then I can do what I please—

Oh, oh, oh! she cried
as the ambulance men lifted
her to the stretcher—
Is this what you call

making me comfortable?
By now her mind was clear—
Oh you think you're smart
you young people,

she said, but I'll tell you
you don't know anything.
Then we started.
On the way

we passed a long row
of elms. She looked at them
awhile out of
the ambulance window and said,

What are all those
fuzzy looking things out there?
Trees? Well, I'm tired
of them, and rolled her head away.

WILLIAM CARLOS WILLIAMS

The Leaden-Eyed

Let not young souls be smothered out before
They do quaint deeds and fully flaunt their pride.
It is the world's one crime its babes grow dull,
Its poor are ox-like, limp and leaden-eyed.

Not that they starve, but starve so dreamlessly,
Not that they sow, but that they seldom reap,
Not that they serve, but have no gods to serve,
Not that they die, but that they die like sheep.

VACHEL LINDSAY

Legend

The blacksmith's boy went out with a rifle
and a black dog running behind.
Cobwebs snatched at his feet,
rivers hindered him,
thorn-branches caught at his eyes to make him blind
and the sky turned into an unlucky opal,
but he didn't mind,

I can break branches, I can swim rivers, I can stare out any
    spider I meet,
said he to his dog and his rifle.

The blacksmith's boy went over the paddocks
with his old black hat on his head.
Mountains jumped in his way,
rocks rolled down on him,
and the old crow cried, 'You'll soon be dead.'
And the rain came down like mattocks.
But he only said
I can climb mountains, I can dodge rocks, I can shoot an old
    crow any day,
and he went on over the paddocks.

When he came to the end of the day the sun began falling.
Up came the night ready to swallow him,
like the barrel of a gun,
like an old black hat,
like a black dog hungry to follow him.
Then the pigeon, the magpie and the dove began wailing
and the grass lay down to pillow him.
His rifle broke, his hat blew away and his dog was gone
and the sun was falling.

But in front of the night the rainbow stood on the mountain,
just as his heart foretold.
He ran like a hare,
he climbed like a fox;
he caught it in his hands, the colours and the cold—
like a bar of ice, like the column of a fountain,
like a ring of gold.
The pigeon, the magpie and the dove flew up to stare,
and the grass stood up again on the mountain.

The blacksmith's boy hung the rainbow on his shoulder
instead of his broken gun.
Lizards ran out to see,

snakes made way for him,
and the rainbow shone as brightly as the sun.
All the world said, Nobody is braver, nobody is bolder,
nobody else has done
anything to equal it. He went home as bold as he could be
with the swinging rainbow on his shoulder.

JUDITH WRIGHT

The Legs

There was this road,
And it led up-hill,
And it led down-hill,
And round and in and out.

And the traffic was legs,
Legs from the knees down,
Coming and going,
Never pausing.

And the gutters gurgled
With the rain's overflow,
And the sticks on the pavement
Blindly tapped and tapped.

What drew the legs along
Was the never-stopping,
And the senseless, frightening
Fate of being legs.

Legs for the road,
The road for legs,
Resolutely nowhere
In both directions.

My legs at least
Were not in that rout:
On grass by the roadside
Entire I stood,

Watching the unstoppable
Legs go by
With never a stumble
Between step and step.

Though my smile was broad
The legs could not see,
Though my laugh was loud
The legs could not hear.

My head dizzied, then:
I wondered suddenly,
Might I too be a walker
From the knees down?

Gently I touched my shins.
The doubt unchained them:
They had run in twenty puddles
Before I regained them.

ROBERT GRAVES

Lepanto

White founts falling in the courts of the sun,
And the Soldan of Byzantium is smiling as they run;
There is laughter like the fountains in that face of all men feared,
It stirs the forest darkness, the darkness of his beard,
It curls the blood–red crescent, the crescent of his lips,
For the inmost sea of all the earth is shaken with his ships.
They have dared the white republics up the capes of Italy,
They have dashed the Adriatic round the Lion of the Sea,
And the Pope has cast his arms abroad for agony and loss,

And called the kings of Christendom for swords about the
    Cross,
The cold queen of England is looking in the glass;
The shadow of the Valois is yawning at the Mass;
From evening isles fantastical rings faint the Spanish gun,
And the Lord upon the Golden Horn is laughing in the sun.

Dim drums throbbing, in the hills half heard,
Where only on a nameless throne a crownless prince has stirred,
Where, risen from a doubtful seat and half-attainted stall,
The last knight of Europe takes weapons from the wall,
The last and lingering troubadour to whom the bird has sung,
That once went singing southward when all the world was
    young,
In that enormous silence, tiny and unafraid,
Comes up along a winding road the noise of the Crusade.
Strong gongs groaning as the guns boom far,
Don John of Austria is going to the war,
Stiff flags straining in the night-blasts cold
In the gloom black-purple, in the glint old-gold,
Torchlight crimson on the copper kettle-drums,
Then the tuckets, then the trumpets, then the cannon, and he
    comes.
Don John laughing in the brave beard curled,
Spurning of his stirrups like the thrones of all the world,
Holding his head up for a flag of all the free.
Love-light of Spain—hurrah!
Death-light of Africa!
Don John of Austria
Is riding to the sea.

Mahound is in his paradise above the evening star,
(*Don John of Austria is going to the war.*)
He moves a mighty turban on the timeless houri's knees,
His turban that is woven of the sunset and the seas.
He shakes the peacock gardens as he rises from his ease,
And he strides among the tree-tops and is taller than the trees,
And his voice through all the garden is a thunder sent to bring
Black Azrael and Ariel and Ammon on the wing.

Giants and the Genii,
Multiplex of wing and eye,
Whose strong obedience broke the sky
When Solomon was king.

They rush in red and purple from the red clouds of the morn,
From temples where the yellow gods shut up their eyes in
    scorn;
They rise in green robes roaring from the green hells of the sea
Where fallen skies and evil hues and eyeless creatures be;
On them the sea-valves cluster and the grey sea-forests curl,
Splashed with a splendid sickness, the sickness of the pearl;
They swell in sapphire smoke out of the blue cracks of the
    ground,—
They gather and they wonder and give worship to Mahound.
And he saith, 'Break up the mountains where the hermit-folk
    may hide,
And sift the red and silver sands lest bone of saint abide,
And chase the Giaours flying night and day, not giving rest,
For that which was our trouble comes again out of the west.
We have set the seal of Solomon on all things under sun,
Of knowledge and of sorrow and endurance of things done,
But a noise is in the mountains, in the mountains, and I know
The voice that shook our palaces—four hundred years ago:
It is he that saith not "Kismet"; it is he that knows not Fate;
It is Richard, it is Raymond, it is Godfrey in the gate!
It is he whose loss is laughter when he counts the wager worth,
Put down your feet upon him, that our peace be on the earth.'
For he heard drums groaning and he heard guns jar,
(*Don John of Austria is going to the war.*)
Sudden and still—hurrah!
Bolt from Iberia!
Don John of Austria
Is gone by Alcalar.

St Michael's on his Mountain in the sea-roads of the north
(*Don John of Austria is girt and going forth.*)
Where the grey seas glitter and the sharp tides shift
And the sea folk labour and the red sails lift.

He shakes his lance of iron and he claps his wings of stone;
The noise is gone through Normandy; the noise is gone alone;
The North is full of tangled things and texts and aching eyes
And dead is all the innocence of anger and surprise,
And Christian killeth Christian in a narrow dusty room,
And Christian dreadeth Christ that hath a newer face of doom,
And Christian hateth Mary that God kissed in Galilee,
But Don John of Austria is riding to the sea.
Don John calling through the blast and the eclipse
Crying with the trumpet, with the trumpet of his lips,
Trumpet that sayeth ha!
Domino gloria!
Don John of Austria
Is shouting to the ships.

King Philip's in his closet with the Fleece about his neck
(*Don John of Austria is armed upon the deck.*)
The walls are hung with velvet that is black and soft as sin,
And little dwarfs creep out of it and little dwarfs creep in.
He holds a crystal phial that has colours like the moon,
He touches, and it tingles, and he trembles very soon,
And his face is as a fungus of a leprous white and grey
Like plants in the high houses that are shuttered from the day,
And death is in the phial, and the end of noble work,
But Don John of Austria has fired upon the Turk.
Don John's hunting, and his hounds have bayed—
Booms away past Italy the rumour of his raid.
Gun upon gun, ha! ha!
Gun upon gun, hurrah!
Don John of Austria
Has loosed the cannonade.

The Pope was in his chapel before day or battle broke,
(*Don John of Austria is hidden in the smoke.*)
The hidden room in a man's house where God sits all the year,
The secret window whence the world looks small and very
   dear.
He sees as in a mirror on the monstrous twilight sea
The crescent of his cruel ships whose name is mystery;

239

They fling great shadows foe-wards, making Cross and Castle
   dark,
They veil the plumèd lions on the galleys of St Mark;
And above the ships are palaces of brown, black-bearded chiefs,
And below the ships are prisons, where the multitudinous
   griefs,
Christian captives sick and sunless, all a labouring race repines
Like a race in sunken cities, like a nation in the mines.
They are lost like slaves that swat, and in the skies of morning
   hung
The stairways of the tallest gods when tyranny was young.
They are countless, voiceless, hopeless as those fallen or fleeing
   on
Before the high Kings' horses in the granite of Babylon.
And many a one grows witless in his quiet room in hell
Where a yellow face looks inward through the lattice of his cell,
And he finds his God forgotten, and he seeks no more a sign—
(But Don John of Austria has burst the battle-line!)
Don John pounding from the slaughter-painted poop,
Purpling all the ocean like a bloody pirate's sloop,
Scarlet running over on the silvers and the golds,
Breaking of the hatches up and bursting of the holds,
Thronging of the thousands up that labour under sea
White for bliss and blind for sun and stunned for liberty.
Vivat Hispania!
Domino Gloria!
Don John of Austria
Has set his people free!

Cervantes on his galley sets the sword back in the sheath
(Don John of Austria rides homeward with a wreath.)
And he sees across a weary land a straggling road in Spain,
Up which a lean and foolish knight forever rides in vain,
And he smiles, but not as Sultans smile, and settles back the
   blade...
(But Don John of Austria rides home from the Crusade.)

G. K. CHESTERTON

The Lie

Go, Soul, the body's guest,
Upon a thankless arrant:
Fear not to touch the best;
The truth shall be thy warrant:
Go, since I needs must die,
And give the world the lie.

Say to the court, it glows
And shines like rotten wood;
Say to the church it shows
What's good, and doth no good:
If church and court reply,
Then give them both the lie.

Tell potentates, they live
Acting by others' action;
Not loved unless they give,
Not strong but by affection:
If potentates reply,
Give potentates the lie.

Tell men of high condition
That manage the estate,
Their purpose is ambition,
Their practice only hate:
And if they once reply,
Then give them all the lie.

Tell them that brave it most
They beg for more by spending,
Who, in their greatest cost,
Seek nothing but commending:
And if they make reply,
Then give them all the lie.

Tell zeal it wants devotion,
Tell love it is but lust;
Tell time it metes but motion,

Tell flesh it is but dust:
And wish them not reply,
For thou must give the lie.

Tell age it daily wasteth;
Tell honour how it alters;
Tell beauty how she blasteth;
Tell favour how it falters:
And as they shall reply,
Give every one the lie.

Tell wit how much it wrangles
In tickle points of niceness;
Tell wisdom she entangles
Herself in over-wiseness:
And when they do reply,
Straight give them both the lie.

Tell physic of her boldness;
Tell skill it is pretension;
Tell charity of coldness;
Tell law it is contention:
And as they do reply,
So give them still the lie.

Tell fortune of her blindness;
Tell nature of decay;
Tell friendship of unkindness;
Tell justice of delay:
And if they will reply,
Then give them all the lie.

Tell arts they have no soundness,
But vary by esteeming;
Tell schools they want profoundness,
And stand too much on seeming:
If arts and schools reply,
Give arts and schools the lie.

Tell faith it's fled the city;
Tell how the country erreth;
Tell manhood shakes off pity
And virtue least preferreth:
And if they do reply,
Spare not to give the lie.

So when thou hast, as I
Commanded thee, done blabbing
—Although to give the lie
Deserves no less than stabbing—
Stab at thee he that will,
No stab thy soul can kill.

SIR WALTER RALEGH

'Like Rain it sounded till it curved'

Like Rain it sounded till it curved
And then I knew 'twas Wind—
It walked as wet as any Wave
But swept as dry as sand—
When it had pushed itself away
To some remotest Plain
A coming as of Hosts was heard
That was indeed the Rain—
It filled the Wells, it pleased the Pools
It warbled in the Road—
It pulled the spigot from the Hills
And let the Floods abroad—
It loosened acres, lifted seas
The sites of Centres stirred
Then like Elijah rode away
Upon a Wheel of Cloud.

EMILY DICKINSON

Lines for an Old Man

The tiger in the tiger-pit
Is not more irritable than I.
The whipping tail is not more still
Than when I smell the enemy
Writhing in the essential blood
Or dangling from the friendly tree.
When I lay bare the tooth of wit
The hissing over the archèd tongue
Is more affectionate than hate,
More bitter than the love of youth,
And inaccessible by the young.
Reflected from my golden eye
The dullard knows that he is mad.

Tell me if I am not glad!

T. S. ELIOT

The Lion for Real

Soyez muette pour moi, Idole contemplative . . .

I came home and found a lion in my living room
Rushed out on the fire-escape screaming Lion! Lion!
Two stenographers pulled their brunette hair and banged the
    window shut
I hurried home to Paterson and stayed two days.

Called up my old Reichian analyst
who'd kicked me out of therapy for smoking marijuana
'It's happened' I panted 'There's a Lion in my room'
'I'm afraid any discussion would have no value' he hung up.

I went to my old boyfriend we got drunk with his girlfriend
I kissed him and announced I had a lion with a mad gleam in my
    eye

244

We wound up fighting on the floor I bit his eyebrow and he
  kicked me out
I ended masturbating in his jeep parked in the street moaning
  'Lion.'

Found Joey my novelist friend and roared at him 'Lion!'
He looked at me interested and read me his spontaneous ignu
  high poetries
I listened for lions all I heard was Elephant Tiglon Hippogryph
  Unicorn Ants
But figured he really understood me when we made it in Ignaz
  Wisdom's bathroom.

But next day he sent me a leaf from his Smokey Mountain
  retreat
'I love you little Bo-Bo with your delicate golden lions
But there being no Self and No Bars therefore the Zoo of your
  dear Father hath no Lion
You said your mother was mad don't expect me to produce the
  Monster for your Bridegroom.'

Confused dazed and exalted bethought me of real lion starved in
  his stink in Harlem
Opened the door the room was filled with the bomb blast of his
  anger
He roaring hungrily at the plaster walls but nobody could hear
  him outside thru the window
My eye caught the edge of the red neighbor apartment building
  standing in deafening stillness

We gazed at each other his implacable yellow eye in the red halo
  of fur
Waxed rheumy on my own but he stopped roaring and bared a
  fang greeting.
I turned my back and cooked broccoli for supper on an iron gas
  stove
boilt water and took a hot bath in the old tub under the sink
  board.

He didn't eat me, tho I regretted him starving in my presence.

Next week he wasted away a sick rug full of bones wheaten hair falling out

enraged and reddening eye as he lay aching huge hairy head on his paws

by the egg-crate bookcase filled up with thin volumes of Plato, and Buddha.

Sat by his side every night averting my eyes from his hungry motheaten face

stopped eating myself he got weaker and roared at night while I had nightmares

Eaten by lion in bookstore on Cosmic Campus, a lion myself starved by Professor Kandisky, dying in a lion's flophouse circus,

I woke up mornings the lion still added dying on the floor— 'Terrible Presence!' I cried 'Eat me or die!'

It got up that afternoon—walked to the door with its paw on the wall to steady its trembling body

Let out a soul rending creak from the bottomless roof of his mouth

thundering from my floor to heaven heavier than a volcano at night in Mexico

Pushed the door open and said in a gravelly voice 'Not this time Baby—but I will be back again.'

Lion that eats my mind now for a decade knowing only your hunger

Not the bliss of your satisfaction O roar of the Universe how am I chosen

In this life I have heard your promise I am ready to die I have served

Your starved and ancient Presence O Lord I wait in my room at your Mercy.

ALLEN GINSBERG

Little Fish

The tiny fish enjoy themselves
in the sea.
Quick little splinters of life,
their little lives are fun to them
in the sea.

D. H. LAWRENCE

The Little Mute Boy

The little boy was looking for his voice.
(The king of the crickets had it.)
In a drop of water
the little boy was looking for his voice.

I do not want it for speaking with;
I will make a ring of it
that my silence may wear
on its little finger.

In a drop of water
the little boy was looking for his voice.

(The captive voice, far away,
put on a cricket's clothes.)

FEDERICO GARCÍA LORCA

From the Spanish (trans. W. S. Merwin)

Little Trotty Wagtail

Little trotty wagtail, he went in the rain,
And tittering, tottering sideways he near got straight again.
He stooped to get a worm, and look'd up to catch a fly,
And then he flew away.ere his feathers they were dry.

Little trotty wagtail, he waddled in the mud,
And left his little footmarks, trample where he would.
He waddled in the water-pudge, and waggle went his tail,
And he chirrup up his wings to dry upon the garden rail.

Little trotty wagtail, you nimble all about,
And in the dimpling water-pudge you waddle in and out;
Your home is nigh at hand, and in the warm pigsty,
So, little Master Wagtail, I'll bid you a goodbye.

JOHN CLARE

Lizard

A lizard ran out on a rock and looked up, listening
no doubt to the sounding of the spheres.
And what a dandy fellow! the right toss of a chin for you
And swirl of a tail!

If men were as much men as lizards are lizards
they'd be worth looking at.

D. H. LAWRENCE

248

The Locust

What is a locust?
Its head, a grain of corn; its neck, the hinge of a knife;
Its horns, a bit of thread; its chest is smooth and burnished;
Its body is like a knife-handle;
Its hock, a saw; its spittle, ink;
Its underwings, clothing for the dead.
On the ground—it is laying eggs;
In flight—it is like the clouds.
Approaching the ground, it is rain glittering in the sun;
Lighting on a plant, it becomes a pair of scissors;
Walking, it becomes a razor;
Desolation walks with it.

ANON

From the Malagasy (trans. A. Marre and Willard R. Trask)

Lollocks

By sloth on sorrow fathered,
These dusty-featured Lollocks
Have their nativity in all disordered
Backs of cupboard drawers.

They play hide and seek
Among collars and novels
And empty medicine bottles,
And letters from abroad
That never will be answered.

Every sultry night
They plague little children,
Gurgling from the cistern,
Humming from the air,
Skewing up the bed-clothes,
Twitching the blind.

249

When the imbecile aged
Are over-long in dying
And the nurse drowses,
Lollocks come skipping
Up the tattered stairs
And are nasty together
In the bed's shadow.

The signs of their presence
Are boils on the neck,
Dreams of vexation suddenly recalled
In the middle of the morning,
Languor after food.

Men cannot see them,
Men cannot hear them,
Do not believe in them—
But suffer the more,
Both in neck and belly.

Women can see them—
O those naughty wives
Who sit by the fireside
Munching bread and honey,
Watching them in mischief
From corners of their eyes,
Slily allowing them to lick
Honey-sticky fingers.

Sovereign against Lollocks
Are hard broom and soft broom,
To well comb the hair,
To well brush the shoe,
And to pay every debt
So soon as it's due.

ROBERT GRAVES

London

I wander thro' each charter'd street,
Near where the charter'd Thames does flow,
And mark in every face I meet
Marks of weakness, marks of woe.

In every cry of every Man,
In every Infant's cry of fear,
In every voice, in every ban,
The mind-forg'd manacles I hear.

How the Chimney-sweeper's cry
Every black'ning Church appalls;
And the hapless Soldier's sigh
Runs in blood down Palace walls.

But most thro' midnight streets I hear
How the youthful Harlot's curse
Blasts the new born Infant's tear,
And blights with plagues the Marriage hearse.

WILLIAM BLAKE
From *Songs of Experience*

'Lonely the sea-bird lies at her rest'

Lonely the sea-bird lies at her rest,
Blown like a dawn-blenched parcel of spray
Upon the wind, or follows her prey
Under a great wave's hollowing crest.

God has not appeared to the birds.

The ger-eagle has chosen his part
In blue-deep of the upper air
Where one-eyed day can meet his stare;
He is content with his savage heart.

God has not appeared to the birds.

251

But where have last-year's cygnets gone?
The lake is empty; why do they fling
White wing out beside white wing?
What can a swan need but a swan?

God has not appeared to the birds.

W. B. YEATS
Song for the Cloth: *Calvary*

Long John Brown and Little Mary Bell

Little Mary Bell had a Fairy in a Nut,
Long John Brown had the Devil in his Gut;
Long John Brown lov'd Little Mary Bell,
And the Fairy drew the Devil into the Nut-shell.

Her Fairy Skip'd out and her Fairy Skip'd in;
He laugh'd at the Devil saying 'Love is a Sin.'
The Devil he raged and the Devil he was wroth,
And the Devil enter'd into the Young Man's broth.

He was soon in the Gut of the loving Young Swain,
For John eat and drank to drive away Love's pain;
But all he could do he grew thinner and thinner,
Tho' he eat and drank as much as ten Men for his dinner.

Some said he had a Wolf in his stomach day and night,
Some said he had the Devil and they guess'd right;
The Fairy skip'd about in his Glory, Joy and Pride,
And he laugh'd at the Devil till poor John Brown died.

Then the Fairy skip'd out of the old Nut-shell,
And woe and alack for Pretty Mary Bell!
For the Devil crept in when the Fairy skip'd out,
And there goes Miss Bell with her fusty old Nut.

WILLIAM BLAKE

Lore

Job Davies, eighty-five
Winters old, and still alive
After the slow poison
And treachery of the seasons.

Miserable? Kick my arse!
It needs more than the rain's hearse,
Wind-drawn, to pull me off
The great perch of my laugh.

What's living but courage?
Paunch full of hot porridge,
Nerves strengthened with tea,
Peat-black, dawn found me

Mowing where the grass grew,
Bearded with golden dew.
Rhythm of the long scythe
Kept this tall frame lithe.

What to do? Stay green.
Never mind the machine,
Whose fuel is human souls.
Live large, man, and dream small.

R. S. THOMAS

'Loveliest of trees, the cherry now'

Loveliest of trees, the cherry now
Is hung with bloom along the bough,
And stands about the woodland ride
Wearing white for Eastertide.

Now, of my threescore years and ten,
Twenty will not come again,
And take from seventy springs a score,
It only leaves me fifty more.

And since to look at things in bloom
Fifty springs are little room,
About the woodlands I will go
To see the cherry hung with snow.

A. E. HOUSMAN
From A Shropshire Lad

'The lowest trees have tops,
the ant her gall'

The lowest trees have tops, the ant her gall,
The fly her spleen, the little spark his heat;
The slender hairs cast shadows, though but small,
And bees have stings, although they be not great;
    Seas have their source, and so have shallow springs:
    And love is love, in beggars and in kings.

Where waters smoothest run, there deepest are the fords;
The dial stirs, yet none perceives it move;
The firmest faith is found in fewest words;
The turtles do not sing, and yet they love;
    True hearts have ears and eyes, no tongues to speak:
    They hear and see, and sigh, and then they break.

SIR EDWARD DYER

Macavity: the Mystery Cat

Macavity's a Mystery Cat: he's called the Hidden Paw—
For he's the master criminal who can defy the Law.
He's the bafflement of Scotland Yard, the Flying Squad's
    despair:
For when they reach the scene of crime—*Macavity's not there!*

Macavity, Macavity, there's no one like Macavity,
He's broken every human law, he breaks the law of gravity.
His powers of levitation would make a fakir stare,
And when you reach the scene of crime—*Macavity's not there!*
You may seek him in the basement, you may look up in the
    air—
But I tell you once and once again, *Macavity's not there!*

Macavity's a ginger cat, he's very tall and thin;
You would know him if you saw him, for his eyes are sunken
    in.
His brow is deeply lined with thought, his head is highly
    domed;
His coat is dusty from neglect, his whiskers are uncombed.
He sways his head from side to side, with movements like a
    snake;
And when you think he's half asleep, he's always wide awake.

Macavity, Macavity, there's no one like Macavity,
For he's a fiend in feline shape, a monster of depravity.
You may meet him in a by-street, you may see him in the
    square—
But when a crime's discovered, then *Macavity's not there!*

He's outwardly respectable. (They say he cheats at cards.)
And his footprints are not found in any file of Scotland Yard's.
And when the larder's looted, or the jewel-case is rifled,
Or when the milk is missing, or another Peke's been stifled,
Or the greenhouse glass is broken, and the trellis past repair—
Ay, there's the wonder of the thing! *Macavity's not there!*

And when the Foreign Office find a Treaty's gone astray,
Or the Admiralty lose some plans and drawings by the way,
There may be a scrap of paper in the hall or on the stair—
But it's useless to investigate—*Macavity's not there!*
And when the loss has been disclosed, the Secret Service say:
'It *must* have been Macavity!'—but he's a mile away.
You'll be sure to find him resting, or a-licking of his thumbs,
Or engaged in doing complicated long division sums.

Macavity, Macavity, there's no one like Macavity,
There never was a Cat of such deceitfulness and suavity.
He always has an alibi, and one or two to spare:
At whatever time the deed took place—MACAVITY WASN'T
    THERE!
And they say that all the Cats whose wicked deeds are widely
    known
(I might mention Mungojerrie, I might mention Griddlebone)
Are nothing more than agents for the Cat who all the time
Just controls their operations: the Napoleon of Crime!

                                              T. S. ELIOT

Mad Gardener's Song

He thought he saw an Elephant,
    That practised on a fife:
He looked again, and found it was
    A letter from his wife.
'At length I realize,' he said,
    'The bitterness of Life!'

He thought he saw a Buffalo
    Upon the chimney-piece:
He looked again, and found it was
    His Sister's Husband's Niece.
'Unless you leave this house,' he said,
    'I'll send for the Police!'

He thought he saw a Rattlesnake
   That questioned him in Greek:
He looked again, and found it was
   The Middle of Next Week.
'The one thing I regret,' he said,
   'Is that it cannot speak!'

He thought he saw a Banker's Clerk
   Descending from the bus:
He looked again, and found it was
   A Hippopotamus:
'If this should stay to dine,' he said,
   'There won't be much for us!'

He thought he saw a Kangaroo
   That worked a coffee-mill:
He looked again, and found it was
   A Vegetable-Pill.
'Were I to swallow this,' he said,
   'I should be very ill!'

He thought he saw a Coach-and-Four
   That stood beside his bed:
He looked again, and found it was
   A Bear without a Head.
'Poor thing,' he said, 'poor silly thing!
   'It's waiting to be fed!'

He thought he saw an Albatross
   That fluttered round the lamp:
He looked again, and found it was
   A Penny-Postage-Stamp.
'You'd best be getting home,' he said:
   'The nights are very damp!'

He thought he saw a Garden-Door
   That opened with a key:
He looked again , and found it was
   A Double Rule of Three:
'And all its mystery,' he said,
   'Is clear as day to me!'

He thought he saw an Argument
   That proved he was the Pope:
He looked again, and found it was
   A Bar of Mottled Soap.
'A fact so dread,' he faintly said,
   'Extinguishes all hope!'

LEWIS CARROLL

Mad Tom's Song

From the hag and hungry goblin
   That into rags would rend ye
The spirit that stands by the naked man
   In the book of moons defend ye,
That of your five sound senses
   Ye never be forsaken
Nor wander from yourselves with Tom
   Abroad to beg your bacon.
      While I do sing: 'Any food, any feeding,
      Feeding, drink, or clothing?
      Come dame, or maid, be not afraid,
      Poor Tom will injure nothing.'

Of thirty bare yeares have I
   Twice twenty been enraged,
And of forty been thrice times fifteen
   In durance soundly caged.
On the lordly lofts of bedlam
   With stubble soft and dainty,
Brave bracelets strong, sweet whips ding-dong,
   And wholesome hunger plenty,
      While I do sing etc.

A thought I took for Maudline
   In a cruse of cockle pottage
With a thing thus tall—God bless you all
   I befell into this dotage.

I've slept not since the Conquest,
    Ere then I never waked
Till the roguish fay of love where I lay
    Me found and stripped me naked.
        While I do sing etc.

When I short have shorn my sow's face
    And snigged my hairy barrel
At an oaken inn I pound my skin
    In a suit of gay apparel.
The moon's my constant mistress
    And the lovely owl my marrow
The flaming drake and the night-crow make
    Me music to my sorrow.
        While I do sing etc.

The palsy plague my pulses
    If I prig your pigs or pullen,
Your culvers take, or matchless make
    Your chanticleer or solan!
When I want provant, with Humphry
    I sup and when benighted
I repose in Paul's with walking souls
    And never am affrighted.
        While I do sing etc.

I know more than Apollo
    For oft when he lies sleeping
I see the stars at bloody wars
    And the wounded welkin weeping,
The moon embrace her shepherd,
    And the Queen of Love her warrior,
When the first doth horn the star of the morn
    And the next the heavenly farrier.
        While I do sing etc.

The gypsies Snap and Pedro
    Are none of Tom's camradoes.
The punk I scorn, and cut-purse sworn
    And the roaring-boy's bravadoes.
        259

The meek, the white, the gentle
    Me handle, touch and spare not,
But those that cross Tom Rhinoceros
    Do what the panther dare not.
        While I do sing etc.

With an host of furious fancies
    Whereof I am commander
With a burning spear and a horse of air
    To the wilderness I wander.
By a knight of ghosts and shadows
    I summoned am to tourney
Ten leagues beyond the wide world's end
    Methinks it is no journey.
        While I do sing etc.

I'll bark against the dog-star
    I'll crow away the morning
I'll chase the moon till it be noon
    And make her leave her horning,
But I'll find merry mad Maudline
    And seek whate'er betides her,
And I will love beneath or above
    The dirty earth that hides her.
        While I do sing etc.

ANON
(version by Robert Graves)

'maggie and milly and molly and may'

maggie and milly and molly and may
went down to the beach(to play one day)

and maggie discovered a shell that sang
so sweetly she couldn't remember her troubles,and

milly befriended a stranded star
whose rays five languid fingers were;

and molly was chased by a horrible thing
which raced sideways while blowing bubbles:and

may came home with a smooth round stone
as small as a world and as large as alone.

For whatever we lose(like a you or a me)
it's always ourselves we find in the sea

E. E. CUMMINGS

The Maldive Shark

About the Shark, phlegmatical one,
Pale sot of the Maldive sea,
The sleek little pilot-fish, azure and slim,
How alert in attendance be.
From his saw-pit of mouth, from his charnel of maw
They have nothing of harm to dread,
But liquidly glide on his ghastly flank
Or before his Gorgonian head;
Or lurk in the port of serrated teeth
In white triple tiers of glittering gates,
And there find a haven when peril's abroad,
An asylum in jaws of the Fates!
They are friends; and friendly they guide him to prey
Yet never partake of the treat—
Eyes and brains to the dotard lethargic and dull,
Pale ravener of horrible meat.

HERMAN MELVILLE

Man and Bat

When I went into my room, at mid-morning,
Say ten o'clock . . .
My room, a crash-box over that great stone rattle
The Via de' Bardi . . .

When I went into my room at mid-morning,
Why? . . . a bird!

A bird
Flying round the room in insane circles.

In insane circles!
. . . A bat!

A disgusting bat
At mid-morning! . . .

Out! Go out!

Round and round and round
With a twitchy, nervous, intolerable flight,
And a neurasthenic lunge,
And an impure frenzy;
A bat, big as a swallow.

Out, out of my room!

The venetian shutters I push wide
To the free, calm upper air;
Loop back the curtains . . .

Now out, out from my room!

So to drive him out, flicking with my white handkerchief: *Go!*
But he will not.

262

Round and round and round
In an impure haste,
Fumbling, a beast in air,
And stumbling, lunging and touching the walls, the bell-wires
About my room!

Always refusing to go out into the air
Above that crash-gulf of the Via de' Bardi,
Yet blind with frenzy, with cluttered fear.

At last he swerved into the window bay,
But blew back, as if an incoming wind blew him in again.
A strong inrushing wind.

And round and round and round!
Blundering more insane, and leaping, in throbs, to clutch at a
    corner,
At a wire, at a bell-rope:
On and on, watched relentless by me, round and round in my
    room,
Round and round and dithering with tiredness and haste and
    increasing delirium
Flicker-splashing round my room.

I would not let him rest;
Not one instant cleave, cling like a blot with his breast to the
    wall
In an obscure corner.
Not an instant!
I flicked him on,
Trying to drive him through the window.

Again he swerved into the window bay
And I ran forward, to frighten him forth.
But he rose, and from a terror worse than me he flew past me
Back into my room, and round, round, round in my room
Clutch, cleave, stagger,
Dropping about the air
Getting tired.

Something seemed to blow him back from the window
Every time he swerved at it;
Back on a strange parabola, then round, round, dizzy in my
    room.

He *could* not go out,
I also realized . . .
It was the light of day, which he could not enter,
Any more than I could enter the white-hot door of a blast
    furnace.

He could not plunge into the daylight that streamed at the
    window
It was asking too much of his nature.

Worse even than the hideous terror of me with my handkerchief
Saying: *Out, go out!* . . .
Was the horror of white daylight in the window!

So I switched on the electric light, thinking: *Now*
The outside will seem brown . . .

But no.
The outside did not seem brown,
And he did not mind the yellow electric light.

Silent!
He was having a silent rest.
But never!
Not in my room.

Round and round and round
Near the ceiling as if in a web,
Staggering;
Plunging, falling out of the web,
Broken in heaviness,
Lunging blindly,
Heavier;
And clutching, clutching for one second's pause,
Always, as if for one drop of rest,
One little drop.

And I!
Never, I say ...
Go out!

Flying slower,
Seeming to stumble, to fall in air.
Blind-weary.

Yet never able to pass the whiteness of light into freedom ...
A bird would have dashed through, come what might.

Fall, sink, lurch, and round and round
Flicker, flicker-heavy;
Even wings heavy:
And cleave in a high corner for a second, like a clot, also a
    prayer.

But no.
Out, you beast.

Till he fell in a corner, palpitating, spent.
And there, a clot, he squatted and looked at me.
With sticking-out, bead-berry eyes, black,
And improper derisive ears,
And shut wings,
And brown, furry body.

Brown, nut-brown, fine fur!
But it might as well have been hair on a spider; thing
With long, black-paper ears.

So, a dilemma!
He squatted there like something unclean.

   No, he must not squat, nor hang, obscene, in my room

 Yet nothing on earth will give him courage to pass the sweet
    fire of day.

 What then?
 Hit him and kill him and throw him away?

Nay,
I didn't create him.
Let the God that created him be responsible for his death . . .
Only, in the bright day, I will not have this clot in my room.

Let the God who is maker of bats watch with them in their
 unclean corners . . .
I admit a God in every crevice,
But not bats in my room;
Nor the God of bats, while the sun shines.

So out, out, you brute! . . .
And he lunged, flight-heavy, away from me sideways, *a
 sghembo!*
And round and round and round my room, a clot with wings,
Impure even in weariness.

Wings dark skinny and flapping the air,
Lost their flicker.
Spent.

He fell again with a little thud
Near the curtain on the floor.
And there lay.

Ah death, death
You are no solution!
Bats must be bats.

Only life has a way out.
And the human soul is fated to wide-eyed responsibility
In life.

So I picked him up in a flannel jacket,
Well covered, lest he should bite me.
For I would have had to kill him if he'd bitten me, the impure
 one . . .
And he hardly stirred in my hand, muffled up.
Hastily, I shook him out of the window.

And away he went!
Fear craven in his tail.
Great haste, and straight, almost bird straight above the Via de'
  Bardi.
Above that crash-gulf of exploding whips,
Towards the Borgo San Jacopo.

And now, at evening, as he flickers over the river
Dipping with petty triumphant flight, and tittering over the
  sun's departure,
I believe he chirps, pipistrello, seeing me here on this terrace
  writing:
There he sits, the long loud one!
But I am greater than he . . .
I escaped him . . .

D. H. LAWRENCE

The Man He Killed

'Had he and I but met
    By some old ancient inn,
We should have sat us down to wet
    Right many a nipperkin!

'But ranged as infantry,
    And staring face to face,
I shot at him as he at me,
    And killed him in his place.

'I shot him dead because—
    Because he was my foe,
Just so: my foe of course he was:
    That's clear enough; although

'He thought he'd 'list, perhaps,
    Off-hand like—just as I—
Was out of work—had sold his traps—
    No other reason why.

'Yes; quaint and curious war is!
You shoot a fellow down
You'd treat if met where any bar is,
Or help to half-a-crown.'

THOMAS HARDY

Manners

for a child of 1918

My grandfather said to me
as we sat on the wagon seat,
'Be sure to remember to always
speak to everyone you meet.'

We met a stranger on foot.
My grandfather's whip tapped his hat.
'Good day, sir. Good day. A fine day.'
And I said it and bowed where I sat.

Then we overtook a boy we knew
with his big pet crow on his shoulder.
'Always offer everyone a ride;
don't forget that when you get older,'

my grandfather said. So Willy
climbed up with us, but the crow
gave a 'Caw!' and flew off. I was worried.
How would he know where to go?

But he flew a little way at a time
from fence post to fence post, ahead;
and when Willy whistled he answered.
'A fine bird,' my grandfather said,

'and he's well brought up. See, he answers
nicely when he's spoken to.
Man or beast, that's good manners.
Be sure that you both always do.'

268

When automobiles went by,
the dust hid the people's faces,
but we shouted 'Good day! Good day!
Fine day!' at the top of our voices.

When we came to Hustler Hill,
he said that the mare was tired,
so we all got down and walked,
as our good manners required.

ELIZABETH BISHOP

The Marvel

A baron of the sea, the great tropic
swordfish, spreadeagled on the thirsty deck
where sailors killed him, in the bright Pacific,

yielded to the sharp enquiring blade
the eye which guided him and found his prey
in the dim place where he was lord.

Which is an instrument forged in semi-darkness;
yet taken from the corpse of this strong traveller
becomes a powerful enlarging glass

reflecting the unusual sun's heat.
With it a sailor writes on the hot wood
the name of a harlot in his last port.

For it is one most curious device
of many, kept by the interesting waves,
for I suppose the querulous soft voice

of mariners who rotted into ghosts
digested by the gluttonous tides
could recount many. Let them be your hosts

and take you where their forgotten ships lie
with fishes going over the tall masts—
all this emerges from the burning eye.

And to engrave that word the sun goes through
with the power of the sea
writing her name and a marvel too.

KEITH DOUGLAS

Mary Stuart

My brother Jamie lost me all,
Fell cleverly to make me fall,
And with a sure reluctant hand
Stole my life and took my land.

It was jealousy of the womb
That let me in and shut him out,
Honesty, kingship, all shut out,
While I enjoyed the royal room.

My father was his, but not my mother,
We were, yet were not, sister, brother,
To reach my mother he had to strike
Me down and leap that deadly dyke.

Over the wall I watched him move
At ease through all the guarded grove,
Then hack, and hack, and hack it down,
Until that ruin was his own.

EDWIN MUIR

The Mask of Anarchy

(*Extracts*)

Written on the Occasion of the Massacre at Manchester

I

As I lay asleep in Italy
There came a voice from over the Sea,
And with great power it forth led me
To walk in the visions of Poesy.

II

I met Murder on the way—
He had a mask like Castlereagh—
Very smooth he looked, yet grim;
Seven blood-hounds followed him:

III

All were fat; and well they might
Be in admirable plight,
For one by one, and two by two,
He tossed them human hearts to chew
Which from his wide cloak he drew.

IV

Next came Fraud, and he had on,
Like Eldon, an ermined gown;
His big tears, for he wept well,
Turned to millstones as they fell.

V

And the little children, who
Round his feet played to and fro,
Thinking every tear a gem,
Had their brains knocked out by them.

VI

Clothed with the Bible, as with light,
And the shadows of the night,
Like Sidmouth, next, Hypocrisy
On a crocodile rode by.

VII

And many more Destructions played
In this ghastly masquerade,
All disguised, even to the eyes,
Like Bishops, lawyers, peers, or spies.

VIII

Last came Anarchy: he rode
On a white horse, splashed with blood;
He was pale even to the lips,
Like Death in the Apocalypse.

IX

And he wore a kingly crown;
And in his grasp a sceptre shone;
On his brow this mark I saw—
'I AM GOD, AND KING, AND LAW!'

X

With a pace stately and fast,
Over English land he passed,
Trampling to a mire of blood
The adoring multitude.

XI

And a mighty troop around,
With their trampling shook the ground,
Waving each a bloody sword,
For the service of their Lord.

XII

And with glorious triumph, they
Rode through England proud and gay,
Drunk with intoxication
Of the wine of desolation.

XIII

O'er fields and towns, from sea to sea,
Passed the Pageant swift and free,
Tearing up, and trampling down;
Till they came to London town.

XIV

And each dweller, panic-stricken,
Felt his heart with terror sicken
Hearing the tempestuous cry
Of the triumph of Anarchy.

XV

For with pomp to meet him came,
Clothed in arms like blood and flame,
The hired murderers, who did sing
'Thou art God, and Law, and King.'...

XVII

Lawyers and priests, a motley crowd,
To the earth their pale brows bowed;
Like a bad prayer not over loud,
Whispering—'Thou art Law and God.'—

XIX

And Anarchy, the Skeleton,
Bowed and grinned to every one,
As well as if his education
Had cost ten millions to the nation.

XX

For he knew the Palaces
Of our Kings were rightly his;
His the sceptre, crown, and globe,
And the gold-inwoven robe.

XXI

So he sent his slaves before
To seize upon the Bank and Tower,
And was proceeding with intent
To meet his pensioned Parliament.

XXII

When one fled past, a maniac maid,
And her name was Hope, she said:
But she looked more like Despair,
And she cried out in the air:

XXIII

'My father Time is weak and gray
With waiting for a better day;
See how idiot-like he stands,
Fumbling with his palsied hands!

XXIV

'He has had child after child,
And the dust of death is piled
Over every one but me—
Misery, oh, Misery!'

XXV

Then she lay down in the street,
Right before the horses' feet,
Expecting, with a patient eye,
Murder, Fraud, and Anarchy.

XXVI

When between her and her foes
A mist, a light, an image rose,
Small at first, and weak, and frail
Like the vapour of a vale . . .

XXVIII

It grew—a Shape arrayed in mail
Brighter than the viper's scale,
And upborne on wings whose grain
Was as the light of sunny rain.

XXIX

On its helm, seen far away,
A planet, like the Morning's, lay;
And those plumes its light rained through
Like a shower of crimson dew.

XXX

With step as soft as wind it passed
O'er the heads of men—so fast
That they knew the presence there,
And looked,—but all was empty air.

XXXI

As flowers beneath May's footstep waken,
As stars from Night's loose hair are shaken,
As waves arise when loud winds call,
Thoughts sprung where'er that step did fall.

XXXII

And the prostrate multitude
Looked—and ankle-deep in blood,
Hope, that maiden most serene,
Was walking with a quiet mien:

XXXIII

And Anarchy, the ghastly birth,
Lay dead earth upon the earth;
The Horse of Death tameless as wind
Fled, and with his hoofs did grind
To dust the murderers thronged behind.

XXXIV

A rushing light of clouds and splendour,
A sense awakening and yet tender
Was heard and felt—and at its close
These words of joy and fear arose.

XXXV

As if their own indignant Earth
Which gave the sons of England birth
Had felt their blood upon her brow,
And shuddering with a mother's throe

XXXVI

Had turnèd every drop of blood
By which her face had been bedewed
To an accent unwithstood,—
As if her heart had cried aloud:

XXXVII

'Men of England, heirs of Glory,
Heroes of unwritten story,
Nurslings of one mighty Mother,
Hopes of her, and one another;

XXXVIII

'Rise like Lions after slumber
In unvanquishable number,
Shake your chains to earth like dew
Which in sleep had fallen on you—
Ye are many—they are few.

XXXIX

'What is Freedom?—ye can tell
That which slavery is, too well—
For its very name has grown
To an echo of your own.

XL

''Tis to work and have such pay
As just keeps life from day to day
In your limbs, as in a cell
For the tyrants' use to dwell...

L

'Asses, swine, have litter spread
And with fitting food are fed;
All things have a home but one—
Thou, Oh, Englishman, has none!

LI

'This is Slavery—savage men,
Or wild beasts within a den
Would endure not as ye do—
But such ills they never knew.

LII

'What art thou Freedom? O! could slaves
Answer from their living graves
This demand—tyrants would flee
Like a dream's dim imagery:

LIII

'Thou art not, as impostors say,
A shadow soon to pass away,
A superstition, and a name
Echoing from the cave of Fame.

LIV

'For the labourer thou art bread,
And a comely table spread
From his daily labour come
In a neat and happy home.

277

LV

'Thou art clothes, and fire, and food
For the trampled multitude—
No—in countries that are free
Such starvation cannot be
As in England now we see...

'Let a great Assembly be
Of the fearless and the free
On some spot of English ground
Where the plains stretch wide around...

'From the workhouse and the prison
Where pale as corpses newly risen,
Women, children, young and old
Groan for pain, and weep for cold—

'From the haunts of daily life
Where is waged the daily strife
With common wants and common cares
Which sows the human heart with tares...

'Let a vast assembly be,
And with great solemnity
Declare with measured words that ye
Are, as God has made ye, free—

'Be your strong and simple words
Keen to wound as sharpened swords,
And wide as targes let them be,
With their shade to cover ye.

LXXV

'Let the tyrants pour around
With a quick and startling sound,
Like the loosening of a sea,
Troops of armed emblazonry.

LXXVI

'Let the charged artillery drive
Till the dead air seems alive
With the clash of clanging wheels,
And the tramp of horses' heels.

LXXVII

'Let the fixèd bayonet
Gleam with sharp desire to wet
Its bright point in English blood
Looking keen as one for food . . .

LXXIX

'Stand ye calm and resolute,
Like a forest close and mute,
With folded arms and looks which are
Weapons of unvanquished war . . .

LXXXI

'Let the laws of your own land,
Good or ill, between ye stand
Hand to hand, and foot to foot,
Arbiters of the dispute,

LXXXII

'The old laws of England—they
Whose reverend heads with age are gray,
Children of a wiser day;
And whose solemn voice must be
Thine own echo—Liberty!

LXXXIII

'On those who first should violate
Such sacred heralds in their state
Rest the blood that must ensue,
And it will not rest on you.

LXXXIV

'And if then the tyrants dare
Let them ride among you there,
Slash, and stab, and maim, and hew,—
What they like, that let them do.

LXXXV

'With folded arms and steady eyes,
And little fear, and less surprise,
Look upon them as they slay
Till their rage has died away.

LXXXVI

'Then they will return with shame
To the place from which they came,
And the blood thus shed will speak
In hot blushes on their cheek.

LXXXVII

'Every woman in the land
Will point at them as they stand—
They will hardly dare to greet
Their acquaintance in the street...

LXXXIX

'And that slaughter to the Nation
Shall steam up like inspiration,
Eloquent, oracular;
A volcano heard afar.

XC

'And these words shall then become
Like Oppression's thundered doom
Ringing through each heart and brain,
Heard again—again—again—

XCI

'Rise like Lions after slumber
In unvanquishable number—
Shake your chains to earth like dew
Which in sleep had fallen on you—
Ye are many—they are few.'

PERCY BYSSHE SHELLEY

Masses

When the battle was over,
And the fighter was dead, a man came toward him
And said to him: 'Do not die; I love you so!'
But the corpse, it was sad! went on dying.

And two came near, and told him again and again:
'Do not leave us! Courage! Return to life!'
But the corpse, it was sad! went on dying.

Twenty arrived, a hundred, a thousand, five hundred thousand,
Shouting: 'So much love, and it can do nothing against death!'
But the corpse, it was sad! went on dying.

Millions of persons stood around him,
All speaking the same thing: 'Stay here, brother!'
But the corpse, it was sad! went on dying.

Then all the men on the earth
Stood around him; the corpse looked at them sadly, deeply
    moved;

281

He sat up slowly,
Put his arms around the first man; started to walk . . .

From the Spanish; from *España, Aparta De Me Este Caliz* . . .

(trans. Robert Bly)

The Meadow Mouse

I

In a shoe box stuffed in an old nylon stocking
Sleeps the baby mouse I found in the meadow,
Where he trembled and shook beneath a stick
Till I caught him up by the tail and brought him in,
Cradled in my hand,
A little quaker, the whole body of him trembling,
His absurd whiskers sticking out like a cartoon-mouse,
His feet like small leaves,
Little lizard-feet,
Whitish and spread wide when he tried to struggle away,
Wriggling like a minuscule puppy.

Now he's eaten his three kinds of cheese and drunk from his
    bottle-cap watering-trough—
So much he just lies in one corner,
His tail curled under him, his belly big
As his head, his bat-like ears
Twitching, tilting toward the least sound.

Do I imagine he no longer trembles
When I come close to him?
He seems no longer to tremble.

II

But this morning the shoe-box house on the back porch is
    empty.
Where has he gone, my meadow mouse,
My thumb of a child that nuzzled in my palm?—

To run under the hawk's wing,
Under the eye of the great owl watching from the elm-tree,
To live by courtesy of the shrike, the snake, the tom-cat.

I think of the nestling fallen into the deep grass,
The turtle gasping in the dusty rubble of the highway,
The paralytic stunned in the tub, and the water rising,—
All things innocent, hapless, forsaken.

THEODORE ROETHKE

Meditation on the A30

A man on his own in a car
   Is revenging himself on his wife;
He opens the throttle and bubbles with dottle
   And puffs at his pitiful life.

'She's losing her looks very fast,
   She loses her temper all day;
That lorry won't let me get past,
   This Mini is blocking my way.

'Why can't you step on it and shift her!
   I can't go on crawling like this!
At breakfast she said that she wished I was dead—
   Thank heavens we don't have to kiss.

'I'd like a nice blonde on my knee
   And one who won't argue or nag.
Who dares to come hooting at *me*?
   I only give way to a Jag.

'You're barmy or plastered, I'll pass you, you bastard—
   I *will* overtake you. I *will* !'
  As he clenches his pipe, his moment is ripe
   And the corner's accepting its kill.

SIR JOHN BETJEMAN

283

Memorabilia

Ah, did you once see Shelley plain,
    And did he stop and speak to you
And did you speak to him again?
    How strange it seems and new!

But you were living before that,
    And also you are living after;
And the memory I started at—
    My starting moves your laughter.

I crossed a moor, with a name of its own
    And a certain use in the world no doubt,
Yet a hand's-breadth of it shines alone
    'Mid the blank miles round about:

For there I picked up on the heather
    And there I put inside my breast
A moulted feather, an eagle-feather!
    Well, I forget the rest.

ROBERT BROWNING

Memories of Verdun

The men laughed and baaed like sheep
and marched across the flashing day
to the flashing valley. A shaved
pig in a uniform led the way.

I crawled down Old Confusion, hid,
and groaned for years about my crime:
was I the proper coward, they
heroically wrong? I lived out their time!,

a hard labor, convict by look and word:
I was the fool and am penitent:
I was afraid of a nothing, a death;
they were afraid of less, its lieutenant.

ALAN DUGAN

Memory of My Father

Every old man I see
Reminds me of my father
When he had fallen in love with death
One time when sheaves were gathered.

That man I saw in Gardner Street
Stumble on the kerb was one,
He stared at me half-eyed,
I might have been his son.

And I remember the musician
Faltering over his fiddle
In Bayswater, London,
He too set me the riddle.

Every old man I see
In October-coloured weather
Seems to say to me:
'I was once your father.'

PATRICK KAVANAGH

Merlin

O Merlin in your crystal cave
Deep in the diamond of the day,
Will there ever be a singer
Whose music will smooth away
The furrow drawn by Adam's finger
Across the meadow and the wave?
Or a runner who'll outrun
Man's long shadow driving on,
Break through the gate of memory
And hang the apple on the tree?
Will your magic ever show
The sleeping bride shut in her bower,
The day wreathed in its mound of snow
And Time locked in his tower?

EDWIN MUIR

'Methought that I had broken from the Tower'

—Methought that I had broken from the Tower,
And was embark'd to cross to Burgundy;
And in my company my brother Gloucester,
Who from my cabin tempted me to walk
Upon the hatches: hence we look'd toward England,
And cited up a thousand heavy times,
During the wars of York and Lancaster,
That had befall'n us. As we pac'd along
Upon the giddy footing of the hatches,
Methought that Gloucester stumbled; and, in falling,
Struck me, that thought to stay him, overboard,
Into the tumbling billows of the main.
Lord, Lord! methought what pain it was to drown:
What dreadful noise of water in mine ears!
What sights of ugly death within mine eyes!
Methought I saw a thousand fearful wracks;
A thousand men that fishes gnaw'd upon;
Wedges of gold, great anchors, heaps of pearl,

Inestimable stones, unvalu'd jewels,
All scatter'd in the bottom of the sea.
Some lay in dead men's skulls; and in those holes
Where eyes did once inhabit, there were crept,
As 'twere in scorn of eyes, reflecting gems,
That woo'd the slimy bottom of the deep,
And mock'd the dead bones that lay scatter'd by.
    —Had you such leisure in the time of death.
To gaze upon those secrets of the deep?
    —Methought I had; and often did I strive
To yield the ghost; but still the envious flood
Stopt in my soul, and would not let it forth
To find the empty, vast, and wandering air;
But smother'd it within my panting bulk,
Which almost burst to belch it in the sea.
    —Awak'd you not with this sore agony?
    —No, no, my dream was lengthen'd after life;
O! then began the tempest to my soul.
I pass'd, methought, the melancholy flood,
With that grim ferryman which poets write of,
Unto the kingdom of perpetual night.
The first that there did greet my stranger soul,
Was my great father-in-law, renowned Warwick;
Who cried aloud, 'What scourge for perjury
Can this dark monarchy afford false Clarence?'
And so he vanish'd: then came wandering by
A shadow like an angel, with bright hair
Dabbled in blood; and he shriek'd out aloud,
'Clarence is come,—false, fleeting, perjur'd Clarence,
That stabb'd me in the field by Tewksbury;—
Seize on him! Furies, take him unto torment.'
With that, methought, a legion of foul fiends
Environ'd me, and howled in mine ears
Such hideous cries, that, with the very noise
I trembling wak'd, and, for a season after
Could not believe but that I was in hell,
Such terrible impression made my dream.

WILLIAM SHAKESPEARE
From *Richard III*, Act 1 Scene 4

The Midnightmouse

It midnights, not a moon is out.
No star lives in the heavenhouse.
Runs twelve times through the heavenhouse
    The Midnightmouse.

She pipes upon her little jaws.
The hellhorse from his nightmare roars . . .
Runs quietly, her allotted course,
    The Midnightmouse.

Her Lord, the Spirit great and white,
Has gone abroad on such a night.
She keeps watch in his heaven; all's right.
    The Midnightmouse.

CHRISTIAN MORGENSTERN
From the German (trans. W. D. Snodgrass and Lore Segal)

The Mill-Pond

The sun blazed while the thunder yet
Added a boom:
A wagtail flickered bright over
The mill-pond's gloom:

Less than the cooing in the alder
Isles of the pool
Sounded the thunder through that plunge
Of waters cool.

Scared starlings on the aspen tip
Past the black mill
Outchattered the stream and the next roar
Far on the hill.

As my feet dangling teased the foam
That slid below
A girl came out. 'Take care!' she said—
Ages ago.

She startled me, standing quite close
Dressed all in white:
Ages ago I was angry till
She passed from sight.

Then the storm burst, and as I crouched
To shelter, how
Beautiful and kind, too, she seemed,
As she does now!

EDWARD THOMAS

The Minimal

I study the lives on a leaf: the little
Sleepers, numb nudgers in cold dimensions,
Beetles in caves, newts, stone-deaf fishes,
Lice tethered to long limp subterranean weeds,
Squirmers in bogs,
And bacterial creepers
Wriggling through wounds
Like elvers in ponds,
Their wan mouths kissing the warm sutures,
Cleaning and caressing,
Creeping and healing.

THEODORE ROETHKE

'Mips and ma the mooly moo'

Mips and ma the mooly moo,
The likes of him is biting who,
A cow's a care and who's a coo?—
What footie does is final.

My dearest dear my fairest fair,
Your father tossed a cat in air.
Though neither you nor I was there,—
What footie does is final.

Be large as an owl, be slick as a frog,
Be good as a goose, be big as a dog.
Be sleek as a heifer, be long as a hog,—
What footie will do will be final.

                    THEODORE ROETHKE
          From 'Praise to the End!'

Monkeyland

Oh for far-off monkeyland,
ripe monkeybread on baobabs,
and the wind strums out monkeytunes
from monkeywindow monkeybars.

Monkeyheroes rise and fight
in monkeyfield and monkeysquare,
And monkeysanatoriums
have monkeypatients crying there.

Monkeygirl monkeytaught
masters monkeyalphabet,
evil monkey pounds his thrawn
feet in monkeyprison yet.

Monkeymill is nearly made,
miles of monkeymayonnaise,
winningly unwinnable
winning monkeymind wins praise.

Monkeyking on monkeypole
harangues the crowd in monkeytongue,
monkeyheaven comes to some,
monkeyhell for those undone.

Macaque, gorilla, chimpanzee,
baboon, orangutan, each beast
reads his monkeynewssheet at
the end of each twilight repast.

With monkeysupper memories
the monkeyouthouse rumbles, hums,
monkeyswaddies start to march,
right turn, left turn, shoulder arms—

monkeymilitary fright
reflected in each monkeyface,
with monkeygun in monkeyfist
the monkeys' world the world we face.

SÁNDOR WEÖRES
From the Hungarian (trans. Edwin Morgan)

The Moon and a Cloud

Sometimes I watch the moon at night,
   No matter be she near or far;
Up high, or in a leafy tree
   Caught laughing like a bigger star.

Tonight the west is full of clouds;
     The east is full of stars that fly
Into the cloud's dark foliage,
     And the moon will follow by and by.

I see a dark brown shabby cloud—
     The moon has gone behind its back;
I looked to see her turn it white—
     She turned it to a lovely black.

A lovely cloud, a jet-black cloud;
     It shines with such a glorious light,
That I am glad with all my heart
     She turned it black instead of white.

                              W. H. DAVIES

Moonrise

I awoke in the Midsummer not-to-call night, in the white and
     the walk of the morning:
The moon, dwindled and thinned to the fringe of a fingernail
     held to the candle,
Or paring of paradisaïcal fruit, lovely in waning but lustreless,
Stepped from the stool, drew back from the barrow, of dark
     Maenefa the mountain;
A cusp still clasped him, a fluke yet fanged him, entangled him,
     not quit utterly.
This was the prized, the desirable sight, unsought, presented so
     easily,
Parted me leaf and leaf, divided me, eyelid and eyelid of
     slumber.

                              GERARD MANLEY HOPKINS

'More Light! More Light!'

For Heinrich Blücher and Hannah Arendt

Composed in the Tower before his execution
These moving verses, and being brought at that time
Painfully to the stake, submitted, declaring thus:
'I implore my God to witness that I have made no crime.'

Nor was he forsaken of courage, but the death was horrible,
The sack of gunpowder failing to ignite.
His legs were blistered sticks on which the black sap
Bubbled and burst as he howled for the Kindly Light.

And that was but one, and by no means one of the worst;
Permitted at least his pitiful dignity;
And such as were by made prayers in the name of Christ,
That shall judge all men, for his soul's tranquillity.

We move now to outside a German wood.
Three men are there commanded to dig a hole
In which the two Jews are ordered to lie down
And be buried alive by the third, who is a Pole.

Not light from the shrine at Weimar beyond the hill
Nor light from heaven appeared. But he did refuse.
A Lüger settled back deeply in its glove.
He was ordered to change places with the Jews.

Much casual death had drained away their souls.
The thick dirt mounted toward the quivering chin.
When only the head was exposed the order came
To dig him out again and to get back in.

No light, no light in the blue Polish eye.
When he finished a riding boot packed down the earth.
The Lüger hovered lightly in its glove.
He was shot in the belly and in three hours bled to death.

No prayers or incense rose up in those hours
Which grew to be years, and every day came mute
Ghosts from the ovens, sifting through crisp air,
And settled upon his eyes in a black soot.

ANTHONY HECHT

Mosquito

When did you start your tricks
Monsieur?

What do you stand on such high legs for?
Why this length of shredded shank
You exaltation?

Is it so that you shall lift your centre of gravity upwards
And weigh no more than air as you alight upon me,
Stand upon me weightless, you phantom?

I heard a woman call you the Winged Victory
In sluggish Venice.
You turn your head towards your tail, and smile.

How can you put so much devilry
Into that translucent phantom shred
Of a frail corpus?

Queer, with your thin wings and your streaming legs
How you sail like a heron, on a dull clot of air,
A nothingness.

Yet what an aura surrounds you;
Your evil little aura, prowling, and casting a numbness on my
      mind.

That is your trick, your bit of filthy magic:
Invisibility, and the anaesthetic power
To deaden my attention in your direction.

But I know your game now, streaky sorcerer.

Queer, how you stalk and prowl the air
In circles and evasions, enveloping me,
Ghoul on wings
Winged Victory.

Settle, and stand on long thin shanks
Eyeing me sideways, and cunningly conscious that I am aware,
You speck.

I hate the way you lurch off sideways into air
Having read my thoughts against you.

Come then, let us play at unawares,
And see who wins in this sly game of bluff,
Man or mosquito.

You don't know that I exist, and I don't know that you exist.
Now then!

It is your trump
It is your hateful little trump
You pointed fiend,
Which shakes my sudden blood to hatred of you:
It is your small, high, hateful bugle in my ear.

Why do you do it?
Surely it is bad policy.

They say you can't help it.

If that is so, then I believe a little in Providence protecting the
    innocent.
But it sounds so amazingly like a slogan,
A yell of triumph as you snatch my scalp.

Blood, red blood
Super-magical
Forbidden liquor.

I behold you stand
For a second enspasmed in oblivion,
Obscenely ecstasied
Sucking live blood,
My blood.

Such silence, such suspended transport,
Such gorging,
Such obscenity of trespass.

You stagger
As well as you may.
Only your accursed hairy frailty
Your own imponderable weightlessness
Saves you, wafts you away on the very draught my anger
    makes in its snatching.

Away with a paean of derision
You winged blood-drop.

Can I not overtake you?
Are you one too many for me,
Winged Victory?
Am I not mosquito enough to out-mosquito you?

Queer, what a big stain my sucked blood makes
Beside the infinitesimal faint smear of you!
Queer, what a dim dark smudge you have disappeared into!

D. H. LAWRENCE

The Mosquito Knows

The mosquito knows full well, small as he is
he's a beast of prey.
But after all
he only takes his bellyful,
he doesn't put my blood in the bank.

D. H. LAWRENCE

Mountain Lion

Climbing through the January snow, into the Lobo canyon
Dark grow the spruce-trees, blue is the balsam, water sounds
   still unfrozen, and the trail is still evident.

Men!
Two men!
Men! The only animal in the world to fear!

They hesitate.
We hesitate.
They have a gun.
We have no gun.

Then we all advance, to meet.

Two Mexicans, strangers, emerging out of the dark and snow
   and inwardness of the Lobo valley.
What are they doing here on this vanishing trail?

What is he carrying?
Something yellow.
A deer?

Qué tiene, amigo?
León—

He smiles, foolishly, as if he were caught doing wrong.
And we smile, foolishly, as if we didn't know.
He is quite gentle and dark-faced.

It is a mountain lion,
A long, long slim cat, yellow like a lioness.
Dead.

He trapped her this morning, he says, smiling foolishly.

Lift up her face,
Her round, bright face, bright as frost.
Her round, fine-fashioned head, with two dead ears;
And stripes in the brilliant frost of her face, sharp, fine dark
    rays,
Dark, keen, fine rays in the brilliant frost of her face.
Beautiful dead eyes.

Hermoso es!

They go out towards the open;
We go on into the gloom of Lobo.
And above the trees I found her lair,
A hole in the blood-orange brilliant rocks that stick up, little
    cave.
And bones, and twigs, and a perilous ascent.

So, she will never leap up that way again, with the yellow flash
    of a mountain lion's long shoot!
And her bright striped frost-face will never watch any more,
    out of the shadow of the cave in the blood-orange rock,
Above the trees of the Lobo dark valley-mouth!

Instead, I look out.
And out to the dim of the desert, like a dream, never real,
To the snow of the Sangre de Cristo mountains, the ice of the
    mountains of Picoris,
And near across at the opposite steep of snow, green trees
    motionless standing in snow, like a Christmas toy.

And I think in this empty world there was room for me and a
   mountain lion.
And I think in the world beyond, how easily we might spare a
   million or two of humans
And never miss them.
Yet what a gap in the world, the missing white frost-face of that
   slim yellow mountain lion!

D. H. LAWRENCE

Mouse's Nest

I found a ball of grass among the hay
And progged it as I passed and went away;
And when I looked I fancied something stirred,
And turned agen and hoped to catch the bird—
When out an old mouse bolted in the wheats
With all her young ones hanging at her teats;
She looked so odd and so grotesque to me,
I ran and wondered what the thing could be,
And pushed the knapweed bunches where I stood;
Then the mouse hurried from the craking brood.
The young ones squeaked, and as I went away
She found her nest again among the hay.
The water o'er the pebbles scarce could run
And broad old cesspools glittered in the sun.

JOHN CLARE

Mushrooms

Overnight, very
Whitely, discreetly,
Very quietly

Our toes, our noses
Take hold on the loam,
Acquire the air.

Nobody sees us,
Stops us, betrays us;
The small grains make room.

Soft fists insist on
Heaving the needles,
The leafy bedding,

Even the paving.
Our hammers, our rams,
Earless and eyeless,

Perfectly voiceless,
Widen the crannies,
Shoulder through holes. We

Diet on water,
On crumbs of shadow,
Bland-mannered, asking

Little or nothing.
So many of us!
So many of us!

We are shelves, we are
Tables, we are meek,
We are edible,

Nudgers and shovers
In spite of ourselves.
Our kind multiplies:

We shall by morning
Inherit the earth.
Our foot's in the door.

SYLVIA PLATH

300

My Cat, Jeoffrey

For I will consider my Cat Jeoffrey.

For he is the servant of the Living God, duly and daily serving him.

For at the First glance of the glory of God in the East he worships in his way.

For is this done by wreathing his body seven times round with elegant quickness.

For then he leaps up to catch the musk, which is the blessing of God upon his prayer.

For he rolls upon prank to work it in.

For having done duty and received blessing he begins to consider himself.

For this he performs in ten degrees.

For first he looks upon his fore-paws to see if they are clean.

For secondly he kicks up behind to clear away there.

For thirdly he works it upon stretch with the fore-paws extended.

For fourthly he sharpens his paws by wood.

For fifthly he washes himself.

For sixthly he rolls upon wash.

For Seventhly he fleas himself, that he may not be interrupted upon the beat.

For Eighthly he rubs himself against a post.

For Ninthly he looks up for his instructions.

For Tenthly he goes in quest of food.

For having consider'd God and himself he will consider his neighbour.

For if he meets another cat he will kiss her in kindness.

For when he takes his prey he plays with it to give it a chance.

For one mouse in seven escapes by his dallying.

For when his day's work is done his business more properly begins.

For he keeps the Lord's watch in the night against the adversary.

How he counteracts the powers of darkness by his electrical skin and glaring eyes.

For he counteracts the Devil, who is death, by brisking about the life.

For in his morning orisons he loves the sun and the sun loves him.

For he is of the tribe of Tiger.

For the Cherub Cat is a term of the Angel Tiger.

For he has the subtlety and hissing of a serpent, which in goodness he suppresses.

For he will not do destruction, if he is well fed, neither will he spit without provocation.

For he purrs in thankfulness, when God tells him he's a good Cat.

For he is an instrument for the children to learn benevolence upon.

For every house is incomplete without him and a blessing is lacking in the spirit.

For the Lord commanded Moses concerning the cats at the departure of the Children of Israel from Egypt.

For every family had one cat at least in the bag.

For the English Cats are the best in Europe.

For he is the cleanest in the use of his fore-paws of any quadrupede.

For the dexterity of his defence is an instance of the love of God to him exceedingly.

For he is the quickest to his mark of any creature.

For he is tenacious of his point.

For he is a mixture of gravity and waggery.

For he knows that God is his Saviour.

For there is nothing sweeter than his peace when at rest.

For there is nothing brisker than his life in motion.

For he is of the Lord's poor and so indeed is he called by benevolence perpetually—Poor Jeoffrey! poor Jeoffrey! the rat has bit thy throat.

For I bless the name of the Lord Jesus that Jeoffrey is better.

For the divine spirit comes about his body to sustain it in complete cat.

For his tongue is exceedingly pure so that it has in purity what it wants in music.

For he is docile and can learn certain things.

For he can set up with gravity which is patience upon approbation.

For he can fetch and carry, which is patience in employment.
For he can jump over a stick which is patience upon proof
    positive.
For he can spraggle upon waggle at the word of command.
For he can jump from an eminence into his master's bosom.
For he can catch the cork and toss it again.
For he is hated by the hypocrite and miser.
For the former is affraid of detection.
For the latter refuses the charge.
For he camels his back to bear the first notion of business.
For he is good to think on, if a man would express himself
    neatly.
For he made a great figure in Egypt for his signal services.
For he killed the Ichneumon-rat very pernicious by land.
For his ears are so acute that they sting again.
For from this proceeds the passing quickness of his attention.
For by stroking of him I have found out electricity.
For I perceived God's light upon him both wax and fire.
For the Electrical fire is the spiritual substance, which God sends
    from heaven to sustain the bodies both of man and beast.
For God has blessed him in the variety of his movements.
For, tho he cannot fly, he is an excellent clamberer.
For his motions upon the face of the earth are more than any
    other quadrupede.
For he can tread to all the measures upon the music.
For he can swim for life.
For he can creep.

CHRISTOPHER SMART
From *Jubilate Agno*

'My father played the melodeon'

My father played the melodeon
Outside at our gate;
There were stars in the morning east
And they danced to his music.

303

Across the wild bogs his melodeon called
To Lennons and Callans.
As I pulled on my trousers in a hurry
I knew some strange thing had happened.

Outside in the cow-house my mother
Made the music of milking;
The light of her stable-lamp was a star
And the frost of Bethlehem made it twinkle.

A water-hen screeched in the bog,
Mass-going feet
Crunched the wafer-ice on the pot-holes,
Somebody wistfully twisted the bellows wheel.

My child poet picked out the letters
On the grey stone,
In silver the wonder of a Christmas townland,
The winking glitter of a frosty dawn.

Cassiopeia was over
Cassidy's hanging hill,
I looked and three whin bushes rode across
The horizon—the Three Wise Kings.

An old man passing said:
'Can't he make it talk'—
The melodeon. I hid in the doorway
And tightened the belt of my box-pleated coat.

I nicked six nicks on the door-post
With my penknife's big blade—
There was a little one for cutting tobacco.
And I was six Christmases of age.

My father played the melodeon,
My mother milked the cows,
And I had a prayer like a white rose pinned
On the Virgin Mary's blouse.

From *A Christmas Childhood*

The Names of the Hare

The man the hare has met
will never be the better of it
except he lay down on the land
what he carries in his hand—
be it staff or be it bow—
and bless him with his elbow
and come out with this litany
with devotion and sincerity
to speak the praises of the hare.
Then the man will better fare.

'The hare, call him scotart,
big-fellow, bouchart,
the O'Hare, the jumper,
the rascal, the racer.

Beat-the-pad, white-face,
funk-the-ditch, shit-ass.

The wimount, the messer,
the skidaddler, the nibbler,
the ill-met, the slabber.

The quick-scut, the dew-flirt,
the grass-biter, the goibert,
the home-late, the do-the-dirt.

The starer, the wood-cat,
the purblind, the furze cat,
the skulker, the bleary-eyed,
the wall-eyed, the glance-aside
and also the hedge-springer.

The stubble-stag, the long lugs,
the stook-deer, the frisky legs,
the wild one, the skipper,
the hug-the-ground, the lurker,

305

the race-the-wind, the skiver,
the shag-the-hare, the hedge-squatter,
the dew-hammer, the dew-hopper,
the sit-tight, the grass-bounder,
the jig-foot, the earth-sitter,
the light-foot, the fern-sitter,
the kail-stag, the herb-cropper.

The creep-along, the sitter-still,
the pintail, the ring-the-hill,
the sudden start,
the shake-the-heart,
the belly-white,
the lambs-in-flight.

The gobshite, the gum-sucker,
the scare-the-man, the faith-breaker,
the snuff-the-ground, the baldy skull,
(his chief name is scoundrel.)

The stag sprouting a suede horn,
the creature living in the corn,
the creature bearing all men's scorn,
the creature no one dares to name.'

When you have got all this said
then the hare's strength has been laid.
Then you might go faring forth—
east and west and south and north,
wherever you incline to go—
but only if you're skilful too.
And now, Sir Hare, good-day to you.
God guide you to a how-d'ye-do
with me: come to me dead
in either onion broth or bread.

ANON
From the Middle English (version by Seamus Heaney)

Napoleon

'What is the world, O soldiers?
        It is I:
I, this incessant snow,
    This northern sky;
Soldiers, this solitude
    Through which we go
        Is I.'

WALTER DE LA MARE

'A narrow Fellow in the Grass'

A narrow Fellow in the Grass
Occasionally rides—
You may have met Him—did you not
His notice sudden is—

The Grass divides as with a Comb—
A spotted shaft is seen—
And then it closes at your feet
And opens further on—

He likes a Boggy Acre
A Floor too cool for Corn—
Yet when a Boy, and Barefoot—
I more than once at Noon
Have passed, I thought, a Whip lash
Unbraiding in the Sun
When stooping to secure it
It wrinkled, and was gone—

Several of Nature's People
I know, and they know me—
I feel for them a transport
Of cordiality—

307

But never met this Fellow
Attended, or alone
Without a tighter breathing
And Zero at the Bone—
EMILY DICKINSON

Nature's Lineaments

When mountain rocks and leafy trees
And clouds and things like these,
With edges,

Caricature the human face,
Such scribblings have no grace
Nor peace—

The bulbous nose, the sunken chin,
The ragged mouth in grin
Of cretin.

Nature is always so: you find
That all she has of mind
Is wind,

Retching among the empty spaces,
Ruffling the idiot grasses,
The sheeps' fleeces.

Whose pleasures are excreting, poking,
Havocking and sucking,
Sleepy licking.

Whose griefs are melancholy,
Whose flowers are oafish,
Whose waters, silly,
Whose birds, raffish,
Whose fish, fish.
ROBERT GRAVES

'nobody loses all the time'

nobody loses all the time

i had an uncle named
Sol who was a born failure and
nearly everybody said he should have gone
into vaudeville perhaps because my Uncle Sol could
sing McCann He Was A Diver on Xmas Eve like Hell Itself which
may or may not account for the fact that my Uncle

Sol indulged in that possibly most inexcusable
of all to use a highfalootin phrase
luxuries that is or to
wit farming and be
it needlessly
added

my Uncle Sol's farm
failed because the chickens
ate the vegetables so
my Uncle Sol had a
chicken farm till the
skunks ate the chickens when

my Uncle Sol
had a skunk farm but
the skunks caught cold and
died and so
my Uncle Sol imitated the
skunks in a subtle manner

or by drowning himself in the watertank
but somebody who'd given my Uncle Sol a Victor
Victrola and records while he lived presented to
him upon the auspicious occasion of his decease a
scrumptious not to mention splendiferous funeral with
tall boys in black gloves and flowers and everything and

i remember we all cried like the Missouri
when my Uncle Sol's coffin lurched because
somebody pressed a button
(and down went
my Uncle
Sol

and started a worm farm)

E. E. CUMMINGS

The North Ship

Legend

I saw three ships go sailing by,
Over the sea, the lifting sea,
And the wind rose in the morning sky,
And one was rigged for a long journey.

The first ship turned towards the west,
Over the sea, the running sea,
And by the wind was all possessed
And carried to a rich country.

The second turned towards the east,
Over the sea, the quaking sea,
And the wind hunted it like a beast
To anchor in captivity.

The third ship drove towards the north,
Over the sea, the darkening sea,
But no breath of wind came forth,
And the decks shone frostily.

The northern sky rose high and black
Over the proud unfruitful sea,
East and west the ships came back
Happily or unhappily:

But the third went wide and far
Into an unforgiving sea
Under a fire-spilling star,
And it was rigged for a long journey.

PHILIP LARKIN

The Nose

(after Gogol)

The nose went away by itself
in the early morning
while its owner was asleep.
It walked along the road
sniffing at everything.

It thought: I have a personality of my own.
Why should I be attached to a body?
I haven't been allowed to flower.
So much of me has been wasted.

And it felt wholly free.
It almost began to dance
The world was so full of scents
it had had no time to notice,

when it was attached to a face
weeping, being blown,
catching all sorts of germs
and changing colour.

But now it was quite at ease
bowling merrily along
like a hoop or a wheel,
a factory packed with scent.

And all would have been well
but that, round about evening,
having no eyes for guides,
it staggered into the path
of a mouth, and it was gobbled
rapidly like a sausage
and chewed by great sour teeth—
and that was how it died.

IAN CRICHTON SMITH

'Now entertain conjecture of a time'

Now entertain conjecture of a time
When creeping murmur and the poring dark
Fills the wide vessel of the universe.
From camp to camp, through the foul womb of night,
The hum of either army stilly sounds,
That the fix'd sentinels almost receive
The secret whispers of each other's watch:
Fire answers fire, and through their paly flames
Each battle sees the other's umber'd face:
Steed threatens steed, in high and boastful neighs
Piercing the night's dull ear; and from the tents
The armourers, accomplishing the knights,
With busy hammers closing rivets up,
Give dreadful note of preparation.
The country cocks do crow, the clocks do toll,
And the third hour of drowsy morning name,
Proud of their numbers, and secure in soul,
The confident and over-lusty French
Do the low-rated English play at dice;
And chide the cripple tardy-gaited night
Who, like a foul and ugly witch, doth limp
So tediously away. The poor condemned English,
Like sacrifices, by their watchful fires

Sit patiently, and inly ruminate
The morning's danger, and their gesture sad
Investing lank-lean cheeks and war-worn coats
Presenteth them unto the gazing moon
So many horrid ghosts. O! now, who will behold
The royal captain of this ruin'd band
Walking from watch to watch, from tent to tent,
Let him cry 'Praise and glory on his head!'
For forth he goes and visits all his host,
Bids them good morrow with a modest smile,
And calls them brothers, friends, and countrymen.
Upon his royal face there is no note
How dread an army hath enrounded him;
Nor doth he dedicate one jot of colour
Unto the weary and all-watched night:
But freshly looks and overbears attaint
With cheerful semblance and sweet majesty;
That every wretch, pining and pale before,
Beholding him, plucks comfort from his looks.
A largess universal, like the sun
His liberal eye doth give to every one,
Thawing cold fear. Then mean and gentle all,
Behold, as may unworthiness define,
A little touch of Harry in the night.
And so our scene must to the battle fly;
Where,—O for pity,—we shall much disgrace,
With four or five most vile and ragged foils,
Right ill dispos'd in brawl ridiculous,
The name of Agincourt.

WILLIAM SHAKESPEARE
From *Henry V*, Act 4 Chorus

Nutting

It seems a day,
(I speak of one from many singled out)
One of those heavenly days which cannot die,
When forth I sallied from our cottage-door,
And with a wallet o'er my shoulder slung,
A nutting crook in hand, I turn'd my steps
Towards the distant woods, a Figure quaint,
Trick'd out in proud disguise of Beggar's weeds
Put on for the occasion, by advice
And exhortation of my frugal Dame.
Motley accoutrement! of power to smile
At thorns, and brakes, and brambles, and, in truth,
More ragged than need was. Among the woods,
And o'er the pathless rocks, I forc'd my way
Until, at length, I came to one dear nook
Unvisited, where not a broken bough
Droop'd with its wither'd leaves, ungracious sign
Of devastation, but the hazels rose
Tall and erect, with milk-white clusters hung,
A virgin scene!—A little while I stood,
Breathing with such suppression of the heart
As joy delights in; and with wise restraint
Voluptuous, fearless of a rival, eyed
The banquet, or beneath the trees I sate
Among the flowers, and with the flowers I play'd;
A temper known to those, who, after long
And weary expectation, have been bless'd
With sudden happiness beyond all hope.—
—Perhaps it was a bower beneath whose leaves
The violets of five seasons re-appear
And fade, unseen by any human eye,
Where fairy water-breaks do murmur on
For ever, and I saw the sparkling foam,
And with my cheek on one of those green stones
That, fleec'd with moss, beneath the shady trees,
Lay round me scatter'd like a flock of sheep,
I heard the murmur and the murmuring sound,

In that sweet mood when pleasure loves to pay
Tribute to ease, and, of its joy secure
The heart luxuriates with indifferent things,
Wasting its kindliness on stocks and stones,
And on the vacant air. Then up I rose,
And dragg'd to earth both branch and bough, with crash
And merciless ravage; and the shady nook
Of hazels, and the green and mossy bower
Deform'd and sullied, patiently gave up
Their quiet being: and unless I now
Confound my present feelings with the past,
Even then, when from the bower I turn'd away,
Exulting, rich beyond the wealth of kings
I felt a sense of pain when I beheld
The silent trees and the intruding sky.—

Then, dearest Maiden! move along these shades
In gentleness of heart with gentle hand
Touch,—for there is a Spirit in the woods.

WILLIAM WORDSWORTH

The Octopus

Tell me, O Octopus, I begs,
Is those things arms, or is they legs?
I marvel at thee, Octopus;
If I were thou, I'd call me Us.

OGDEN NASH

Ode to a Nightingale

I

My heart aches, and a drowsy numbness pains
  My sense, as though of hemlock I had drunk,
Or emptied some dull opiate to the drains
  One minute past, and Lethe-wards had sunk.
'Tis not through envy of thy happy lot,
  But being too happy in thine happiness—
    That thou, light-winged Dryad of the trees,
      In some melodious plot
Of beechen green, and shadows numberless,
  Singest of summer in full-throated ease.

II

Oh, for a draught of vintage that hath been
  Cooled a long age in the deep-delvèd earth,
Tasting of Flora and the country green,
  Dance, and Provençal song, and sunburnt mirth!
Oh, for a beaker full of the warm South,
  Full of the true, the blushful Hippocrene,
    With beaded bubbles winking at the brim,
      And purple-stained mouth,
That I might drink, and leave the world unseen,
  And with thee fade away into the forest dim—

III

Fade far away, dissolve, and quite forget
  What thou among the leaves hast never known,
The weariness, the fever, and the fret
  Here, where men sit and hear each other groan;
Where palsy shakes a few, sad, last gray hairs,
  Where youth grows pale, and spectre-thin, and dies;
    Where but to think is to be full of sorrow
      And leaden-eyed despairs;
Where Beauty cannot keep her lustrous eyes,
  Or new Love pine at them beyond to-morrow.

Away! away! For I will fly to thee,
  Not charioted by Bacchus and his pards,
But on the viewless wings of Poesy,
  Though the dull brain perplexes and retards.
Already with thee! Tender is the night,
    And haply the Queen-Moon is on her throne,
      Clustered around by all her starry fays;
        But here there is no light,
    Save what from heaven is with the breezes blown
      Through verdurous glooms and winding mossy ways.

V

I cannot see what flowers are at my feet,
  Nor what soft incense hangs upon the boughs,
But, in embalmèd darkness, guess each sweet
  Wherewith the seasonable month endows
The grass, the thicket, and the fruit-tree wild—
    White hawthorn, and the pastoral eglantine;
      Fast-fading violets covered up in leaves;
        And mid-May's eldest child,
    The coming musk-rose, full of dewy wine,
      The murmurous haunt of flies on summer eves.

VI

Darkling, I listen; and, for many a time
  I have been half in love with easeful Death,
Called him soft names in many a musèd rhyme,
  To take into the air my quiet breath;
Now more than ever seems it rich to die,
    To cease upon the midnight with no pain,
      While thou art pouring forth thy soul abroad
        In such an ecstasy.
    Still wouldst thou sing, and I have ears in vain—
      To thy high requiem become a sod.

VII

Thou wast not born for death, immortal bird!
  No hungry generations tread thee down;

The voice I hear this passing night was heard
    In ancient days by emperor and clown:
Perhaps the self-same song that found a path
        Through the sad heart of Ruth, when, sick for home,
            She stood in tears amid the alien corn;
                The same that oft-times hath
            Charmed magic casements, opening on the foam
                Of perilous seas in fairy lands forlorn.

VIII

Forlorn! The very word is like a bell
    To toll me back from thee to my sole self!
Adieu! The fancy cannot cheat so well
    As she is famed to do, deceiving elf.
Adieu! adieu! Thy plaintive anthem fades
    Past the near meadows, over the still stream,
        Up the hill-side; and now 'tis buried deep
            In the next valley-glades:
        Was it a vision, or a waking dream?
            Fled is that music . . . Do I wake or sleep?

JOHN KEATS

Of Poor B.B.

I

I, Bertolt Brecht, came out of the black forests.
My mother moved me into the cities as I lay
Inside her body. And the coldness of the forests
Will be inside me till my dying day.

II

In the asphalt city I'm at home. From the very start
Provided with every last sacrament:
With newspapers. And tobacco. And brandy.
To the end mistrustful, lazy and content.

III

I'm polite and friendly to people. I put on
A hard hat because that's what they do.
I say: they are animals with a quite peculiar smell
And I say: does it matter? I am too.

IV

Before noon on my empty rocking chairs
I'll sit a woman or two, and with an untroubled eye
Look at them steadily and say to them:
Here you have someone on whom you can't rely.

V

Towards evening it's men that I gather round me
And then we address one another as 'gentlemen'.
They're resting their feet on my table tops
And say: things will get better for us. And I don't ask when.

VI

In the grey light before morning the pine trees piss
And their vermin, the birds, raise their twitter and cheep.
At that hour in the city I drain my glass, then throw
The cigar butt away and worriedly go to sleep.

VII

We have sat, an easy generation
In houses held to be indestructible
(Thus we built those tall boxes on the island of Manhattan
And those thin aerials that amuse the Atlantic swell).

VIII

Of those cities will remain what passed through them, the
    wind!
The house makes glad the eater: he clears it out.
We know that we're only tenants, provisional ones
And after us there will come: nothing worth talking about.

319

In the earthquakes to come, I very much hope
I shall keep my cigar alight, embittered or no
I, Bertolt Brecht, carried off to the asphalt cities
From the black forests inside my mother long ago.

BERTOLT BRECHT

From the German (trans. Michael Hamburger)

The Old Familiar Faces

I have had playmates, I have had companions
In my days of childhood, in my joyful schooldays;
   All, all are gone, the old familiar faces.

I have been laughing, I have been carousing,
Drinking late, sitting late, with my bosom cronies;
   All, all are gone, the old familiar faces.

I loved a love once, fairest among women:
Closed are her doors on me, I must not see her—
   All, all are gone, the old familiar faces.

I have a friend, a kinder friend has no man:
Like an ingrate, I left my friend abruptly;
   Left him, to muse on the old familiar faces.

Ghost-like I paced round the haunts of my childhood,
Earth seem'd a desert I was bound to traverse,
   Seeking to find the old familiar faces.

Friend of my bosom, thou more than a brother,
Why wert not thou born in my father's dwelling?
   So might we talk of the old familiar faces.

How some they have died, and some they have left me,
And some are taken from me; all are departed;
   All, all are gone, the old familiar faces.

CHARLES LAMB

'An old man stirs the fire to a blaze'

'An old man stirs the fire to a blaze,
In the house of a child, of a friend, of a brother.
He has over-lingered his welcome; the days,
Grown desolate, whisper and sigh to each other;
He hears the storm in the chimney above,
And bends to the fire and shakes with the cold,
While his heart still dreams of battle and love,
And the cry of the hounds on the hills of old.

'But we are apart in the grassy places,
Where care cannot trouble the least of our days,
Or the softness of youth be gone from our faces,
Or love's first tenderness die in our gaze.
The hare grows old as she plays in the sun
And gazes around her with eyes of brightness;
Before the swift things that she dreamed of were done
She limps along in an aged whiteness;
A storm of birds in the Asian trees
Like tulips in the air a-winging,
And the gentle waves of the summer seas,
That raise their heads and wander singing,
Must murmur at last, "Unjust, unjust";
And "My speed is a weariness," falters the mouse,
And the kingfisher turns to a ball of dust,
And the roof falls in of his tunnelled house.
But the love-dew dims our eyes till the day
When God shall come from the sea with a sigh
And bid the stars drop down from the sky,
And the moon like a pale rose wither away.'

W. B. YEATS
From *The Wanderings of Oisin*

Old Men

People expect old men to die,
They do not really mourn old men.
Old men are different. People look
At them with eyes that wonder when . . .
People watch with unshocked eyes;
But the old men know when an old man dies.

OGDEN NASH

Omens

Early on the morning of Monday,
I heard the bleating of a lamb,

And the kid-like cry of snipe,
While gently sitting bent,

And the grey-blue cuckoo,
And no food on my stomach.

On the fair evening of Tuesday,
I saw on the smooth stone,
The snail slimy, pale,

And the ashy wheatear
On the top of the dyke of holes,

The foal of the old mare
Of sprauchly gait and its back to me.

And I knew from these
That the year would not go well with me.

ANON
From the Gaelic (trans. A. Carmichael)

On a Tree Fallen Across the Road

(To Hear Us Talk)

The tree the tempest with a crash of wood
Throws down in front of us is not to bar
Our passage to our journey's end for good,
But just to ask us who we think we are

Insisting always on our own way so.
She likes to halt us in our runner tracks,
And make us get down in a foot of snow
Debating what to do without an axe.

And yet she knows obstruction is in vain:
We will not be put off the final goal
We have it hidden in us to attain,
Not though we have to seize earth by the pole

And, tired of aimless circling in one place,
Steer straight off after something into space.

ROBERT FROST

On Buying a Horse

One white foot, try him;
Two white feet, buy him;
Three white feet, put him in the dray;
Four white feet, give him away;
Four white feet, and a white nose,
Take off his hide and feed him to the crows.

ANON

On My First Sonne

Farewell, thou child of my right hand, and joy;
My sinne was too much hope of thee, lov'd boy,
Seven yeeres tho'wert lent to me, and I thee pay,
Exacted by thy fate, on the just day.
O, could I loose all father, now. For why
Will man lament the state he should envie?
To have so soone scap'd worlds, and fleshes rage,
And, if no other miserie, yet age?
Rest in soft peace, and, ask'd, say here doth lye
Ben. Jonson his best piece of poetrie.
For whose sake, hence-forth, all his bowes be such,
As what he loves may never like too much.

BEN JONSON

On the Beach at Fontana

Wind whines and whines the shingle,
The crazy pierstakes groan;
A senile sea numbers each single
Slimesilvered stone.

From whining wind and colder
Grey sea I wrap him warm
And touch his trembling fineboned shoulder
And boyish arm.

Around us fear, descending
Darkness of fear above
And in my heart how deep unending
Ache of love!

JAMES JOYCE

324

On the Cards and Dice

Before the sixth day of the next new year,
Strange wonders in this kingdom shall appear.
Four kings shall be assembled in this isle,
Where they shall keep great tumult for a while.
Many men then shall have an end of crosses,
And many likewise shall sustain great losses.
Many that now full joyful are and glad,
Shall at that time be sorrowful and sad.
Full many a Christian's heart shall quake for fear,
The dreadful sound of trump when he shall hear.
Dead bones shall then be tumbled up and down,
In every city and in every town.
By day or night this tumult shall not cease,
Until an herald shall proclaim a peace,
An herald strange, the like was never born
Whose very beard is flesh, and mouth is horn.

SIR WALTER RALEGH

On the Congo

Our ship, the Sea Smithy, swerved out of the tradewinds
and began to creep up the Congo River.
Vines trailed along the deck like ropes.
We met the famous iron barges of the Congo,
whose hot steeldecks swarmed with negroes from the
    tributaries.

They put their hands to their mouths
and shouted, 'Go to hell' in a Bantu language.
We slid marveling and depressed through the tunnels of
    vegetation
and cook in his galley thought:
'now I am peeling potatoes in the middle of the Congo.'

At night the Sea Smithy
goggled with its red eyes into the jungle,
an animal roared, a jungle rat plopped into the water,
a millet mortar coughed sharply,
and a drum was beating softly in a village somewhere where the
    rubber negroes were going on with their slave lives.

HARRY EDMUND MARTINSON
From the Swedish (trans. Robert Bly)

On Wenlock Edge

On Wenlock Edge the wood's in trouble;
His forest fleece the Wrekin heaves;
The gale, it plies the saplings double,
And thick on Severn snow the leaves.

'Twould blow like this through hold and hangar
When Uricon the city stood:
'Tis the old wind in the old anger,
But then it threshed another wood.

Then, 'twas before my time, the Roman
At yonder, heaving hill would stare:
The blood that warms an English yeoman,
The thoughts that hurt him, they were there.

There, like the wind through woods in riot,
Through him the gale of life blew high;
The tree of man was never quiet:
Then 'twas the Roman, now 'tis I.

The gale; it plies the saplings double,
It blows so hard, 'twill soon be gone:
Today the Roman and his trouble
Are ashes under Uricon.

A. E. HOUSMAN

'One Christmas-time'

One Christmas-time,

The day before the holidays began,
Feverish and tired, and restless, I went forth
Into the fields, impatient for the sight
Of those two horses which should bear us home;
My brothers and myself. There was a crag,
An eminence, which from the meeting-point
Of two highways ascending, overlook'd
At least a long half-mile of those two roads,
By each of which the expected steeds might come,
The choice uncertain. Thither I repair'd
Up to the highest summit; 'twas a day
Stormy, and rough, and wild, and on the grass
I sat, half-sheltered by a naked wall;
Upon my right hand was a single sheep,
A whistling hawthorn on my left, and there,
With those companions at my side, I watch'd,
Straining my eyes intensely, as the mist
Gave intermitting prospect of the wood
And plain beneath. Ere I to school return'd
That dreary time, ere I had been ten days
A dweller in my father's house, he died,
And I and my two brothers, orphans then,
Followed his body to the grave. The event
With all the sorrow which it brought appeared
A chastisement; and when I called to mind
That day so lately pass'd, when from the crag
I look'd in such anxiety of hope,
With trite reflections of morality,
Yet in the deepest passion, I bow'd low
To God, who thus corrected my desires;
And afterwards, the wind and sleety rain
And all the business of the elements,
The single sheep and the one blasted tree,
And the bleak music of that old stone wall,
The noise of wood and water, and the mist
Which on the line of each of those two roads

Advanced in such indisputable shapes,
All these were spectacles and sounds to which
I often would repair and thence would drink,
As at a fountain; and I do not doubt
That in this later time, when storm and rain
Beat on my roof at midnight, or by day
When I am in the woods, unknown to me
The workings of my spirit thence are brought.

WILLIAM WORDSWORTH
From *The Prelude*, Book XI

'Our revels now are ended'

Our revels now are ended. These our actors,
As I foretold you, were all spirits and
Are melted into air, into thin air:
And, like the baseless fabric of this vision,
The cloud-capp'd towers, the gorgeous palaces,
The solemn temples, the great globe itself,
Yea, all which it inherit, shall dissolve
And, like this insubstantial pageant faded,
Leave not a rack behind. We are such stuff
As dreams are made on, and our little life
Is rounded with a sleep.

WILLIAM SHAKESPEARE
From *The Tempest*, Act 4 Scene 1

Out in the Dark

Out in the dark over the snow
The fallow fawns invisible go
With the fallow doe;
And the winds blow
Fast as the stars are slow.

Stealthily the dark haunts round
And, when the lamp goes, without sound
At a swifter bound
Than the swiftest hound,
Arrives, and all else is drowned;

And star and I and wind and deer
Are in the dark together, —near,
Yet far, —and fear
Drums on my ear
In that sage company drear.

How weak and little is the light,
All the universe of sight,
Love and delight,
Before the might,
If you love it not, of night.

EDWARD THOMAS

'Out, Out —'

The buzz saw snarled and rattled in the yard
And made dust and dropped stove-length sticks of wood,
Sweet-scented stuff when the breeze drew across it.
And from there those that lifted eyes could count
Five mountain ranges one behind the other
Under the sunset far into Vermont.
And the saw snarled and rattled, snarled and rattled,

329

As it ran light, or had to bear a load.
And nothing happened; day was all but done.
Call it a day, I wish they might have said
To please the boy by giving him the half hour
That a boy counts so much when saved from work.
His sister stood beside them in her apron
To tell them 'Supper'. At the word, the saw,
As if to prove saws knew what supper meant,
Leaped out at the boy's hand, or seemed to leap—
He must have given the hand. However it was,
Neither refused the meeting. But the hand!
The boy's first outcry was a rueful laugh,
As he swung toward them holding up the hand
Half in appeal, but half as if to keep
The life from spilling. Then the boy saw all—
Since he was old enough to know, big boy
Doing a man's work, though a child at heart—
He saw all spoiled. 'Don't let him cut my hand off—
The doctor, when he comes. Don't let him, sister!'
So. But the hand was gone already.
The doctor put him in the dark of ether.
He lay and puffed his lips out with his breath.
And then—the watcher at his pulse took fright.
No one believed. They listened at his heart.
Little—less—nothing!—and that ended it.
No more to build on there. And they, since they
Were not the one dead, turned to their affairs.

ROBERT FROST

The Owl

Downhill I came, hungry, and yet not starved;
Cold, yet had heat within me that was proof
Against the North wind; tired, yet so that rest
Had seemed the sweetest thing under a roof.

330

Then at the inn I had food, fire, and rest,
Knowing how hungry, cold, and tired was I.
All of the night was quite barred out except
An owl's cry, a most melancholy cry

Shaken out long and clear upon the hill,
No merry note, nor cause of merriment,
But one telling me plain what I escaped
And others could not, that night, as in I went.

And salted was my food, and my repose,
Salted and sobered, too, by the bird's voice
Speaking for all who lay under the stars,
Soldiers and poor, unable to rejoice.

EDWARD THOMAS

The Oxen

Christmas Eve, and twelve of the clock.
   'Now they are all on their knees,'
An elder said as we sat in a flock
   By the embers in hearthside ease.

We pictured the meek mild creatures where
   They dwelt in their strawy pen,
Nor did it occur to one of us there
   To doubt they were kneeling then.

So fair a fancy few would weave
   In these years! Yet, I feel,
If someone said on Christmas Eve,
   'Come; see the oxen kneel

'In the lonely barton by yonder coomb
   Our childhood used to know,'
I should go with him in the gloom,
   Hoping it might be so.

THOMAS HARDY

The Ox-Tamer

In a far-away northern county in the placid pastoral region,
Lives my farmer friend, the theme of my recitative, a famous
  tamer of oxen,
There they bring him the three-year-olds and the four-year-olds
  to break them,
He will take the wildest steer in the world and break him and
  tame him,
He will go fearless without any whip where the young bullock
  chafes up and down the yard,
The bullock's head tosses restless high in the air with raging
  eyes,
Yet see you! how soon his rage subsides—how soon this tamer
  tames him;
See you! on the farms hereabouts a hundred oxen young and
  old, and he is the man who has tamed them,
They all know him, all are affectionate to him;
See you! some are such beautiful animals, so lofty looking;
Some are buff-color'd, some mottled, one has a white line
  running along his back, some are brindled,
Some have wide flaring horns (a good sign)—see you! the
  bright hides,
See, the two with stars on their foreheads—see, the round
  bodies and broad backs,
How straight and square they stand on their legs—what fine
  sagacious eyes!
How they watch their tamer—they wish him near them—how
  they turn to look after him!
What yearning expression! how uneasy they are when he moves
  away from them;
Now I marvel what it can be he appears to them, (books,
  politics, poems, depart—all else departs,)
I confess I envy only his fascination—my silent, illiterate friend,
Whom a hundred oxen love there in his life on farms,
In the northern county far, in the placid pastoral region.

WALT WHITMAN

Ozymandias

I met a traveller from an antique land
Who said: Two vast and trunkless legs of stone
Stand in the desert. Near them on the sand,
Half sunk, a shatter'd visage lies, whose frown
And wrinkled lip and sneer of cold command
Tell that its sculptor well those passions read
Which yet survive, stamp'd on these lifeless things,
The hand that mock'd them and the heart that fed;
And on the pedestal these words appear:
'My name is Ozymandias, king of kings:
Look on my works, ye Mighty, and despair!'
Nothing beside remains. Round the decay
Of that colossal wreck, boundless and bare,
The lone and level sands stretch far away.

PERCY BYSSHE SHELLEY

Pangur Bán

*Written by a student of the monastery of Carinthia on a copy of
St Paul's Epistles, in the eighth century*

I and Pangur Bán, my cat,
'Tis a like task we are at;
Hunting mice is his delight,
Hunting words I sit all night.

Better far than praise of men
'Tis to sit with book and pen;
Pangur bears me no ill-will,
He too plies his simple skill.

'Tis a merry thing to see
At our tasks how glad are we,
When at home we sit and find
Entertainment to our mind.

Oftentimes a mouse will stray
In the hero Pangur's way;
Oftentimes my keen thought set
Takes a meaning in its net.

'Gainst the wall he sets his eye
Full and fierce and sharp and sly;
'Gainst the wall of knowledge I
All my little wisdom try.

When a mouse darts from its den,
O how glad is Pangur then!
O what gladness do I prove
When I solve the doubts I love!

So in peace our tasks we ply,
Pangur Bán, my cat, and I;
In our arts we find our bliss,
I have mine and he has his.

Practice every day has made
Pangur perfect in his trade;
I get wisdom day and night
Turning darkness into light.

ANON
From the Gaelic (trans. Robin Flower)

The Passionate Man's Pilgrimage

Give me my scallop-shell of quiet,
My staff of faith to walk upon,
My scrip of joy, immortal diet,
My bottle of salvatión,
My gown of glory, hope's true gage:
And thus I'll take my pilgrimage.

Blood must be my body's balmer;
No other balm will there be given,
Whilst my soul, like a white palmer,
Travels to the land of heaven,
Over the silver mountains
Where spring the nectar fountains.
And there I'll kiss
The bowl of bliss,
And drink my eternal fill
On every milken hill.
My soul will be a-dry before,
But after it will ne'er thirst more.

And by the happy blissful way
More peaceful pilgrims I shall see
That have shook off their gowns of clay
And go apparelled fresh like me.
I'll bring them first
To slake their thirst
And then to taste those nectar suckets
At the clear wells
Where sweetness dwells,
Drawn up by saints in crystal buckets.

And when our bottles and all we
Are filled with immortality,
Then the holy paths we'll travel,
Strewed with rubies thick as gravel;
Ceilings of diamonds, sapphire floors,
High walls of coral and pearly bowers.

From thence to heaven's bribeless hall,
Where no corrupted voices brawl,
·No conscience molten into gold,
No forged accusers bought and sold,
No cause deferred, no vain-spent journey—
For there Christ is the King's Attorney,
Who pleads for all without degrees,
And He hath angels, but no fees.

When the grand twelve million jury
Of our sins and sinful fury
'Gainst our souls black verdicts give,
Christ pleads His death, and then we live.
Be Thou my speaker, taintless pleader,
Unblotted lawyer, true proceeder!
Thou movest salvation even for alms,
Not with a bribèd lawyer's palms.

And this is my eternal plea
To Him that made heaven, earth, and sea:
Seeing my flesh must die so soon
And want a head to dine next noon,
Just at the stroke, when my veins start and spread,
Set on my soul an everlasting head!
Then am I ready, like a palmer fit,
To tread those blest paths which before I writ.

SIR WALTER RALEGH

The Passionate Shepherd to His Love

Come live with me and be my Love,
And we will all the pleasures prove
That valleys, groves, hills, and fields,
Woods, or steepy mountains yields.

And we will sit upon the rocks
Seeing the shepherds feed their flocks,
By shallow rivers, to whose falls
Melodious birds sing madrigals.

And I will make thee beds of roses
And a thousand fragrant posies,
A cap of flowers, and a kirtle
Embroidered all with leaves of myrtle;

A gown made of the finest wool,
Which from our pretty lambs we pull;
Fair linëd slippers for the cold,
With buckles of the purest gold;

A belt of straw and ivy buds
With coral clasps and amber studs;
And if these pleasures may thee move,
Come live with me and be my Love.

The shepherd swains shall dance and sing
For thy delight each May morning:
If these delights thy mind may move,
Then live with me and be my Love.

                                    CHRISTOPHER MARLOWE

The Nymph's Reply to the Shepherd

If all the world and love were young,
And truth in every shepherd's tongue,
These pretty pleasures might me move
To live with thee and be thy Love.

Time drives the flocks from field to fold,
When rivers rage and rocks grow cold;
And Philomel becometh dumb;
The rest complains of cares to come.

The flowers do fade, and wanton fields
To wayward winter reckoning yields:
A honey tongue, a heart of gall,
Is fancy's spring, but sorrow's fall.

Thy gowns, thy shoes, thy beds of roses,
Thy cap, thy kirtle, and thy posies
Soon break, soon wither, soon forgotten,
In folly ripe, in reason rotten.

Thy belt of straw and ivy buds,
Thy coral clasps and amber studs,
All these in me no means can move
To come to thee and be thy Love.

But could youth last, and love still breed,
Had joys no date, nor age no need,
Then these delights my mind might move
To live with thee and be thy Love.

SIR WALTER RALEGH

The Baite

Come live with mee, and bee my love,
And we will some new pleasures prove
Of golden sands, and christall brookes,
With silken lines, and silver hookes.

There will the river whispering runne
Warm'd by thy eyes, more then the Sunne.
And there th' inamor'd fish will stay,
Begging themselves they may betray.

When thou wilt swimme in that live bath,
Each fish, which every channell hath,
Will amorously to thee swimme,
Gladder to catch thee, then thou him.

If thou, to be so seene, beest loath,
By Sunne, or Moone, thou darknest both,
And if my selfe have leave to see,
I need not their light, having thee.

Let others freeze with angling reeds,
And cut their legges, with shells and weeds,
Or treacherously poore fish beset,
With strangling snare, or windowie net:

Let coarse bold hands, from slimy nest
The bedded fish in banks out-wrest,
Or curious traitors, sleavesilke flies
Bewitch poore fishes wandring eyes.

For thee, thou needst no such deceit,
For thou thy selfe art thine owne bait;
That fish, that is not catch'd thereby,
Alas, is wiser farre then I.

JOHN DONNE

Pat Cloherty's Version of The Maisie

I've no tooth to sing you the song
   Tierney made at the time
      but I'll tell the truth

It happened on St John's Day
   sixty-eight years ago
      last June the twenty-fourth

The Maisie sailed from Westport Quay
   homeward on a Sunday
      missing Mass to catch the tide

John Kerrigan sat at her helm
   Michael Barrett stood at her mast
      and Kerrigan's wife lay down below

The men were two stepbrothers
   drownings in the family
      and all through the family

Barrett kept a shop in the island
   Kerrigan plied the hooker
      now deeply laden with flour

339

She passed Clare and she came to Cahir
   two reefs tied in the mainsail
      she bore a foresail but no jib

South-east wind with strong ebb-tide
   still she rode this way that way
      hugging it hugging it O my dear

And it blew and blew hard and blew hard
   but Kerrigan kept her to it
      as long as he was there he kept her to it

Rain fell in a cloudburst
   hailstones hit her deck
      there was no return for him once he'd put out

At Inishturk when the people saw
   The Maisie smothered up in darkness
      they lit candles in the church

What more could Kerrigan do?
   he put her jaw into the hurricane
      and the sea claimed him

Barrett was not a sailor
   to take a man from the water
      the sea claimed him too

At noon the storm ceased
   and we heard *The Maisie*'d foundered
      high upon a Mayo strand

The woman came from the forecastle
   she came up alone on deck
      and a great heave cast her out on shore

And another heave came while she drowned
   and put her on her knees
      like a person'd be in prayer

340

That's the way the people found her
and the sea never came in
near that mark no more

John Kerrigan was found
far down at Achill Sound
he's buried there

Michael Barrett was taken
off Murrisk Pier
he's buried there

Kerrigan's wife was brought from Cross
home to Inishbofin
and she's buried there

RICHARD MURPHY

'Pensive, on her dead gazing, I heard the Mother of All'

Pensive, on her dead gazing, I heard the Mother of All,
Desperate, on the torn bodies, on the forms covering the
    battle-fields gazing;
(As the last gun ceased—but the scent of the powder-smoke
    linger'd;)
As she call'd to her earth with mournful voice while she stalk'd:
Absorb them well, O my earth, she cried—I charge you, lose
    not my sons! lose not an atom;
And you streams, absorb them well, taking their dear blood;
And you local spots, and you airs that swim above lightly,
And all you essences of soil and growth—and you, my rivers'
    depths;
And you, mountain sides—and the woods where my dear
    children's blood, trickling, redden'd;
And you trees, down in your roots, to bequeath to all future
    trees,

341

My dead absorb—my young men's beautiful bodies
    absorb—and their precious, precious, precious blood;
Which holding in trust for me, faithfully back again give me
    many a year hence,
In unseen essence and odor of surface and grass, centuries hence;
In blowing airs from the fields, back again give me my
    darlings—give my immortal heroes;
Exhale me them centuries hence—breathe me their breath—let
    not an atom be lost;
O years and graves! O air and soil! O my dead, an aroma sweet!
Exhale them perennial, sweet death, years, centuries hence.

WALT WHITMAN

Perfect

On the Western Seaboard of South Uist

Los muertos abren los ojos a los que viven

I found a pigeon's skull on the machair,
All the bones pure white and dry, and chalky,
But perfect,
Without a crack or a flaw anywhere.

At the back, rising out of the beak,
Were domes like bubbles of thin bone,
Almost transparent, where the brain had been
That fixed the tilt of the wings.

HUGH MACDIARMID

With the exception of the first line, the words of 'Perfect' were taken
from 'Porth-y-Rhyd', a short story in a collection by Glyn Jones entitled
The Blue Bed, published by Jonathan Cape in 1937.

Pheasant

You said you would kill it this morning.
Do not kill it. It startles me still,
The jut of that odd, dark head, pacing

342

Through the uncut grass on the elm's hill.
It is something to own a pheasant,
Or just to be visited at all.

I am not mystical: it isn't
As if I thought it had a spirit.
It is simply in its element.

That gives it a kingliness, a right.
The print of its big foot last winter,
The tail-track, on the snow in our court—

The wonder of it, in that pallor,
Through crosshatch of sparrow and starling.
Is it its rareness, then? It is rare.

But a dozen would be worth having,
A hundred, on that hill—green and red,
Crossing and recrossing: a fine thing!

It is such a good shape, so vivid.
It's a little cornucopia.
It unclaps, brown as a leaf, and loud,

Settles in the elm, and is easy.
It was sunning in the narcissi.
I trespass stupidly. Let be, let be.

SYLVIA PLATH

Piano

Softly, in the dusk, a woman is singing to me;
Taking me back down the vista of years, till I see
A child sitting under the piano, in the boom of the tingling
    strings
And pressing the small, poised feet of a mother who smiles as
    she sings.

In spite of myself, the insidious mastery of song
Betrays me back, till the heart of me weeps to belong
To the old Sunday evenings at home, with winter outside
And hymns in the cosy parlour, the tinkling piano our guide.

So now it is vain for the singer to burst into clamour
With the great black piano appassionato. The glamour
Of childish days is upon me, my manhood is cast
Down in the flood of remembrance, I weep like a child for the
    past.

D. H. LAWRENCE

Pied Beauty

Glory be to God for dappled things—
    For skies of couple-colour as a brinded cow;
        For rose-moles all in stipple upon trout that swim;
Fresh-firecoal chestnut-falls; finches' wings;
    Landscape plotted and pieced—fold, fallow, and plough;
        And áll trádes, their gear and tackle and trim.

All things counter, original, spare, strange;
    Whatever is fickle, freckled (who knows how?)
        With swift, slow; sweet, sour; adazzle, dim;
He fathers-forth whose beauty is past change:
                    Praise him.

GERARD MANLEY HOPKINS

The Pig

The pig, if I am not mistaken,
Supplies us sausage, ham, and bacon.
Let others say his heart is big—
I call it stupid of the pig.

OGDEN NASH

The Pilgrim

I fasted for some forty days on bread and buttermilk,
For passing round the bottle with girls in rags or silk,
In country shawl or Paris cloak, had put my wits astray,
And what's the good of women, for all that they can say
Is fol de rol de rolly O.

Round Lough Derg's holy island I went upon the stones,
I prayed at all the Stations upon my marrow-bones,
And there I found an old man, and though I prayed all day
And that old man beside me, nothing would he say
But fol de rol de rolly O.

All know that all the dead in the world about that place are
    stuck,
And that should mother seek her son she'd have but little luck
Because the fires of Purgatory have ate their shapes away;
I swear to God I questioned them, and all they had to say
Was fol de rol de rolly O.

A great black ragged bird appeared when I was in the boat;
Some twenty feet from tip to tip had it stretched rightly out,
With flopping and with flapping it made a great display,
But I never stopped to question, what could the boatman say
But fol de rol de rolly O.

Now I am in the public-house and lean upon the wall,
So come in rags or come in silk, in cloak or country shawl,
And come with learned lovers or with what men you may,
For I can put the whole lot down, and all I have to say
Is fol de rol de rolly O.

W. B. YEATS

Ploughing on Sunday

The white cock's tail
Tosses in the wind.
The turkey-cock's tail
Glitters in the sun.

Water in the fields.
The wind pours down.
The feathers flare
And bluster in the wind.

Remus, blow your horn!
I'm ploughing on Sunday,
Ploughing North America.
Blow your horn!

Tum-ti-tum,
Ti-tum-tum-tum!
The turkey-cock's tail
Spreads to the sun.

The white cock's tail
Streams to the moon.
Water in the fields.
The wind pours down.

WALLACE STEVENS

Poem in October

It was my thirtieth year to heaven
Woke to my hearing from harbour and neighbour wood
And the mussel pooled and the heron
Priested shore
The morning beckon
With water praying and call of seagull and rook
And the knock of sailing boats on the net webbed wall
Myself to set foot
That second
In the still sleeping town and set forth.

My birthday began with the water-
Birds and the birds of the winged trees flying my name
Above the farms and the white horses
And I rose
In rainy autumn
And walked abroad in a shower of all my days.
High tide and the heron dived when I took the road
Over the border
And the gates
Of the town closed as the town awoke.

A springful of larks in a rolling
Cloud and the roadside bushes brimming with whistling
Blackbirds and the sun of October
Summery
On the hill's shoulder,
Here were fond climates and sweet singers suddenly
Come in the morning where I wandered and listened
To the rain wringing
Wind blow cold
In the wood faraway under me.

Pale rain over the dwindling harbour
And over the sea wet church the size of a snail
With its horns through mist and the castle
Brown as owls

But all the gardens
Of spring and summer were blooming in the tall tales
Beyond the border and under the lark full cloud.
There could I marvel
My birthday
Away but the weather turned around.

It turned away from the blithe country
And down the other air and the blue altered sky
Streamed again a wonder of summer
With apples
Pears and red currants
And I saw in the turning so clearly a child's
Forgotten mornings when he walked with his mother
Through the parables
Of sun light
And the legends of the green chapels

And the twice told fields of infancy
That his tears burned my cheeks and his heart moved in mine.
These were the woods the river and sea
Where a boy
In the listening
Summertime of the dead whispered the truth of his joy
To the trees and the stones and the fish in the tide.
And the mystery
Sang alive
Still in the water and singingbirds.

And there could I marvel my birthday
Away but the weather turned around. And the true
Joy of the long dead child sang burning
In the sun.
It was my thirtieth
Year to heaven stood there then in the summer noon
Though the town below lay leaved with October blood.
O may my heart's truth
Still be sung
On this high hill in a year's turning.

DYLAN THOMAS

A Poison Tree

I was angry with my friend:
I told my wrath, my wrath did end.
I was angry with my foe:
I told it not, my wrath did grow.

And I water'd it in fears,
Night and morning with my tears;
And I sunned it with smiles,
And with soft deceitful wiles.

And it grew both day and night,
Till it bore an apple bright;
And my foe beheld it shine,
And he knew that it was mine,

And into my garden stole
When the night had veil'd the pole:
In the morning glad I see
My foe outstretch'd beneath the tree.

WILLIAM BLAKE
From *Songs of Experience*

Poor but Honest

She was poor, but she was honest,
  Victim of the squire's whim:
First he loved her, then he left her,
  And she lost her honest name.

Then she ran away to London,
  For to hide her grief and shame,
There she met another squire,
  And she lost her name again.

See her riding in her carriage,
    In the Park and all so gay:
All the nibs and nobby persons
    Come to pass the time of day.

See the little old-world village
    Where her aged parents live,
Drinking the champagne she sends them;
    But they never can forgive.

In the rich man's arms she flutters,
    Like a bird with broken wing:
First he loved her, then he left her,
    And she hasn't got a ring.

See him in the splendid mansion,
    Entertaining with the best,
While the girl that he has ruined,
    Entertains a sordid guest.

See him in the House of Commons,
    Making laws to put down crime,
While the victim of his passions
    Trails her way through mud and slime.

Standing on the bridge at midnight,
    She says: 'Farewell, blighted Love.'
There's a scream, a splash—Good Heavens!
    What is she a-doing of?

Then they drag her from the river,
    Water from her clothes they wrang,
For they thought that she was drownded;
    But the corpse got up and sang:

'It's the same the whole world over;
    It's the poor that gets the blame,
It's the rich that get the pleasure.
    Isn't it a blooming shame?'

                                    ANON

350

Poppies in July

Little poppies, little hell flames,
Do you do no harm?

You flicker. I cannot touch you.
I put my hands among the flames. Nothing burns.

And it exhausts me to watch you
Flickering like that, wrinkly and clear red, like the skin of a
    mouth.

A mouth just bloodied.
Little bloody skirts!

There are fumes that I cannot touch.
Where are your opiates, your nauseous capsules?

If I could bleed, or sleep!—
If my mouth could marry a hurt like that!

Or your liquors seep to me, in this glass capsule,
Dulling and stilling.

But colorless. Colorless.

SYLVIA PLATH

Praise of a Collie

She was a small dog, neat and fluid—
Even her conversation was tiny:
She greeted you with *bow*, never *bow-wow*.

Her sons stood monumentally over her
But did what she told them. Each grew grizzled
Till it seemed he was his own mother's grandfather.

Once, gathering sheep on a showery day,
I remarked how dry she was. Pollóchan said, 'Ah,
It would take a very accurate drop to hit Lassie.'

And her tact—and tactics! When the sheep bolted
In an unforeseen direction, over the skyline
Came—who but Lassie, and not even panting.

She sailed in the dinghy like a proper sea–dog.
Where's a burn?—she's first on the other side.
She flowed through fences like a piece of black wind.

But suddenly she was old and sick and crippled . . .
I grieved for Pollóchan when he took her a stroll
And put his gun to the back of her head.

NORMAN MACCAIG

The Properties of a Good Greyhound

A greyhound should be headed like a Snake,
And necked like a Drake,
Footed like a Cat,
Tailed like a Rat,
Sidèd like a Team,
Chined like a Beam.

The first year he must learn to feed,
The second year to field him lead,
The third year he is fellow-like,
The fourth year there is none sike,
The fifth year he is good enough,
The sixth year he shall hold the plough,
The seventh year he will avail
Great bitches for to assail,
The eighth year lick ladle,

The ninth year cart saddle,
And when he is comen to that year
Have him to the tanner,
For the best hound that ever bitch had
At nine year he is full bad.

DAME JULIANA BERNERS

Raleigh Was Right

We cannot go to the country
for the country will bring us no peace
What can the small violets tell us
that grow on furry stems in
the long grass among lance shaped leaves?

Though you praise us
and call to mind the poets
who sung of our loveliness
it was long ago!
long ago! when country people
would plow and sow with
flowering minds and pockets at ease—
if ever this were true.

Not now. Love itself a flower
with roots in a parched ground.
Empty pockets make empty heads.
Cure it if you can but
do not believe that we can live
today in the country
for the country will bring us no peace.

WILLIAM CARLOS WILLIAMS

Range-Finding

The battle rent a cobweb diamond-strung
And cut a flower beside a ground bird's nest
Before it stained a single human breast.
The stricken flower bent double and so hung.
And still the bird revisited her young.
A butterfly its fall had dispossessed
A moment sought in air his flower of rest,
Then lightly stooped to it and fluttering clung.

On the bare upland pasture there had spread
O'ernight 'twixt mullein stalks a wheel of thread
And straining cables wet with silver dew.
A sudden passing bullet shook it dry.
The indwelling spider ran to greet the fly,
But finding nothing, sullenly withdrew.

ROBERT FROST

The Rattle Bag

As I lay, fullness of praise,
On a summer day under
Trees between field and mountain
Awaiting my soft-voiced girl,
She came, there's no denying,
Where she vowed, a very moon.
Together we sat, fine theme,
The girl and I, debating,
Trading, while I had the right,
Words with the splendid maiden.

And so we were, she was shy,
Learning to love each other,
Concealing sin, winning mead,
An hour lying together,

And then, cold comfort, it came,
A blare, a bloody nuisance,
A sack's bottom's foul seething
From an imp in shepherd's shape,
Who had, public enemy,
A harsh-horned sag-cheeked rattle.
He played, cramped yellow belly,
This bag, curse its scabby leg.
So before satisfaction
The sweet girl panicked: poor me!
When she heard, feeble-hearted,
The stones whir, she would not stay.

By Christ, no Christian country,
Cold harsh tune, has heard the like.
Noisy pouch perched on a pole,
Bell of pebbles and gravel,
Saxon rocks making music
Quaking in a bullock's skin,
Crib of three thousand beetles,
Commotion's cauldron, black bag,
Field-keeper, comrade of straw,
Black-skinned, pregnant with splinters,
Noise that's an old buck's loathing,
Devil's bell, stake in its crotch,
Scarred pebble-bearing belly,
May it be sliced into thongs.
May the churl be struck frigid,
Amen, who scared off my girl.

DAFYDD AP GWILYM
From the Welsh (trans. Joseph Clancy)

Reflection on Ingenuity

Here's a good rule of thumb:
Too clever is dumb.

OGDEN NASH

'Repeat that, repeat'

Repeat that, repeat,
Cuckoo, bird, and open ear wells, heart-springs, delightfully
    sweet,
With a ballad, with a ballad, a rebound
Off trundled timber and scoops of the hillside ground, hollow
    hollow hollow ground:
The whole landscape flushes on a sudden at a sound.

GERARD MANLEY HOPKINS
Fragment 146

The Return

See, they return; ah, see the tentative
    Movements, and the slow feet,
    The trouble in the pace and the uncertain
Wavering!

See, they return, one, and by one,
With fear, as half-awakened;
As if the snow should hesitate
And murmur in the wind,
        and half turn back;
These were the 'Wing'd-with-Awe',
    Inviolable.

356

Gods of the wingèd shoe!
With them the silver hounds,
                sniffing the trace of air!

Haie! Haie!
        These were the swift to harry;
These the keen-scented;
These were the souls of blood.

Slow on the leash,
                pallid the leash-men!

EZRA POUND

The River-Merchant's Wife: A Letter

While my hair was still cut straight across my forehead
I played about the front gate, pulling flowers.
You came by on bamboo stilts, playing horse,
You walked about my seat, playing with blue plums.
And we went on living in the village of Chokan:
Two small people, without dislike or suspicion.

At fourteen I married My Lord you.
I never laughed, being bashful.
Lowering my head, I looked at the wall.
Called to, a thousand times, I never looked back.

At fifteen I stopped scowling,
I desired my dust to be mingled with yours
Forever and forever and forever.
Why should I climb the look out?

At sixteen you departed,
You went into far Ku-to-en, by the river of swirling eddies,
And you have been gone five months.
The monkeys make sorrowful noise overhead.

357

You dragged your feet when you went out.
By the gate now, the moss is grown, the different mosses,
Too deep to clear them away!
The leaves fall early this autumn, in wind.
The paired butterflies are already yellow with August
Over the grass in the West garden;
They hurt me. I grow older.
If you are coming down through the narrows of the river
    Kiang,
Please let me know beforehand,
And I will come out to meet you
                As far as Cho-fu-Sa.

                                        EZRA POUND

'Running lightly over spongy ground'

Running lightly over spongy ground,
Past the pasture of flat stones,
The three elms,
The sheep strewn on a field,
Over a rickety bridge
Toward the quick-water, wrinkling and rippling.

Hunting along the river,
Down among the rubbish, the bug-riddled foliage,
By the muddy pond-edge, by the bog-holes,
By the shrunken lake, hunting, in the heat of summer.

The shape of a rat?
    It's bigger than that.
    It's less than a leg
    And more than a nose,
    Just under the water
    It usually goes.

Is it soft like a mouse?
Can it wrinkle its nose?
Could it come in the house
On the tips of its toes?

Take the skin of a cat
And the back of an eel,
Then roll them in grease,—
That's the way it would feel.

It's sleek as an otter
With wide webby toes
Just under the water
It usually goes.

THEODORE ROETHKE

The Sad Boy

Ay, his mother was a mad one
And his father was a bad one:
The two begot this sad one.

Alas for the single boot
The Sad Boy pulled out of the rank green pond,
Fishing for happiness
On the gloomy advice
Of a professional lover of small boys.

Pity the lucky Sad Boy
With but a single happy boot
And an extra foot
With no boot for it.

This was how the terrible hopping began
That wore the Sad Boy down
To a single foot
And started the great fright in the province
Where the Sad Boy became half of himself.

Wherever he went thumping and hopping,
Pounding a whole earth into a half-heaven,
Things split all around
Into a left side for the left magic,
Into no side for the missing right boot.

Mercy be to the Sad Boy,
Mercy be to the melancholy folk
On the Sad Boy's right.

It was not for clumsiness
He lost the left boot
And the knowledge of his left side,
But because one awful Sunday
This dear boy dislimbed
Went back to the old pond
To fish up the other boot
And was quickly (being too light for his line)
Fished in.

Gracious how he kicks now—
And the almost-ripples show
Where the Sad Boy went in
And his mad mother
And his bad father after him.

LAURA RIDING

The Saginaw Song

In Saginaw, in Saginaw,
    The wind blows up your feet,
When the ladies' guild puts on a feed,
    There's beans on every plate,
And if you eat more than you should,
    Destruction is complete.

Out Hemlock Way there is a stream
  That some have called Swan Creek;
The turtles have bloodsucker sores,
  And mossy filthy feet;
The bottoms of migrating ducks
  Come off it much less neat.

In Saginaw, in Saginaw,
  Bartenders think no ill;
But they've ways of indicating when
  You are not acting well:
They throw you through the front plate glass
  And then send you the bill.

The Morleys and the Burrows are
  The aristocracy;
A likely thing for they're no worse
  Than the likes of you or me,—
A picture window's one you can't
  Raise up when you would pee.

In Shaginaw, in Shaginaw
  I went to Shunday Shule;
The only thing I ever learned
  Was called the Golden Rhule,—
But that's enough for any man
  What's not a proper fool.

I took the pledge cards on my bike;
  I helped out with the books;
The stingy members when they signed
  Made with their stingy looks,—
The largest contributions came
  From the town's biggest crooks.

In Saginaw, in Saginaw,
  There's never a household fart,
For if it did occur,
  It would blow the place apart,—
I met a woman who could break wind
  And she is my sweet-heart.

O, I'm the genius of the world,—
    Of that you can be sure,
But alas, alack, and me achin' back,
    I'm often a drunken boor;
But when I die—and that won't be soon—
    I'll sing with dear Tom Moore,
    With that lovely man, Tom Moore.

Coda:
    My father never used a stick,
        He slapped me with his hand;
    He was a Prussian through and through
        And knew how to command;
    I ran behind him every day
        He walked our greenhouse land.

    I saw a figure in a cloud,
        A child upon her breast,
    And it was O, my mother O,
        And she was half-undressed,
    All women, O, are beautiful
        When they are half-undressed.

THEODORE ROETHKE

Saint Francis and the Sow

The bud
stands for all things,
even for those things that don't flower,
for everything flowers, from within, of self-blessing;
though sometimes it is necessary
to reteach a thing its loveliness,
to put a hand on its brow
of the flower

and retell it in words and in touch
it is lovely
until it flowers again from within, of self-blessing;
as Saint Francis
put his hand on the creased forehead
of the sow, and told her in words and in touch
blessings of earth on the sow, and the sow
began remembering all down her thick length,
from the earthen snout all the way
through the fodder and slops to the spiritual curl of the tail,
from the hard spininess spiked out from the spine
down through the great broken heart
to the blue milken dreaminess spurting and shuddering
from the fourteen teats into the fourteen mouths sucking and
    blowing beneath them:
the long, perfect loveliness of sow.

GALWAY KINNELL

Sandpiper

The roaring alongside he takes for granted,
and that every so often the world is bound to shake.
He runs, he runs to the south, finical, awkward,
in a state of controlled panic, a student of Blake.

The beach hisses like fat. On his left, a sheet
of interrupting water comes and goes
and glazes over his dark and brittle feet.
He runs, he runs straight through it, watching his toes.

—Watching, rather, the spaces of sand between them,
where (no detail too small) the Atlantic drains
rapidly backwards and downwards. As he runs,
he stares at the dragging grains.

363

The world is a mist. And then the world is
minute and vast and clear. The tide
is higher or lower. He couldn't tell you which.
His beak is focused; he is preoccupied,

looking for something, something, something.
Poor bird, he is obsessed!
The millions of grains are black, white, tan, and gray,
mixed with quartz grains, rose and amethyst.

ELIZABETH BISHOP

The Scholar

Summer delights the scholar
With knowledge and reason.
Who is happy in hedgerow
Or meadow as he is?

Paying no dues to the parish,
He argues in logic
And has no care of cattle
But a satchel and stick.

The showery airs grow softer,
He profits from his ploughland
For the share of the schoolmen
Is a pen in hand.

When midday hides the reaping,
He sleeps by a river
Or comes to the stone plain
Where the saints live.

But in winter by the big fires,
The ignorant hear his fiddle,
And he battles on the chessboard,
As the land lords bid him.

AUSTIN CLARKE

Scotland Small?

Scotland small? Our multiform, our infinite Scotland *small?*
Only as a patch of hillside may be a cliché corner
To a fool who cries 'Nothing but heather!' Where in September
   another
Sitting there and resting and gazing round
Sees not only heather but blaeberries
With bright green leaves and leaves already turned scarlet,
Hiding ripe blue berries; and amongst the sage-green leaves
Of the bog-myrtle the golden flowers of the tormentil shining;
And on the small bare places, where the little Blackface sheep
Found grazing, milkworts blue as summer skies;
And down in neglected peat-hags, not worked
In living memory, sphagnum moss in pastel shades
Of yellow, green, and pink; sundew and butterwort
And nodding harebells vying in their colour
With the blue butterflies that poise themselves delicately upon
   them,
And stunted rowans with harsh dry leaves of glorious colour
'Nothing but heather!'—How marvellously descriptive! And
   incomplete!

HUGH MACDIARMID

Sea-Change

'Goneys an' gullies an' all o' the birds o' the sea
   They ain't no birds, not really,' said Billy the Dane.
'Not mollies, nor gullies, nor goneys at all,' said he,
   'But simply the sperrits of mariners livin' again.

'Them birds goin' fishin' is nothin' but souls o' the drowned,
   Souls o' the drowned an' the kicked as are never no more
An' that there haughty old albatross cruisin' around,
   Belike he's Admiral Nelson or Admiral Noah.

365

'An' merry 's the life they are living. They settle and dip,
   They fishes, they never stands watches, they waggle their
      wings;
When a ship comes by, they fly to look at the ship
   To see how the nowaday mariners manages things.

'When freezing aloft in a snorter, I tell you I wish—
   (Though maybe it ain't like a Christian)—I wish I could be
A haughty old copper-bound albatross dipping for fish
   And coming the proud over all o' the birds o' the sea.'

JOHN MASEFIELD

A Sea-Chantey

Là, tout n'est qu'ordre et beauté,
Luxe, calme, et volupté.

Anguilla, Adina,
Antigua, Cannelles,
Andreuille, all the l's,
Voyelles, of the liquid Antilles,
The names tremble like needles
Of anchored frigates,
Yachts tranquil as lilies,
In ports of calm coral,
The lithe, ebony hulls
Of strait-stitching schooners,
The needles of their masts
That thread archipelagoes
Refracted embroidery
In feverish waters
Of the sea-farer's islands,
Their shorn, leaning palms,
Shaft of Odysseus,
Cyclopic volcanoes,
Creak their own histories,

366

In the peace of green anchorage;
Flight, and Phyllis,
Returned from the Grenadines,
Names entered this sabbath,
In the port-clerk's register;
Their baptismal names,
The sea's liquid letters,
Repos donnez a cils . . .
And their blazing cargoes
Of charcoal and oranges;
Quiet, the fury of their ropes.
Daybreak is breaking
On the green chrome water,
The white herons of yachts
Are at sabbath communion,
The histories of schooners
Are murmured in coral,
Their cargoes of sponges
On sandspits of islets
Barques white as white salt
Of acrid Saint Maarten,
Hulls crusted with barnacles,
Holds foul with great turtles,
Whose ship-boys have seen
The blue heave of Leviathan,
A sea-faring, Christian,
And intrepid people.

Now an apprentice washes his cheeks
With salt water and sunlight.

In the middle of the harbour
A fish breaks the Sabbath
With a silvery leap.
The scales fall from him
In a tinkle of church-bells;
The town streets are orange
With the week-ripened sunlight,
Balanced on the bowsprit

A young sailor is playing
His grandfather's chantey
On a trembling mouth-organ.
The music curls, dwindling
Like smoke from blue galleys,
To dissolve near the mountains.
The music uncurls with
The soft vowels of inlets,
The christening of vessels,
The titles of portages,
The colours of sea-grapes,
The tartness of sea-almonds,
The alphabet of church-bells,
The peace of white horses,
The pastures of ports,
The litany of islands,
The rosary of archipelagoes,
Anguilla, Antigua,
Virgin of Guadeloupe,
And stone-white Grenada
Of sunlight and pigeons,
The amen of calm waters,
The amen of calm waters,
The amen of calm waters.

DEREK WALCOTT

The Seafarer

May I, for my own self, song's truth reckon,
Journey's jargon, how I in harsh days
Hardship endured oft.
Bitter breast-cares have I abided,
Known on my keel many a care's hold,
And dire sea-surge, and there I oft spent
Narrow nightwatch nigh the ship's head

While she tossed close to cliffs. Coldly afflicted,
My feet were by frost benumbed.
Chill its chains are; chafing sighs
Hew my heart round and hunger begot
Mere-weary mood. Lest man know not
That he on dry land loveliest liveth,
List how I, care-wretched, on ice-cold sea,
Weathered the winter, wretched outcast
Deprived of my kinsmen;
Hung with hard ice-flakes, where hail-scur flew,
There I heard naught save the harsh sea
And ice-cold wave, at whiles the swan cries,
Did for my games, the gannet's clamour,
Sea-fowls' loudness was for me laughter,
The mews' singing all my mead-drink.
Storms, on the stone-cliffs beaten, fell on the stern
In icy feathers; full oft the eagle screamed
With spray on his pinion.
                              Not any protector
May make merry man faring needy.
This he little believes, who aye in winsome life
Abides 'mid burghers some heavy business,
Wealthy and wine-flushed, how I weary oft
Must bide above brine.
Neareth nightshade, snoweth from north,
Frost froze the land, hail fell on earth then,
Corn of the coldest. Nathless there knocketh now
The heart's thought that I on high streams
The salt-wavy tumult traverse alone.
Moaneth alway my mind's lust
That I fare forth, that I afar hence
Seek out a foreign fastness.
For this there's no mood-lofty man over earth's midst,
Not though he be given his good, but will have in his youth
      greed;
Nor his deed to the daring, nor his king to the faithful
But shall have his sorrow for sea-fare
Whatever his lord will.
He hath not heart for harping, nor in ring-having

369

Nor winsomeness to wife, nor world's delight
Nor any whit else save the wave's slash,
Yet longing comes upon him to fare forth on the water.
Bosque taketh blossom, cometh beauty of berries,
Fields to fairness, land fares brisker,
All this admonisheth man eager of mood,
The heart turns to travel so that he then thinks
On flood-ways to be far departing.
Cuckoo calleth with gloomy crying,
He singeth summerward, bodeth sorrow,
The bitter heart's blood. Burgher knows not—
He the prosperous man—what some perform
Where wandering them widest draweth.
So that but now my heart burst from my breastlock,
My mood 'mid the mere-flood,
Over the whale's acre, would wander wide.
On earth's shelter cometh oft to me,
Eager and ready, the crying lone-flyer,
Whets for the whale-path the heart irresistibly,
O'er tracks of ocean; seeing that anyhow
My lord deems to me this dead life
On loan and on land, I believe not
That any earth-weal eternal standeth
Save there be somewhat calamitous
That, ere a man's tide go, turn it to twain.
Disease or oldness or sword-hate
Beats out the breath from doom-gripped body.
And for this, every earl whatever, for those speaking after—
Laud of the living, boasteth some last word,
That he will work ere he pass onward,
Frame on the fair earth 'gainst foes his malice,
Daring ado, . . .
So that all men shall honour him after
And his laud beyond them remain 'mid the English,
Aye, for ever, a lasting life's-blast,
Delight 'mid the doughty.
                                    Days little durable,
And all arrogance of earthen riches,
There come now no kings nor Caesars

Nor gold-giving lords like those gone.
Howe'er in mirth most magnified,
Whoe'er lived in life most lordliest,
Drear all this excellence, delights undurable!
Waneth the watch, but the world holdeth.
Tomb hideth trouble. The blade is layed low.
Earthly glory ageth and seareth.
No man at all going the earth's gait,
But age fares against him, his face paleth,
Grey-haired he groaneth, knows gone companions,
Lordly men, are to earth o'ergiven,
Nor may he then the flesh-cover, whose life ceaseth,
Nor eat the sweet nor feel the sorry,
Nor stir hand nor think in mid heart,
And though he strew the grave with gold,
His born brothers, their buried bodies
Be an unlikely treasure hoard.

ANON
From the Anglo-Saxon (version by Ezra Pound)

Sea-Hawk

The six-foot nest of the sea-hawk,
Almost inaccessible,
Surveys from the headland the lonely, the violent waters.

I have driven him off,
Somewhat foolhardily,
And look into the fierce eye of the offspring.

It is an eye of fire,
An eye of icy crystal,
A threat of ancient purity,

Power of an immense reserve,
An agate-well of purpose,
Life before man, and maybe after.

How many centuries of sight
In this piercing, inhuman perfection
Stretch the gaze off the rocky promontory,

To make the mind exult
At the eye of a sea-hawk,
A blaze of grandeur, permanence of the impersonal.

RICHARD EBERHART

Season Song

Here's a song—
stags give tongue
winter snows
summer goes.

High cold blow
sun is low
brief his day
seas give spray.

Fern clumps redden
shapes are hidden
wildgeese raise
wonted cries.

Cold now girds
wings of birds
icy time—
that's my rime.

ANON
From the Irish (version by Flann O'Brien)

Sea-Weed

Sea-weed sways and sways and swirls
as if swaying were its form of stillness;
and if it flushes against fierce rock
it slips over it as shadows do, without hurting itself.

D. H. LAWRENCE

Self-Pity

I never saw a wild thing
sorry for itself.
A small bird will drop frozen dead from a bough
without ever having felt sorry for itself.

D. H. LAWRENCE

The Self-Unseeing

Here is the ancient floor,
Footworn and hollowed and thin,
Here was the former door
Where the dead feet walked in.

She sat here in her chair,
Smiling into the fire;
He who played stood there,
Bowing it higher and higher.

Childlike, I danced in a dream;
Blessings emblazoned that day;
Everything glowed with a gleam;
Yet we were looking away!

THOMAS HARDY

The Send-Off

Down the close, darkening lanes they sang their way
To the siding-shed,
And lined the train with faces grimly gay.

Their breasts were stuck all white with wreath and spray
As men's are, dead.

Dull porters watched them, and a casual tramp
Stood staring hard,
Sorry to miss them from the upland camp.
Then, unmoved, signals nodded, and a lamp
Winked to the guard.

So secretly, like wrongs hushed-up, they went.
They were not ours:
We never heard to which front these were sent.

Nor there if they yet mock what women meant
Who gave them flowers.

Shall they return to beatings of great bells
In wild train-loads?
A few, a few, too few for drums and yells,
May creep back, silent, to village wells
Up half-known roads.

WILFRED OWEN

Senex

Oh would I could subdue the flesh
    Which sadly troubles me!
And then perhaps could view the flesh
As though I never knew the flesh
    And merry misery.

374

To see the golden hiking girl
   With wind about her hair,
The tennis-playing, biking girl,
The wholly-to-my-liking girl,
   To see and not to care.

At sundown on my tricycle
   I tour the Borough's edge,
And icy as an icicle
See bicycle by bicycle
   Stacked waiting in the hedge.

Get down from me! I thunder there,
   You spaniels! Shut your jaws!
Your teeth are stuffed with underwear,
Suspenders torn asunder there
   And buttocks in your paws!

Oh whip the dogs away my Lord,
   They make me ill with lust.
Bend bare knees down to pray, my Lord,
Teach sulky lips to say, my Lord,
   That flaxen hair is dust.

SIR JOHN BETJEMAN

The Seven

They are 7 in number, just 7
In the terrible depths they are 7
Bow down, in the sky they are 7

In the terrible depths, the dark houses
They swell, they grow tall

375

They are neither female nor male
They are a silence heavy with seastorms
They bear off no women their loins are empty of children
They are strangers to pity, compassion is far from them
They are deaf to men's prayers, entreaties can't reach them
They are horses that grow to great size that feed on mountains
They are the enemies of our friends
They feed on the gods
They tear up the highways they spread out over the roads
They are the faces of evil they are the faces of evil

They are 7 they are 7 they are 7 times 7
In the name of Heaven let them be torn from our sight
In the name of the Earth let them be torn from our sight

ANON

From the Sumerian (trans. Jerome K. Rothenberg)

'Seventy feet down'

Seventy feet down
The sea explodes upwards,
Relapsing, to slaver
Off landing-stage steps—
Running suds, rejoice!

Rocks writhe back to sight.
Mussels, limpets,
Husband their tenacity
In the freezing slither—
Creatures, I cherish you!

By day, sky builds
Grape-dark over the salt
Unsown stirring fields.
Radio rubs its legs,
Telling me of elsewhere:

Barometers falling,
Ports wind-shuttered,
Fleets pent like hounds,
Fires in humped inns
Kippering sea-pictures—

Keep it all off!
By night, snow swerves
(O loose moth world)
Through the stare travelling
Leather-black waters.

Guarded by brilliance
I set plate and spoon,
And after, divining-cards.
Lit shelved liners
Grope like mad worlds westward.

PHILIP LARKIN
From *Livings*

The Seventh

If you set out in this world,
better be born seven times.
Once, in a house on fire,
once, in a freezing flood,
once, in a wild madhouse,
once, in a field of ripe wheat,
once, in an empty cloister,
and once among pigs in a sty.
Six babes crying, not enough:
you yourself must be the seventh.

When you must fight to survive,
let your enemy see seven.
One, away from work on Sunday,
one, starting his work on Monday,
one, who teaches without payment,

377

one, who learned to swim by drowning,
one, who is the seed of a forest,
and one, whom wild forefathers protect,
but all their tricks are not enough:
you yourself must be the seventh.

If you want to find a woman,
let seven men go for her.
One, who gives his heart for words,
one, who takes care of himself,
one, who claims to be a dreamer,
one, who through her skirt can feel her,
one, who knows the hooks and snaps,
one, who steps upon her scarf:
let them buzz like flies around her.
You yourself must be the seventh.

If you write and can afford it,
let seven men write your poem.
One, who builds a marble village,
one, who was born in his sleep,
one, who charts the sky and knows it,
one, whom words call by his name,
one, who perfected his soul,
one, who dissects living rats.
Two are brave and four are wise;
you yourself must be the seventh.

And if all went as was written,
you will die for seven men.
One, who is rocked and suckled,
one, who grabs a hard young breast,
one, who throws down empty dishes,
one, who helps the poor to win,
one, who works till he goes to pieces,
one, who just stares at the moon.
The world will be your tombstone:
you yourself must be the seventh.

ATTILA JÓZSEF
From the Hungarian (trans. John Batki)

Sheep

When I was once in Baltimore,
   A man came up to me and cried,
'Come, I have eighteen hundred sheep,
   And we will sail on Tuesday's tide.

'If you will sail with me, young man,
   I'll pay you fifty shillings down;
These eighteen hundred sheep I take
   From Baltimore to Glasgow town.'

He paid me fifty shillings down,
   I sailed with eighteen hundred sheep;
We soon had cleared the harbour's mouth,
   We soon were in the salt sea deep.

The first night we were out at sea
   Those sheep were quiet in their mind;
The second night they cried with fear—
   They smelt no pastures in the wind.

They sniffed, poor things, for their green fields,
   They cried so loud I could not sleep:
For fifty thousand shillings down
   I would not sail again with sheep.

W. H. DAVIES

She and I

She and I, we thought and fought
And each of us won by the other's defeat;
She and I, we danced and pranced
And lost by neglect the use of our feet;
She and I caught ills and chills
And were cured or dead before we could cough;
She and I, we walked and talked
Half an hour after our heads were cut off.

NORMAN CAMERON

'She is the fairies' midwife, and she comes'

She is the fairies' midwife, and she comes
In shape no bigger than an agate-stone
On the fore-finger of an alderman,
Drawn with a team of little atomies
Athwart men's noses as they lie asleep:
Her waggon-spokes made of long spinners' legs;
The cover, of the wings of grasshoppers;
The traces, of the smallest spider's web;
The collars, of the moonshine's watery beams;
Her whip, of cricket's bone; the lash, of film;
Her waggoner, a small grey-coated gnat,
Not half so big as a round little worm
Prick'd from the lazy finger of a maid;
Her chariot is an empty hazel-nut,
Made by the joiner squirrel or old grub,
Time out o' mind the fairies' coach-makers.
And in this state she gallops night by night
Through lovers' brains, and then they dream of love;
O'er courtiers' knees, that dream on curtsies straight;
O'er lawyers' fingers, who straight dream on fees;
O'er ladies' lips, who straight on kisses dream;
Which oft the angry Mab with blisters plagues,
Because their breaths with sweetmeats tainted are.
Sometimes she gallops o'er a courtier's nose,
And then dreams he of smelling out a suit;
And sometimes comes she with a tithe-pig's tail,
Tickling a parson's nose as a' lies asleep,
Then dreams he of another benefice;
Sometimes she driveth o'er a soldier's neck,
And then dreams he of cutting foreign throats,
Of breaches, ambuscadoes, Spanish blades,
Of healths five fathom deep; and then anon
Drums in his ear, at which he starts and wakes;
And, being thus frighted, swears a prayer or two,
And sleeps again. This is that very Mab
That plats the manes of horses in the night;
And bakes the elf-locks in foul sluttish hairs,

Which once untangled much misfortune bodes;
This is the hag, when maids lie on their backs,
That presses them and learns them first to bear,
Making them women of good carriage:
This is she—

WILLIAM SHAKESPEARE
From *Romeo and Juliet*, Act 1 Scene 4

The Shooting of Dan McGrew

A bunch of the boys were whooping it up in the Malamute
    saloon;
The kid that handles the music-box was hitting a rag-time tune;
Back of the bar, in a solo game, sat Dangerous Dan McGrew,
And watching his luck was his light-o'-love, the lady that's
    known as Lou.

When out of the night, which was fifty below, and into the din
    and the glare,
There stumbled a miner fresh from the creeks, dog-dirty and
    loaded for bear.
He looked like a man with a foot in the grave, and scarcely the
    strength of a louse,
Yet he tilted a poke of dust on the bar, and he called for drinks
    for the house.
There was none could place the stranger's face, though we
    searched ourselves for a clue;
But we drank his health, and the last to drink was Dangerous
    Dan McGrew.

There's men that somehow just grip your eyes, and hold them
    hard like a spell;
And such was he, and he looked to me like a man who had lived
    in hell;
With a face most hair, and the dreary stare of a dog whose day is
    done,

As he watered the green stuff in his glass, and the drops fell one
   by one.
Then I got to figgering who he was, and wondering what he'd
   do,
And I turned my head—and there watching him was the lady
   that's known as Lou.

His eyes went rubbering round the room, and he seemed in a
   kind of daze,
Till at last that old piano fell in the way of his wandering
   gaze.
The rag-time kid was having a drink; there was no one else on
   the stool,
So the stranger stumbles across the room, and flops down there
   like a fool.
In a buckskin shirt that was glazed with dirt he sat, and I saw
   him sway;
Then he clutched the keys with his talon hands—my God! but
   that man could play!

Were you ever out in the Great Alone, when the moon was
   awful clear,
And the icy mountains hemmed you in with a silence you most
   could *hear*;
With only the howl of a timber wolf, and you camped there in
   the cold,
A half-dead thing in a stark, dead-world, clean mad for the
   muck called gold;
While high overhead, green, yellow, and red, the North Light
   swept in bars—
Then you've a hunch what the music meant . . . hunger and
   night and the stars.

And hunger not of the belly kind, that's banished with bacon
   and beans;
But the gnawing hunger of lonely men for a home and all that it
   means;
For a fireside far from the cares that are, four walls and a roof
   above;

But oh! so cramful of cosy joy, and crowned with a woman's
    love:
A woman dearer than all the world, and true as Heaven is
    true—
(God! how ghastly she looks through her rouge,—the lady
    that's known as Lou.)

Then on a sudden the music changed, so soft that you scarce
    could hear;
But you felt that your life had been looted clean of all that it
    once held dear;
That someone had stolen the woman you loved; that her love
    was a devil's lie;
That your guts were gone, and the best for you was to crawl
    away and die.
'Twas the crowning cry of a heart's despair, and it thrilled you
    through and through—
'I guess I'll make it a spread misere,' said Dangerous Dan
    McGrew.

The music almost died away ... then it burst like a pent-up
    flood;
And it seemed to say, 'Repay, repay,' and my eyes were blind
    with blood.
The thought came back of an ancient wrong, and it stung like a
    frozen lash,
And the lust awoke to kill, to kill ... then the music stopped
    with a crash.

And the stranger turned, and his eyes they burned in a most
    peculiar way;
In a buckskin shirt that was glazed with dirt he sat, and I saw
    him sway;
Then his lips went in in a kind of grin, and he spoke, and his
    voice was calm;
And, 'Boys,' says he, 'you don't know me, and none of you care
    a damn;
But I want to state, and my words are straight, and I'll bet my
    poke they're true,

That one of you is a hound of hell . . . and that one is Dan
    McGrew.'

Then I ducked my head, and the lights went out, and two guns
    blazed in the dark;
And a woman screamed, and the lights went up, and two men
    lay stiff and stark.
Pitched on his head, and pumped full of lead, was Dangerous
    Dan McGrew,
While the man from the creeks lay clutched to the breast of the
    lady that's known as Lou.

These are the simple facts of the case, and I guess I ought to
    know;
They say that the stranger was crazed with 'hooch', and I'm not
    denying it's so.
I'm not so wise as the lawyer guys, but strictly between us
    two—
The woman that kissed him and—pinched his poke—was the
    lady that's known as Lou.

ROBERT SERVICE

The Shooting of John Dillinger Outside the Biograph Theater, July 22 1934

Chicago ran a fever of a hundred and one that groggy Sunday.
A reporter fried an egg on a sidewalk; the air looked shaky.
And a hundred thousand people were in the lake like shirts in a
    laundry.
Why was Johnny lonely?
Not because two dozen solid citizens, heat-struck, had keeled
    over backward.
Not because those lawful souls had fallen out of their sockets
    and melted.

But because the sun went down like a lump in a furnace or a bull
  in the Stockyards.
Where was Johnny headed?
Under the Biograph Theater sign that said, 'Our Air is
  Refrigerated.'
Past seventeen FBI men and four policemen who stood in
  doorways and sweated.
Johnny sat down in a cold seat to watch Clark Gable get
  electrocuted.
Had Johnny been mistreated?
Yes, but Gable told the D.A. he'd rather fry than be shut up
  forever.
Two women sat by Johnny. One looked sweet, one looked like
  J. Edgar Hoover.
Polly Hamilton made him feel hot, but Anna Sage made him
  shiver.
Was Johnny a good lover?
Yes, but he passed out his share of squeezes and pokes like a
  jittery masher
While Agent Purvis sneaked up and down the aisle like an extra
  usher,
Trying to make sure they wouldn't slip out till the show was
  over.
Was Johnny a fourflusher?
No, not if he knew the game. He got it up or got it
  back.
But he liked to take snapshots of policemen with his own
  Kodak,
And once in a while he liked to take them with an automatic.
Why was Johnny frantic?
Because he couldn't take a walk or sit down in a movie
Without being afraid he'd run smack into somebody
Who'd point at his rearranged face and holler, 'Johnny!'
Was Johnny ugly?
Yes, because Dr Wilhelm Loeser had given him a new profile
With a baggy jawline and squint eyes and an erased dimple,
With kangaroo-tendon cheekbones and a gigolo's mustache that
  should've been illegal.
Did Johnny love a girl?

Yes, a good-looking, hard-headed Indian named Billie
    Frechette.
He wanted to marry her and lie down and try to get over it,
But she was locked in jail for giving him first-aid and comfort.
Did Johnny feel hurt?
He felt like breaking a bank or jumping over a railing
Into some panicky teller's cage to shout, 'Reach for the ceiling!'
Or like kicking some vice president in the bum checks and
    smiling.
What was he really doing?
Going up the aisle with the crowd and into the lobby
With Polly saying, 'Would *you* do what Clark done?' And
    Johnny saying, 'Maybe.'
And Anna saying, 'If he'd been smart, he'd of acted like Bing
    Crosby.'
Did Johnny look flashy?
Yes, his white-on-white shirt and tie were luminous.
His trousers were creased like knives to the tops of his shoes,
And his yellow straw hat came down to his dark glasses.
Was Johnny suspicious?
Yes, and when Agent Purvis signalled with a trembling cigar,
Johnny ducked left and ran out of the theater,
And innocent Polly and squealing Anna were left nowhere.
Was Johnny a fast runner?
No, but he crouched and scurried past a friendly liquor store
Under the coupled arms of double-daters, under awnings,
    under stars,
To the curb at the mouth of an alley. He hunched there.
Was Johnny a thinker?
No, but he was thinking more or less of Billie Frechette
Who was lost in prison for longer than he could possibly wait,
And then it was suddenly too hard to think around a bullet.
Did anyone shoot straight?
Yes, but Mrs Etta Natalsky fell out from under her picture
    hat.
Theresa Paulus sprawled on the sidewalk, clutching her left
    foot.
And both of them groaned loud and long under the streetlight.
Did Johnny like that?

No, but he lay down with those strange women, his face in the alley,
One shoe off, cinders in his mouth, his eyelids heavy.
When they shouted questions at him, he talked back to nobody.
Did Johnny lie easy?
Yes, holding his gun and holding his breath as a last trick,
He waited, but when the Agents came close, his breath wouldn't work.
Clark Gable walked his last mile; Johnny ran half a block.
Did he run out of luck?
Yes, before he was cool, they had him spread out on dished-in marble
In the Cook County Morgue, surrounded by babbling people
With a crime reporter presiding over the head of the table.
Did Johnny have a soul?
Yes, and it was climbing his slippery wind-pipe like a trapped burglar.
It was beating the inside of his ribcage, hollering, 'Let me out of here!'
Maybe it got out, and maybe it just stayed there.
Was Johnny a money-maker?
Yes, and thousands paid 25¢ to see him, mostly women,
And one said, 'I wouldn't have come, except he's a moral lesson,'
And another, 'I'm disappointed. He feels like a dead man.'
Did Johnny have a brain?
Yes, and it always worked best through the worst of dangers,
Through flat-footed hammerlocks, through guarded doors, around corners,
But it got taken out in the morgue and sold to some doctors.
Could Johnny take orders?
No, but he stayed in the wicker basket carried by six men
Through the bulging crowd to the hearse and let himself be locked in,
And he stayed put as it went driving south in a driving rain.
And he didn't get stolen?
No, not even after his old hard-nosed dad refused to sell
The quick-drawing corpse for $10,000 to somebody in a carnival.

He figured he'd let *Johnny* decide how to get to Hell.
Did anyone wish him well?
Yes, half of Indiana camped in the family pasture,
And the minister said, 'With luck, he could have been a
    minister.'
And up the sleeve of his oversized gray suit, Johnny twitched a
    finger.
Does anyone remember?
Everyone still alive. And some dead ones. It was a new kind of
    holiday
With hot and cold drinks and hot and cold tears. They planted
    him in a cemetery
With three unknown vice presidents, Benjamin Harrison, and
    James Whitcomb Riley,
Who never held up anybody.

DAVID WAGONER

Shroud

Seven threads make the shroud,
The white thread,
A green corn thread,
A blue fish thread,
A red stitch, rut and rieving and wrath,
A gray thread
(All winter failing hand falleth on wheel)
The black thread,
And a thread too bright for the eye.

GEORGE MACKAY BROWN

The Sick Rose

O rose, thou art sick!
The invisible worm
That flies in the night,
In the howling storm,

Has found out thy bed
Of crimson joy,
And his dark secret love
Does thy life destroy.

WILLIAM BLAKE
From *Songs of Experience*

'The silver swan, who living had no note'

The silver swan, who living had no note,
When death approached unlocked her silent throat;
Leaning her breast against the reedy shore,
Thus sung her first and last, and sung no more:
Farewell, all joys; O death, come close mine eyes;
More geese than swans now live, more fools than wise.

ORLANDO GIBBONS

Similes for Two Political Characters of 1819

I

As from an ancestral oak
    Two empty ravens sound their clarion,
Yell by yell, and croak by croak,
When they scent the noonday smoke
    Of fresh human carrion:—

389

II

As two gibbering night-birds flit
   From their bowers of deadly yew
Through the night to frighten it,
When the moon is in a fit,
      And the stars are none, or few:—

III

As a shark and dog-fish wait
   Under an Atlantic isle,
For the negro-ship, whose freight
Is the theme of their debate,
      Wrinkling their red gills the while—

IV

Are ye, two vultures sick for battle
   Two scorpions under one wet stone
Two bloodless wolves whose dry throats rattle,
Two crows perched on the murrained cattle,
      Two vipers tangled into one.

PERCY BYSSHE SHELLEY

'Since there's no help, come, let us kiss and part'

Since there's no help, come, let us kiss and part—
Nay, I have done: you get no more of me;
And I am glad, yea, glad with all my heart
That thus so cleanly I myself can free.
Shake hands forever, cancel all our vows,
And when we meet at any time again,
Be it not seen in either of our brows
That we one jot of former love retain.
Now at the last gasp of love's latest breath,
When, his pulse failing, Passion speechless lies,
When Faith is kneeling by his bed of death,

And Innocence is closing up his eyes,—
   Now, if thou wouldst, when all have given him over,
  From death to life thou mightst him yet recover.

MICHAEL DRAYTON

Sir Patrick Spens

The King sits in Dunfermline toun,
   A drinking at the wine.
'O where shall I get a skilly skipper
   To sail this ship o mine?'

Then up and spak an eldern carle
   Stood by the King's right knee.
'Sir Patrick Spens is the best sailor
   That ever sailed the sea.'

The King has written a lang letter
   And signed it wi his hand,
And sent it to young Patrick Spens
   Was walking on Leith sands.

The first line that Sir Patrick read
   A loud laugh laughèd he.
The next line that Sir Patrick read
   The tear blinded his ee.

'Tae Norrowa, tae Norrowa,
   Tae Norrowa o'er the faem,
The King's daughter frae Norrowa,
   'Tis ye maun brang her hame.'

'O Wha is this done this ill deed,
   And telled the King o me?
Although it were my ain father
   An ill death may he dee.'

391

They hadna been in Norrowa
    A week but barely three
When all the Lords o Norrowa
    They up and spak sae free.

'These outland Scots waste our King's gold
    And swalla our Queen's fee.'
Wearie fa the tongue that spak
    Sicca mortal lee.

'Tak tent, tak tent, my good men all,
    Our good ship sails the morne.'
'O say na sae, my master dear,
    For I fear a deadly storm.

'Late late yestreen I saw the new moon
    Wi the auld moon in her arm.
I fear, I fear, my dear master
    That we shall come to harm.'

O laith laith were those good Scots Lords
    To wet their cork-heeled shoon,
But long e'er all the play was played
    They wet their hats aboon.

O lang lang may their ladies sit
    Wi their gold fans in their hand
Waiting for Sir Patrick Spens
    Come sailing to the land.

O lang lang may their ladies sit
    Wi the gold combs in their hair
Waiting for their own dear lords,
    They'll see them never mair.

Haf owre, haf owre, by Aberdour,
    Where the sea's sae wide and deep,
It's there it lies Sir Patrick Spens
    Wi the Scots Lords at his feet.

ANON

Sir Walter Ralegh to His Son

Three things there be that prosper up apace
And flourish, whilst they grow asunder far;
But on a day, they meet all in one place,
And when they meet, they one another mar.
And they be these: the wood, the weed, the wag.
The wood is that which makes the gallow tree;
The weed is that which strings the hangman's bag;
The wag, my pretty knave, betokeneth thee.
Mark well, dear boy, whilst these assemble not,
Green springs the tree, hemp grows, the wag is wild;
But when they meet, it makes the timber rot,
It frets the halter, and it chokes the child.
  Then bless thee, and beware, and let us pray
  We part not with thee at this meeting day.

SIR WALTER RALEGH

The Six Strings

The guitar
makes dreams cry.
The crying of lost
souls
escapes from its round
mouth.
And like the tarantula
it weaves a huge star
to catch sighs
that float on its black
wooden tank.

FEDERICO GARCÍA LORCA
(trans. Donald Hall)

'Slow, slow, fresh fount, keepe time with my salt teares'

Slow, slow, fresh fount, keepe time with my salt teares;
Yet slower, yet, o faintly gentle springs:
List to the heavy part the musique beares,
    'Woe weepes out her division,' when shee sings.
      Droupe hearbs, and flowers,
      Fall griefe in showers;
      'Our beauties are not ours:
            O, I could still
(Like melting snow upon some craggie hill,)
      drop, drop, drop, drop,
Since natures pride is, now, a wither'd Daffodill.

BEN JONSON

The Smile

There is a Smile of Love.
And there is a Smile of Deceit,
And there is a Smile of Smiles
In which these two Smiles meet.

And there is a Frown of Hate,
And there is a Frown of Disdain,
And there is a Frown of Frowns
Which you strive to forget in vain,

For it sticks in the Heart's deep Core
And it sticks in the deep Back bone;
And no Smile that ever was smil'd,
But only one Smile alone,

That betwixt the Cradle and Grave
It only once Smil'd can be;
But, when it once is Smil'd,
There's an end to all Misery.

WILLIAM BLAKE

Snake

A snake came to my water-trough
On a hot, hot day, and I in pyjamas for the heat,
To drink there.

In the deep, strange-scented shade of the great dark carob tree
I came down the steps with my pitcher
And must wait, must stand and wait, for there he was at the
trough before me.

He reached down from a fissure in the earth-wall in the gloom
And trailed his yellow-brown slackness soft-bellied down, over
the edge of the stone trough
And rested his throat upon the stone bottom,
And where the water had dripped from the tap, in a small
clearness,
He sipped with his straight mouth,
Softly drank through his straight gums, into his slack long
body,
Silently.

Someone was before me at my water-trough,
And I, like a second-comer, waiting.

He lifted his head from his drinking, as cattle do,
And looked at me vaguely, as drinking cattle do,
And flickered his two-forked tongue from his lips, and mused a
moment,
And stooped and drank a little more,
Being earth-brown, earth-golden from the burning bowels of
the earth
On the day of Sicilian July, with Etna smoking.

The voice of my education said to me
He must be killed,
For in Sicily the black, black snakes are innocent, the gold are
venomous.

And voices in me said, If you were a man
You would take a stick and break him now, and finish him off.

But must I confess how I liked him,
How glad I was he had come like a guest in quiet, to drink at my
    water-trough
And depart peaceful, pacified, and thankless,
Into the burning bowels of this earth?

Was it cowardice, that I dared not kill him?
Was it perversity, that I longed to talk to him?
Was it humility, to feel so honoured?
I felt so honoured.

And yet those voices:
If you were not afraid, you would kill him!

And truly I was afraid, I was most afraid,
But even so, honoured still more
That he should seek my hospitality
From out the dark door of the secret earth.

He drank enough
And lifted his head, dreamily, as one who has drunken,
And flickered his tongue like a forked night on the air, so black,
Seeming to lick his lips,
And looked around like a god, unseeing, into the air,
And slowly turned his head,
And slowly, very slowly, as if thrice adream,
Proceeded to draw his slow length curving round
And climb again the broken bank of my wall-face.

And as he put his head into that dreadful hole,
And as he slowly drew up, snake-easing his shoulders, and
    entered farther,
A sort of horror, a sort of protest against his withdrawing into
    that horrid black hole,
Deliberately going into the blackness, and slowly drawing
    himself after,
Overcame me now his back was turned.

I looked round, I put down my pitcher,
I picked up a clumsy log
And threw it at the water-trough with a clatter.

I think it did not hit him,
But suddenly that part of him that was left behind convulsed in
    undignified haste,
Writhed like lightning, and was gone
Into the black hole, the earth-lipped fissure in the wallfront,
At which, in the intense still noon, I stared with fascination.

And immediately I regretted it.
I thought how paltry, how vulgar, what a mean act!
I despised myself and the voices of my accursed human
    education.

And I thought of the albatross,
And I wished he would come back, my snake.
For he seemed to me again like a king,
Like a king in exile, uncrowned in the underworld,
Now due to be crowned again.

And so, I missed my chance with one of the lords
Of life.
And I have something to expiate:
A pettiness.

D. H. LAWRENCE

Solitude

I

Right here I was nearly killed one night in February.
My car slewed on the ice, sideways,
into the other lane. The oncoming cars—
their headlights—came nearer.

My name, my daughters, my job
slipped free and fell behind silently,
farther and farther back. I was anonymous,
like a schoolboy in a lot surrounded by enemies.

The approaching traffic had powerful lights.
They shone on me while I turned and turned
the wheel in a transparent fear that moved like eggwhite.
The seconds lengthened out—making more room—
they grew long as hospital buildings.

It felt as if you could just take it easy
and loaf a bit
before the smash came.

Then firm land appeared: a helping sandgrain
or a marvelous gust of wind. The car took hold
and fish-tailed back across the road.
A signpost shot up, snapped off—a ringing sound—
tossed into the dark.

Came all quiet. I sat there in my seatbelt
and watched someone tramp through the blowing snow
to see what had become of me.

II

I have been walking a while
on the frozen Swedish fields
and I have seen no one.

In other parts of the world
people are born, live, and die
in a constant human crush.

To be visible all the time—to live
in a swarm of eyes—
surely that leaves its mark on the face.
Features overlaid with clay.

The low voices rise and fall
as they divide up
heaven, shadows, grains of sand.

I have to be by myself
ten minutes every morning,
ten minutes every night,
—and nothing to be done!

We all line up to ask each other for help.

Millions.

One.

TOMAS TRANSTROMER
From the Swedish (trans. Robert Bly)

Song: I Hid My Love

I hid my love when young while I
Couldn't bear the buzzing of a fly;
I hid my love to my despite
Till I could not bear to look at light:
I dare not gaze upon her face
But left her memory in each place;
Where'er I saw a wild flower lie
I kissed and bade my love good-bye.

I met her in the greenest dells,
Where dewdrops pearl the wood bluebells;
The lost breeze kissed her bright blue eye,
The bee kissed and went singing by,
A sunbeam found a passage there,
A gold chain round her neck so fair;
As secret as the wild bee's song
She lay there all the summer long.

I hid my love in field and town
Till e'en the breeze would knock me down;
The Bees seemed singing ballads o'er,
The flyes buzz turned a Lion's roar;
And even silence found a tongue,
To haunt me all the summer long;
The riddle nature could not prove
Was nothing else but secret love.

JOHN CLARE

Song for the Clatter-Bones

God rest that wicked woman,
Queen Jezebel, the bitch
Who peeled the clothes from her shoulder-bones
Down to her spent teats
As she stretched out of the window
Among the geraniums, where
She chaffed and laughed like one half daft
Titivating her painted hair—

King Jehu he drove to her,
She tipped him a fancy beck;
But he from his knacky side-car spoke,
'Who'll break that dewlapped neck?'
And so she was thrown from the window;
Like Lucifer she fell
Beneath the feet of the horses and they beat
The light out of Jezebel.

That corpse wasn't planted in clover;
Ah, nothing of her was found

400

Save those grey bones that Hare-foot Mike
Gave me for their lovely sound;
And as once her dancing body
Made star-lit princes sweat,
So I'll just clack: though her ghost lacks a back
There's music in the old bones yet.

F. R. HIGGINS

Song for the Head

(Enter Zantippa with a pitcher to the well. A head comes up with ears of corn, and she combs them in her lap.)

Voice

Gently dip, but not too deep.
For fear you make the golden beard to weep.
Fair maiden, white and red.
Comb me smooth, and stroke my head.
And thou shalt have some cockell-bread.

(A second head comes up full of gold, which she combs in her lap.)

Second Head

Gently dip, but not too deep,
For fear thou make the golden beard to weep.
Fair maiden, white and red,
Comb me smooth and stroke my head,
And every hair a sheaf shall be,
And every sheaf a golden tree.

GEORGE PEELE

Songs for a Colored Singer

I

A washing hangs upon the line,
    but it's not mine.
None of the things that I can see
    belong to me.
The neighbors got a radio with an aerial;
    we got a little portable.
They got a lot of closet space;
    we got a suitcase.

I say, 'Le Roy, just how much are we owing?
Something I can't comprehend,
the more we got the more we spend. . . .'
He only answers, 'Let's get going.'
Le Roy, you're earning too much money now.

I sit and look at our backyard
    and find it very hard.
What have we got for all his dollars and cents?
    —A pile of bottles by the fence.
He's faithful and he's kind
    but he sure has an inquiring mind.
He's seen a lot; he's bound to see the rest,
    and if I protest

Le Roy answers with a frown,
'Darling, when I earns I spends.
The world is wide; it still extends. . . .
I'm going to get a job in the next town.'
Le Roy, you're earning too much money now.

II

The time has come to call a halt;
    and so it ends.
    He's gone off with his other friends.
    He needn't try to make amends,
    this occasion's all his fault.

Through rain and dark I see his face
across the street at Flossie's place.
He's drinking in the warm pink glow
to th' accompaniment of the piccolo.

The time has come to call a halt.
I met him walking with Varella
and hit him twice with my umbrella.
Perhaps that occasion was my fault,
but the time has come to call a halt.

Go drink your wine and go get tight.
    Let the piccolo play.
    I'm sick of all your fussing anyway.
    Now I'm pursuing my own way.
I'm leaving on the bus tonight.
    Far down the highway wet and black
    I'll ride and ride and not come back.
    I'm going to go and take the bus
    and find someone monogamous.

The time has come to call a halt.
I've borrowed fifteen dollars fare
and it will take me anywhere.
For this occasion's all his fault.
The time has come to call a halt.

ELIZABETH BISHOP

Sonnet

Guido, I wish that you and Lapo and I
Were carried off by magic
And put in a boat, which, every time there was wind,
Would sail on the ocean exactly where we wanted.

In this way storms and other dangerous weather
Wouldn't be able to harm us—
And I wish that, since we all were of one mind,
We'd go on wanting more and more to be together.

And I wish that Vanna and Lagia too
And the girl whose name on the list is number thirty
Were put in the boat by the magician too

And that we all did nothing but talk about love
And I wish that they were just as glad to be there
As I believe the three of us would be.

DANTE
From the Italian (trans. Kenneth Koch)

Sounds of the Day

When a clatter came,
It was horses crossing the ford.
When the air creaked, it was
A lapwing seeing us off the premises
Of its private marsh. A snuffling puff
Ten yards from the boat was the tide blocking,
unblocking a hole in a rock.
When the black drums rolled, it was water
Falling sixty feet into itself.

When the door
Scraped shut, it was the end
Of all the sounds there are.

You left me
Beside the quietest fire in the world.

I thought I was hurt in my pride only,
Forgetting that,
When you plunge your hand in freezing water,
You feel
A bangle of ice round your wrist
Before the whole hand goes numb.

NORMAN MACCAIG

Spring

Nothing is so beautiful as Spring—
   When weeds, in wheels, shoot long and lovely and lush;
   Thrush's eggs look little low heavens, and thrush
Through the echoing timber does so rinse and wring
The ear, it strikes like lightnings to hear him sing;
   The glassy peartree leaves and blooms, they brush
   The descending blue; that blue is all in a rush
With richness; the racing lambs too have fair their fling.

What is all this juice and all this joy?
   A strain of the earth's sweet being in the beginning
In Eden garden.—Have, get, before it cloy,

   Before it cloud, Christ, lord, and sour with sinning,
Innocent mind and Mayday in girl and boy,
   Most, O maid's child, thy choice and worthy the winning.

GERARD MANLEY HOPKINS

Spring and Fall

to a young child

   Márgarét, áre you gríeving
   Over Goldengrove unleaving?
   Leáves, líke the things of man, you
   With your fresh thoughts care for, can you?
   Áh! ás the heart grows older
   It will come to such sights colder
   By and by, nor spare a sigh
   Though worlds of wanwood leafmeal lie;
   And yet you *will* weep and know why.
   Now no matter, child, the name:
   Sórrow's spríngs áre the same.

Nor mouth had, no nor mind, expressed
What heart heard of, ghost guessed:
It is the blight man was born for,
It is Margaret you mourn for.

GERARD MANLEY HOPKINS

'Stop all the clocks, cut off the telephone'

Stop all the clocks, cut off the telphone,
Prevent the dog from barking with a juicy bone,
Silence the pianos and with muffled drum
Bring out the coffin, let the mourners come.

Let aeroplanes circle moaning overhead
Scribbling on the sky the message He Is Dead,
Put crêpe bows round the white necks of the public doves,
Let the traffic policemen wear black cotton gloves.

He was my North, my South, my East and West,
My working week and my Sunday rest,
My noon, my midnight, my talk, my song;
I thought that love would last for ever: I was wrong.

The stars are not wanted now: put out every one;
Pack up the moon and dismantle the sun;
Pour away the ocean and sweep up the wood;
For nothing now can ever come to any good.

W. H. AUDEN

Stopping by Woods on a Snowy Evening

Whose woods these are I think I know,
His house is in the village though;
He will not see me stopping here
To watch his woods fill up with snow.

My little horse must think it queer
To stop without a farmhouse near
Between the woods and frozen lake
The darkest evening of the year.

He gives his harness bells a shake
To ask if there is some mistake.
The only other sound's the sweep
Of easy wind and downy flake.

The woods are lovely, dark and deep,
But I have promises to keep,
And miles to go before I sleep,
And miles to go before I sleep.

ROBERT FROST

Strange Meeting

It seemed that out of battle I escaped
Down some profound dull tunnel, long since scooped
Through granites which titanic wars had groined.
Yet also there encumbered sleepers groaned,
Too fast in thought or death to be bestirred.
Then, as I probed them, one sprang up, and stared
With piteous recognition in fixed eyes,
Lifting distressful hands as if to bless.
And by his smile, I knew that sullen hall,
By his dead smile I knew we stood in Hell.
With a thousand pains that vision's face was grained;

Yet no blood reached there from the upper ground,
And no guns thumped, or down the flues made moan.
'Strange friend,' I said, 'here is no cause to mourn.'
'None,' said the other, 'save the undone years,
The hopelessness. Whatever hope is yours,
Was my life also; I went hunting wild
After the wildest beauty in the world,
Which lies not calm in eyes, or braided hair,
But mocks the steady running of the hour,
And if it grieves, grieves richlier than here.
For by my glee might many men have laughed,
And of my weeping something had been left,
Which must die now. I mean the truth untold,
The pity of war, the pity war distilled.
Now men will go content with what we spoiled.
Or, discontent, boil bloody, and be spilled.
They will be swift with swiftness of the tigress,
None will break ranks, though nations trek from progress.
Courage was mine, and I had mystery,
Wisdom was mine, and I had mastery;
To miss the march of this retreating world
Into vain citadels that are not walled.
Then, when much blood had clogged their chariot-wheels
I would go up and wash them from sweet wells,
Even with truths that lie too deep for taint.
I would have poured my spirit without stint
But not through wounds; not on the cess of war.
Foreheads of men have bled where no wounds were.
I am the enemy you killed, my friend.
I knew you in this dark; for so you frowned
Yesterday through me as you jabbed and killed.
I parried; but my hands were loath and cold.
Let us sleep now. . . .'

WILFRED OWEN

The Streets of Laredo

As I walked out in the streets of Laredo,
As I walked out in Laredo one day,
I spied a young cowboy all wrapped in white linen,
All wrapped in white linen as cold as the clay.

'I see by your outfit that you are a cowboy'—
These words he did say as I boldly stepped by,
'Come sit down beside me and hear my sad story;
I'm shot in the breast and I know I must die.

'It was once in the saddle I used to go dashing,
Once in the saddle I used to go gay;
First to the ale-house and then to the jail-house,
Got shot in the breast and I'm dying today.

'Get six jolly cowboys to carry my coffin;
Get six pretty maidens to carry my pall;
Put bunches of roses all over my coffin,
Roses to deaden the clods as they fall.

'Oh, beat the drum slowly and play the fife lowly,
Play the dead march as you carry me along;
Take me to the green valley and lay the sod o'er me,
For I'm a young cowboy and I know I've done wrong.

'Go gather around you a crowd of young cowboys
And tell them the story of this, my sad fate;
Tell one and the other before they go further
To stop their wild roving before it's too late.

'Go fetch me a cup, a cup of cold water
To cool my parched lips,' the cowboy then said.
Before I returned, the spirit had left him
And gone to its Maker—the cowboy was dead.

We beat the drum slowly and played the fife lowly,
And bitterly wept as we carried him along;
For we all loved our comrade, so brave, young and handsome,
We all loved our comrade although he'd done wrong.

ANON

409

A Strong Wind

All day a strong wind blew
Across the green and brown from Kerry.
The leaves hurrying, two
By three, over the road, collected
In chattering groups. New berry
Dipped with old branch. Careful insects
Flew low behind their hedges.
Held back by her pretty petticoat,
Butterfly struggled. A bit of
Paper, on which a schoolgirl had written
'Máire loves Jimmy', jumped up
Into a tree. Tapping in haste,
The wind was telegraphing, hundreds
Of miles. All Ireland raced.

AUSTIN CLARKE

A Survey

Down in the Frantic Mountains
they say a canyon winds
crammed with hysterical water
hushed by placid sands.

They tried to map that country,
sent out a field boot crew,
but the river surged at night
and ripped the map in two.

So they sent out wildcats, printed
with intricate lines of fur,
to put their paws with such finesse
the ground was unaware.

Now only the wildcats know it,
patting a tentative paw,
soothing the hackles of ridges,
pouring past rocks and away.

The sun rakes that land each morning;
the mountains buck and scream.
By night the wildcats pad by
gazing it quiet again.

WILLIAM STAFFORD

Swedes

They have taken the gable from the roof of clay
On the long swede pile. They have let in the sun
To the white and gold and purple of curled fronds
Unsunned. It is a sight more tender-gorgeous
At the wood-corner where Winter moans and drips
Than when, in the Valley of the Tombs of Kings,
A boy crawls down into a Pharaoh's tomb
And, first of Christian men, beholds the mummy,
God and monkey, chariot and throne and vase,
Blue pottery, alabaster, and gold.

But dreamless long-dead Amen-hotep lies.
This is a dream of Winter, sweet as Spring.

EDWARD THOMAS

Sweeney Praises the Trees

The branchy leafy oak-tree
is highest in the wood,
the shooting hazel bushes
hide sweet hazel-nuts.

411

The alder is my darling,
all thornless in the gap,
some milk of human kindness
coursing in its sap.

The blackthorn is a jaggy creel,
stippled with dark sloes;
green watercress is thatch on wells
where the drinking blackbird goes.

Sweetest of the leafy stalks,
the vetches strew the pathway;
the oyster-grass is my delight
and the wild strawberry.

Low-set clumps of apple-trees
drum down fruit when shaken;
scarlet berries clot like blood
on mountain rowan.

Briars curl in sideways,
arch a stickle back,
draw blood, and curl back innocent
to sneak the next attack.

The yew-tree in each churchyard
wraps night in its dark hood.
ivy is a shadowy
genius of the wood.

Holly rears its windbreak,
a door in winter's face;
life-blood on a spear-shaft
darkens the grain of ash.

Birch-tree, smooth and pale-skinned,
delicious to the breeze,
high twigs plait and crown it
the queen of trees.

The aspen pales
and whispers, hesitates:
a thousand frightened scuts
race in its leaves.

But what disturbs me most
in the living wood
is the swishing to and fro
of an oak-rod.

ANON

From the Irish (trans. Seamus Heaney)

Sweet Suffolk Owl

Sweet Suffolk owl, so trimly dight
With feathers like a lady bright,
Thou singest alone, sitting by night,
Te whit, te whoo, te whit, te whit.
Thy note, that forth so freely rolls,
With shrill command the mouse controls,
And sings a dirge for dying souls,
Te whit, te whoo, te whit, te whit.

THOMAS VAUTOR

Taboo to Boot

One bliss for which
There is no match
Is when you itch
To up and scratch.

Yet doctors and dowagers deprecate scratching,
Society ranks it with spitting and snatching,
And medical circles consistently hold
That scratching's as wicked as feeding a cold.
Hell's flame burns unquenched 'neath how many a stocking
On account of to scratch in a salon is shocking!

> 'Neath tile or thatch
> That man is rich
> Who has a scratch
> For every itch.

Ho, squirmers and writhers, how long will ye suffer
The medical tyrant, the social rebuffer!

On the edge of the door let our shoulder blades rub,
Let the drawing room now be as free as the tub!

> I'm greatly attached
> To Barbara Frietchie.
> I bet she scratched
> When she was itchy.

OGDEN NASH

Taffy was a Welshman

Taffy was a Welshman, Taffy was a thief,
Taffy came to my house and stole a piece of beef,
I went to Taffy's house, Taffy wasn't in,
I jumped upon his Sunday hat, and poked it with a pin.

Taffy was a Welshman, Taffy was a sham,
Taffy came to my house and stole a leg of lamb,
I went to Taffy's house, Taffy was away,
I stuffed his socks with sawdust and filled his shoes with clay.

Taffy was a Welshman, Taffy was a cheat,
Taffy came to my house and stole a piece of meat,
I went to Taffy's house, Taffy wasn't there,
I hung his coat and trousers to roast before a fire.

ANON

Tails and Heads

The cormorant has
Fourteen feathers in its tail;
Almost identical, the shag has twelve.
One cannot fail
To differentiate at once between
Bird and bird sharing the sea and wind.

Here—
Take these two non-feathers of the shag
To ornament your mind,
As Pocahontas put
Feathers from tameless eagles in her hair,
And Henri de Navarre a great white
Plume upon his helmet for a flag.

SUZANNE KNOWLES

Taking Leave of a Friend

Blue mountains to the north of the walls,
White river winding about them;
Here we must make separation
And go out through a thousand miles of dead grass,

Mind like a floating wide cloud,
Sunset like the parting of old acquaintances
Who bow over their clasped hands at a distance.
Our horses neigh to each other
　　　　　as we are departing.

RIHAKU
From the Chinese (version by Ezra Pound)

Tarantella

Do you remember an Inn,
Miranda?
Do you remember an Inn?
And the tedding and the spreading
Of the straw for a bedding,
And the fleas that tease in the High Pyrenees,
And the wine that tasted of the tar?
And the cheers and the jeers of the young muleteers
(Under the vine of the dark verandah)?
Do you remember an Inn, Miranda,
Do you remember an Inn?
And the cheers and the jeers of the young muleteers
Who hadn't got a penny,
And who weren't paying any,
And the hammer at the doors and the Din?
And the Hip! Hop! Hap!
Of the clap
Of the hands to the twirl and the swirl
Of the girl gone chancing,
Glancing,
Dancing,
Backing and advancing,
Snapping of a clapper to the spin
Out and in—
And the Ting, Tong, Tang of the Guitar
Do you remember an Inn,

Miranda?
Do you remember an Inn?

　　　Never more;
　　　Miranda,
　　　Never more.
　　　Only the high peaks hoar:
　　　And Aragon a torrent at the door.
　　　No sound
　　　In the walls of the Halls where falls
　　　The tread
　　　Of the feet of the dead to the ground
　　　No sound:
　　　But the boom
　　　Of the far Waterfall like Doom.

                              HILAIRE BELLOC

'There came a Wind like a Bugle'

There came a Wind like a Bugle—
It quivered through the Grass
And a Green Chill upon the Heat
So ominous did pass
We barred the Windows and the Doors
As from an Emerald Ghost—
The Doom's electric Moccasin
That very instant passed—
On a strange Mob of panting Trees
And Fences fled away
And Rivers where the Houses ran
Those looked that lived—that Day—
The Bell within the steeple wild
The flying tidings told—
How much can come
And much can go,
And yet abide the World!

                              EMILY DICKINSON

'There is a willow grows aslant a brook'

There is a willow grows aslant a brook,
That shows his hoar leaves in the glassy stream;
There with fantastic garlands did she come,
Of crow-flowers, nettles, daisies, and long purples,
That liberal shepherds give a grosser name,
But our cold maids do dead men's fingers call them:
There, on the pendent boughs her coronet weeds
Clambering to hang, an envious sliver broke,
When down her weedy trophies and herself
Fell in the weeping brook. Her clothes spread wide,
And, mermaid-like, awhile they bore her up;
Which time she chanted snatches of old tunes,
As one incapable of her own distress,
Or like a creature native and indu'd
Unto that element; but long it could not be
Till that her garments, heavy with their drink,
Pull'd the poor wretch from her melodious lay
To muddy death.

WILLIAM SHAKESPEARE
From *Hamlet*, Act 4 Scene 7

'There's a certain Slant of Light'

There's a certain Slant of light,
Winter Afternoons—
That oppresses, like the Heft
Of Cathedral Tunes—

Heavenly Hurt, it gives us—
We can find no scar,
But internal difference,
Where the Meanings, are—

None may teach it—Any—
'Tis the Seal Despair—
An imperial affliction
Sent us of the Air—

When it comes, the Landscape listens—
Shadows—hold their breath—
When it goes, 'tis like the Distance
On the look of Death—

EMILY DICKINSON

There Was a Boy

There was a Boy, ye knew him well, ye Cliffs
And Islands of Winander! many a time,
At evening, when the stars had just begun
To move along the edges of the hills,
Rising or setting, would he stand alone,
Beneath the trees, or by the glimmering lake,
And there, with fingers interwoven, both hands
Press'd closely palm to palm and to his mouth
Uplifted, he, as through an instrument,
Blew mimic hootings to the silent owls
That they might answer him. And they would shout
Across the wat'ry vale and shout again
Responsive to his call, with quivering peals,
And long halloos, and screams, and echoes loud
Redoubled and redoubled, a wild scene
Of mirth and jocund din. And, when it chanced
That pauses of deep silence mock'd his skill,
Then, sometimes, in that silence, while he hung
Listening, a gentle shock of mild surprize
Has carried far into his heart the voice
Of mountain torrents, or the visible scene
Would enter unawares into his mind
With all its solemn imagery, its rocks,

Its woods, and that uncertain heaven, receiv'd
Into the bosom of the steady lake.
    Fair are the woods, and beauteous is the spot,
The vale where he was born: the Church-yard hangs
Upon a slope above the village school,
And there along the bank when I have pass'd
At evening, I believe, that near his grave
A full half-hour together I have stood,
Mute—looking at the grave in which he lies.

WILLIAM WORDSWORTH
From The Prelude, Book V

'There was a man and he was mad'

There was a man and he was mad
    And he ran up the steeple,
And there he cut his nose off
    And flung it at the people.

ANON

'There was a man of double deed'

There was a man of double deed
Who sowed his garden full of seed.
When the seed began to grow,
'Twas like a garden full of snow.
When the snow began to melt,
'Twas like a ship without a bell.
When the ship began to sail,
'Twas like a bird without a tail.
When the bird began to fly,
'Twas like an eagle in the sky.
When the sky began to roar,

'Twas like a lion at the door.
When the door began to crack,
'Twas like a stick across my back.
When my back began to smart,
'Twas like a penknife in my heart.
When my heart began to bleed,
'Twas death, and death, and death indeed.

ANON

Thirteen Ways of Looking at a Blackbird

I

Among twenty snowy mountains
The only moving thing
Was the eye of the blackbird.

II

I was of three minds,
Like a tree
In which there are three blackbirds.

III

The blackbird whirled in the autumn winds.
It was a small part of the pantomime.

IV

A man and a woman
Are one.
A man and a woman and a blackbird
Are one.

V

I do not know which to prefer,
The beauty of inflexions
Or the beauty of innuendos,
The blackbird whistling
Or just after.

VI

Icicles filled the long window
With barbaric glass.
The shadow of the blackbird
Crossed it, to and fro.
The mood
Traced in the shadow
An indecipherable cause.

VII

O thin men of Haddam,
Why do you imagine golden birds?
Do you not see how the blackbird
Walks around the feet
Of the women about you?

VIII

I know noble accents
And lucid, inescapable rhythms;
But I know, too,
That the blackbird is involved
In what I know.

IX

When the blackbird flew out of sight,
It marked the edge
Of one of many circles.

X

At the sight of blackbirds
Flying in a green light
Even the bawds of euphony
Would cry out sharply.

XI

He rode over Connecticut
In a glass coach.
Once, a fear pierced him,

In that he mistook
The shadow of his equipage
For blackbirds.

XII

The river is moving.
The blackbird must be flying.

XIII

It was evening all afternoon.
It was snowing
And it was going to snow.
The blackbird sat
In the cedar limbs.

WALLACE STEVENS

'This lunar beauty'

This lunar beauty
Has no history,
Is complete and early;
If beauty later
Bear any feature,
It had a lover
And is another.

This like a dream
Keeps other time,
And daytime is
The loss of this;
For time is inches
And the heart's changes,
Where ghost has haunted
Lost and wanted.

423

But this was never
A ghost's endeavour
Nor, finished this,
Was ghost at ease;
And till it pass
Love shall not near
The sweetness here,
Nor sorrow take
His endless look.

Thistle

They brought a bouquet of thistles
And set it on the table,
And at once there was ferment and fire
And a crimson roundelay of flames.
These bristling stars,
These splashes of a northern dawn,
Jingle and moan like bells,
Blazing like lamps from within.
Here too is an image of the universe,
An organism woven out of rays,
The raging of undecided battle,
The flashing of uplifted blades.
Here is a tower of fury and of glory,
Where lance is laid on lance,
Where bunches of bloody-headed flowers
Are graven on my heart.
I dreamt of a vast dungeon
And barred windows black as night,
Behind the bars the legendary bird
Whose plight no man can help.
But clearly I too am poor in spirit
For I have not the strength to help,
And the wall of thistles rises

Between me and my happiness.
And the thorn blade has pierced my breast,
And already the sad, lovely gaze
Of its undimmed eyes
Shines on me for the last time.

NIKOLAI ALEKSEEVICH ZABOLOTSKY

From the Russian (trans. Daniel Weissbort)

Thomas Rymer

True Thomas lay on Huntlie bank,
   A ferlie he spied wi' his ee,
And there he saw a lady bright,
   Come riding down by the Eildon Tree.

Her shirt was o the grass-green silk,
   Her mantle o the velvet fyne,
At ilka tett of her horse's mane
   Hang fifty siller bells and nine.

True Thomas, he pulld aff his cap,
   And louted low down to his knee:
'All hail, thou mighty Queen of Heaven!
   For thy peer on earth I never did see.'

'O no, O no, Thomas,' she said,
   'That name does not belang to me;
I am but the queen of fair Elfland,
   That am hither come to visit thee.

'Harp and carp, Thomas,' she said,
   'Harp and carp along wi me,
And if ye dare to kiss my lips,
   Sure of your bodie I will be.'

'Betide me weal, betide me woe,
    That weird shall never daunton me;'
Syne he has kissed her rosy lips,
    All underneath the Eildon Tree.

'Now, ye maun go wi me,' she said,
    'True Thomas, ye maun go wi me,
And ye maun serve me seven years,
    Thro weal or woe, as may chance to be.'

She mounted on her milk-white steed,
    She's taen True Thomas up behind,
And aye wheneer her bridle rung,
    The steed flew swifter than the wind.

O they rade on, and farther on—
    The steed gaed swifter than the wind—
Untill they reached a desart wide,
    And living land was left behind.

'Light down, light down, now, True Thomas,
    And lean your head upon my knee;
Abide and rest a little space,
    And I will show you ferlies three.

'O see ye not yon narrow road,
    So thick beset with thorns and briers?
That is the path of righteousness,
    Tho after it but few enquires.

'And see not ye that braid braid road,
    That lies across that lily leven?
That is the path of wickedness,
    Tho some call it the road to heaven.

'And see not ye that bonny road,
    That winds about the fernie brae?
That is the road to fair Elfland,
    Where thou and I this night maun gae.

'But, Thomas, ye maun hold your tongue,
    Whatever ye may hear or see,
For, if you speak word in Elflyn land,
    Ye'll neer get back to your ain countrie.'

O they rade on, and farther on,
    And they waded thro rivers aboon the knee,
And they saw neither sun nor moon,
    But they heard the roaring of the sea.

It was mirk mirk night, and there was nae stern light,
    And they waded thro red blude to the knee;
For a' the blude that's shed on earth
    Rins thro the springs o that countrie.

Syne they came on to a garden green,
    And she pu'd an apple frae a tree:
'Take this for thy wages, True Thomas,
    It will give the tongue that can never lie.'

'My tongue is mine ain,' True Thomas said;
    'A gudely gift ye wad gie to me!
I neither dought to buy nor sell,
    At fair or tryst where I may be.

'I dought neither speak to prince or peer,
    Nor ask of grace from fair ladye:'
'Now hold thy peace,' the lady said,
    'For as I say, so must it be.'

He has gotten a coat of the even cloth,
    And a pair of shoes of velvet green,
And till seven years were gane and past
    True Thomas on earth was never seen.

ANON

Three Riddles from the Exeter Book

Clothes make no sound when I tread ground
Or dwell in dwellings or disturb the flow.
   And lofty air and gear at times
   Above men's towns will lift me:
   Brisk breezes bear me far, and then
   My frettings loudly rush and ring
   Above the people and most clearly sing
     When I forth-fare on air
      And feel and know
       No fold, no flow.

                            (*The Swan*)

White is my neck, head yellow, sides
The same. Weapons I wear, am hurried, and along
My back as on my cheek stands hair. Two ears
Above my eyes, through greenest grass
On claws I go. If in my house sharp
Fighter finds me where my children
Live, my part is grief, this stranger bringing
Doom of dying to my door.
I must be cool then, and
Take off my dear ones: To wait for
His fierceness (on ribs crawling
Closer) would be most witless, I
Would not chance it. But working with forefeet
A way through the steep hill, with ease I shall
Lead out my dears through the down
By a tunnel in secret. I shall not fear then
To fight with the death dog. And if close behind me
He follows a pathway up on the hilltop
I shall turn, and go for him,
And viciously spear this creature I hate
       Who has followed me there.

                            (*The Badger*)

I puff my breast out, my neck swells,
I have a high tail and a head,
One foot and eyes and ears,
A back, my beak is hard,
My neck is high, I have two sides,
A rod inside me. Pains afflict me
When the tree-mover moves me
Rain in my placing beats me, hard
Hail hits me, hoar-frost clothes me, cold
Snow sits on me, holed
  In my belly.

     (*The Weathercock*)
     GEOFFREY GRIGSON

'Thrice the brinded cat hath mew'd'

Thrice the brinded cat hath mew'd.
Thrice and once the hedge-pig whin'd.
Harper cries: 'Tis time, 'tis time.
Round about the cauldron go;
In the poison'd entrails throw.
Toad, that under cold stone
Days and nights hast thirty-one
Swelter'd venom sleeping got,
Boil thou first i' the charmed pot.
 Double, double toil and trouble;
 Fire burn and cauldron bubble.

Fillet of a fenny snake,
In the cauldron boil and bake;
Eye of newt, and toe of frog,
Wool of bat, and tongue of dog,
Adder's fork, and blind-worm's sting,
Lizard's leg, and howlet's wing,
For a charm of powerful trouble,
Like a hell-broth boil and bubble.
 Double, double toil and trouble;
 Fire burn and cauldron bubble.

Scale of dragon, tooth of wolf,
Witches' mummy, maw and gulf
Of the ravin'd salt-sea shark,
Root of hemlock digg'd i' the dark,
Liver of blaspheming Jew,
Gall of goat, and slips of yew
Sliver'd in the moon's eclipse,
Nose of Turk, and Tartar's lips,
Finger of birth-strangled babe
Ditch-deliver'd by a drab,
Make the gruel thick and slab:
Add thereto a tiger's chaudron,
For the ingredients of our cauldron.
  Double, double toil and trouble;
  Fire burn and cauldron bubble.
  Cool it with a baboon's blood,
  Then the charm is firm and good.

WILLIAM SHAKESPEARE
From *Macbeth*, Act 4 Scene 1

Tiger

At noon the paper tigers roar—Miroslav Holub

The paper tigers roar at noon;
The sun is hot, the sun is high.
They roar in chorus, not in tune,
Their plaintive, savage hunting cry.

O, when you hear them, stop your ears
And clench your lids and bite your tongue.
The harmless paper tiger bears
Strong fascination for the young.

His forest is the busy street;
His dens the forum and the mart;
He drinks no blood, he tastes no meat:
He riddles and corrupts the heart.

430

But when the dusk begins to creep
From tree to tree, from door to door,
The jungle tiger wakes from sleep
And utters his authentic roar.

It bursts the night and shakes the stars
Till one breaks blazing from the sky;
Then listen! If to meet it soars
Your heart's reverberating cry,

My child, then put aside your fear:
Unbar the door and walk outside!
The real tiger waits you there;
His golden eyes shall be your guide.

And, should he spare you in his wrath,
The world and all the worlds are yours;
And should he leap the jungle path
And clasp you with his bloody jaws,

Then say, as his divine embrace
Destroys the mortal parts of you:
I too am of that royal race
Who do what we are born to do.

A. D. HOPE

Tilly

He travels after a winter sun,
Urging the cattle along a cold red road,
Calling to them, a voice they know,
He drives his beasts above Cabra.

The voice tells them home is warm.
They moo and make brute music with their hoofs.
He drives them with a flowering branch before him,
Smoke pluming their foreheads.

Boor, bond of the herd,
Tonight stretch full by the fire!
I bleed by the black stream
For my torn bough!

JAMES JOYCE

Timothy Winters

Timothy Winters comes to school
With eyes as wide as a football pool,
Ears like bombs and teeth like splinters:
A blitz of a boy is Timothy Winters.

His belly is white, his neck is dark,
And his hair is an exclamation mark.
His clothes are enough to scare a crow
And through his britches the blue winds blow.

When teacher talks he won't hear a word
And he shoots down dead the arithmetic-bird,
He licks the patterns off his plate
And he's not even heard of the Welfare State.

Timothy Winters has bloody feet
And he lives in a house on Suez Street,
He sleeps in a sack on the kitchen floor
And they say there aren't boys like him any more.

Old Man Winters likes his beer
And his missus ran off with a bombardier,
Grandma sits in the grate with a gin
And Timothy's dosed with an aspirin.

The Welfare Worker lies awake
But the law's as tricky as a ten-foot snake,
So Timothy Winters drinks his cup
And slowly goes on growing up.

At Morning Prayers the Headmaster helves
For children less fortunate than ourselves,
And the loudest response in the room is when
Timothy Winters roars 'Amen!'

So come one angel, come on ten:
Timothy Winters says 'Amen'
Amen amen amen amen.
Timothy Winters, Lord.

Amen.

CHARLES CAUSLEY

To a Schoolboy

Ploughman ploughing a level field
His plough a magic tree
An oleaster tree

Ploughing a level field
His ploughshare a grey dove
His goad a sprig of basil
His oxen two stags

Instead of wheat
He's sowing small pearls
Ploughing with a magic feather
A peacock feather

ANON

From the Serbian (trans. Anne Pennington)

To Autumn

I

Season of mists and mellow fruitfulness,
   Close bosom friend of the maturing sun,
Conspiring with him how to load and bless
   With fruit the vines that round the thatch-eves run:
To bend with apples the mossed cottage-trees,
   And fill all fruit with ripeness to the core;
     To swell the gourd, and plump the hazel shells
   With a sweet kernel; to set budding more,
And still more, later flowers for the bees,
Until they think warm days will never cease,
     For summer has o'er-brimmed their clammy
     cells.

II

Who hath not seen thee oft amid thy store?
   Sometimes whoever seeks abroad may find
Thee sitting careless on a granary floor,
   Thy hair soft-lifted by the winnowing wind;
Or on a half-reaped furrow sound asleep,
   Drowsed with the fume of poppies, while thy hook
     Spares the next swath and all its twinèd flowers;
And sometimes like a gleaner thou dost keep
   Steady thy laden head across a brook;
   Or by a cyder-press, with patient look,
     Thou watchest the last oozings hours by hours.

III

Where are the songs of spring? Aye, where are they?
   Think not of them, thou hast thy music too—
While barrèd clouds bloom the soft-dying day,
   And touch the stubble-plains with rosy hue.
Then in a wailful choir the small gnats mourn
   Among the river sallows, borne aloft
     Or sinking as the light wind lives or dies;

And full-grown lambs loud bleat from hilly bourn;
   Hedge-crickets sing; and now with treble soft
The red-breast whistles from a garden-croft;
   And gathering swallows twitter in the skies.

JOHN KEATS

To the Foot from its Child

The child's foot is not yet aware it's a foot,
and would like to be a butterfly or an apple.

But in time, stones and bits of glass,
streets, ladders,
and the paths in the rough earth
go on teaching the foot that it cannot fly,
cannot be a fruit bulging on the branch.
Then, the child's foot
is defeated, falls
in the battle,
is a prisoner
condemned to live in a shoe.

Bit by bit, in that dark,
it grows to know the world in its own way,
out of touch with its fellow, enclosed,
feeling out life like a blind man.

These soft nails
of quartz, bunched together,
grow hard, and change themselves
into opaque substance, hard as horn,
and the tiny, petalled toes of the child
grow bunched and out of trim,
take on the form of eyeless reptiles
with triangular heads, like worms.
Later, they grow calloused

and are covered
with the faint volcanoes of death,
a coarsening hard to accept.

But this blind thing walks
without respite, never stopping
for hour after hour,
the one foot, the other,
now the man's,
now the woman's,
up above,
down below,
through fields, mines,
markets and ministries,
backwards,
far afield, inward,
forward,
this foot toils in its shoe,
scarcely taking time
to bare itself in love or sleep;
it walks, they walk,
until the whole man chooses to stop.

And then it descended
underground, unaware,
for there, everything, everything was dark.
It never knew it had ceased to be a foot
or if they were burying it so that it could fly
or so that it could become
an apple.

PABLO NERUDA

From the Spanish (trans. Alistair Reid)

Track

2 a.m.: moonlight. The train has stopped
out in a field. Far off sparks of light from a town,
flickering coldly on the horizon.

As when a man goes so deep into his dream
he will never remember that he was there
when he returns again to his room.

Or when a person goes so deep into a sickness
that his days all become some flickering sparks, a swarm,
feeble and cold on the horizon.

The train is entirely motionless.
2 o'clock: strong moonlight, few stars.

TOMAS TRANSTRÖMER
From the Swedish (trans. Robert Bly)

Transformations

Portion of this yew
Is a man my grandsire knew,
Bosomed here at its foot:
This branch may be his wife,
A ruddy human life
Now turned to a green shoot.

These grasses must be made
Of her who often prayed,
Last century, for repose;
And the fair girl long ago
Whom I often tried to know
May be entering this rose.

So, they are not underground,
But as nerves and veins abound
In the growths of upper air,
And they feel the sun and rain,
And the energy again
That made them what they were!

THOMAS HARDY

A True Account of Talking to the Sun at Fire Island

The Sun woke me this morning loud
and clear, saying 'Hey! I've been
trying to wake you up for fifteen
minutes. Don't be so rude, you are
only the second poet I've ever chosen
to speak to personally
                              so why
aren't you more attentive? If I could
burn you through the window I would
to wake you up. I can't hang around
here all day.'
                    'Sorry, Sun, I stayed
up late last night talking to Hal.'

'When I woke up Mayakovsky he was
a lot more prompt' the Sun said
petulantly. 'Most people are up
already waiting to see if I'm going
to put in an appearance.'
                              I tried
to apologize 'I missed you yesterday.'
'That's better' he said. 'I didn't
know you'd come out.' 'You may be
wondering why I've come so close?'
'Yes' I said beginning to feel hot

438

wondering if maybe he wasn't burning me
anyway.
         'Frankly I wanted to tell you
I like your poetry. I see a lot
on my rounds and you're okay. You may
not be the greatest thing on earth, but
you're different. Now, I've heard some
say you're crazy, they being excessively
calm themselves to my mind, and other
crazy poets think that you're a boring
reactionary. Not me.
                Just keep on
like I do and pay no attention. You'll
find that people always will complain
about the atmosphere, either too hot
or too cold too bright or too dark, days
too short or too long.
                If you don't appear
at all one day they think you're lazy
or dead. Just keep right on, I like it.

And don't worry about your lineage
poetic or natural. The Sun shines on
the jungle, you know, on the tundra
the sea, the ghetto. Wherever you were
I knew it and saw you moving. I was waiting
for you to get to work.

                And now that you
are making your own days, so to speak,
even if no one reads you but me
you won't be depressed. Not
everyone can look up, even at me. It
hurts their eyes.'
                'Oh Sun, I'm so grateful to you!'

'Thanks and remember I'm watching. It's
easier for me to speak to you out
here. I don't have to slide down

between buildings to get your ear.
I know you love Manhattan, but
you ought to look up more often.
                                    And
always embrace things, people earth
sky stars, as I do, freely and with
the appropriate sense of space. That
is your inclination, known in the heavens
and you should follow it to hell, if
necessary, which I doubt.
                                    Maybe we'll
speak again in Africa, of which I too
am specially fond. Go back to sleep now
Frank, and I may leave a tiny poem
in that brain of yours as my farewell.'

'Sun, don't go!' I was awake
at last. 'No, go I must, they're calling
me.'
        'Who are they?'
                                    Rising he said 'Some
day you'll know. They're calling to you
too.' Darkly he rose, and then I slept.

                                    FRANK O'HARA

The Twa Corbies

As I was walking all alane
I heard twa corbies making a mane;
The tane unto the t'other say,
'Where sall we gang and dine to–day?'

'—In behint yon auld fail dyke,
I wot there lies a new–slain Knight;
And naebody kens that he lies there,
But his hawk, his hound, and lady fair.

'His hound is to the hunting gane,
His hawk to fetch the wild-fowl hame,
His lady's ta'en another mate,
So we may make our dinner sweet.

'Ye'll sit on his white hause-bane,
And I'll pick out his bonny blue een:
Wi' ae lock o' his gowden hair
We'll theek our nest when it grows bare.

'Mony a one for him makes mane,
But nane sall ken where he is gane;
O'er his white banes, when they are bare,
The wind sall blaw for evermair.'

ANON

Two Drops

No time to grieve for roses, when the forests are burning—Slowacki

The forests were on fire—
they however
wreathed their necks with their hands
like bouquets of roses

People ran to the shelters—
he said his wife had hair
in whose depths one could hide

Covered by one blanket
they whispered shameless words
the litany of those who love

When it got very bad
they leapt into each other's eyes
and shut them firmly

441

So firmly they did not feel the flames
when they came up to the eyelashes

To the end they were brave
To the end they were faithful
To the end they were similar
like two drops
stuck at the edge of a face

ZBIGNIEW HERBERT

From the Polish (trans. Peter Dale Scott)

Two Performing Elephants

He stands with his forefeet on the drum
and the other, the old one, the pallid hoary female
must creep her great bulk beneath the bridge of him.

On her knees, in utmost caution
all agog, and curling up her trunk
she edges through without upsetting him.
Triumph! the ancient pig-tailed monster!

When her trick is to climb over him
with what shadow-like slow carefulness
she skims him, sensitive
as shadows from the ages gone and perished
in touching him, and planting her round feet.

While the wispy, modern children, half-afraid
watch silent. The looming of the hoary, far-gone ages
is too much for them.

D. H. LAWRENCE

Two Songs of a Fool

I

A speckled cat and a tame hare
Eat at my hearthstone
And sleep there;
And both look up to me alone
For learning and defence
As I look up to Providence.

I start out of my sleep to think
Some day I may forget
Their food and drink;
Or, the house door left unshut,
The hare may run till it's found
The horn's sweet note and the tooth of the hound.

I bear a burden that might well try
Men that do all by rule,
And what can I
That am a wandering-witted fool
But pray to God that He ease
My great responsibilities?

II

I slept on my three-legged stool by the fire,
The speckled cat slept on my knee;
We never thought to enquire
Where the brown hare might be,
And whether the door were shut.
Who knows how she drank the wind
Stretched up on two legs from the mat,
Before she had settled her mind
To drum with her heel and to leap?
Had I but awakened from sleep
And called her name, she had heard,
It may be, and had not stirred,
That now, it may be, has found
The horn's sweet note and the tooth of the hound.

W. B. YEATS

The Tyger

Tyger! Tyger! burning bright
In the forests of the night,
What immortal hand or eye
Could frame thy fearful symmetry?

In what distant deeps or skies
Burnt the fire of thine eyes?
On what wings dare he aspire?
What the hand dare seize the fire?

And what shoulder, and what art,
Could twist the sinews of thy heart?
And when thy heart began to beat,
What dread hand? and what dread feet?

What the hammer? what the chain?
In what furnace was thy brain?
What the anvil? what dread grasp
Dare its deadly terrors clasp?

When the stars threw down their spears,
And water'd heaven with their tears,
Did he smile his work to see?
Did he who made the Lamb make thee?

Tyger! Tyger! burning bright
In the forests of the night,
What immortal hand or eye,
Dare frame thy fearful symmetry?

WILLIAM BLAKE
From *Songs of Experience*

The Unknown Bird

Three lovely notes he whistled, too soft to be heard
If others sang; but others never sang
In the great beech-wood all that May and June.
No one saw him: I alone could hear him
Though many listened. Was it but four years
Ago? or five? He never came again.

Oftenest when I heard him I was alone,
Nor could I ever make another hear.
La-la-la! he called, seeming far off—
As if a cock crowed past the edge of the world,
As if the bird or I were in a dream.
Yet that he travelled through the trees and sometimes
Neared me, was plain, though somehow distant still
He sounded. All the proof is—I told men
What I had heard.

               I never knew a voice,
Man, beast, or bird, better than this. I told
The naturalists; but neither had they heard
Anything like the notes that did so haunt me;
I had them clear by heart and have them still.
Four years, or five, have made no difference. Then
As now that La-la-la! was bodiless sweet:
Sad more than joyful it was, if I must say
That it was one or other, but if sad
'Twas sad only with joy too, too far off
For me to taste it. But I cannot tell
If truly never anything but fair
The days were when he sang, as now they seem.
This surely I know, that I who listened then,
Happy sometimes, sometimes suffering
A heavy body and a heavy heart,
Now straightway, if I think of it, become
Light as that bird wandering beyond my shore.

EDWARD THOMAS

445

The Unquiet Grave

'The wind doth blow today, my love,
  And a few small drops of rain;
I never had but one true-love,
  In cold grave she was lain.

'I'll do as much for my true-love
  As any young man may;
I'll sit and mourn all at her grave
  For a twelvemonth and a day.'

The twelvemonth and a day being up,
  The dead began to speak:
'Oh who sits weeping on my grave,
  And will not let me sleep?'

' 'Tis I, my love, sits on your grave,
  And will not let you sleep;
For I crave one kiss of your clay-cold lips,
  And that is all I seek.'

'You crave one kiss of my clay-cold lips;
  But my breath smells earthy strong;
If you have one kiss of my clay-cold lips,
  Your time will not be long.

' 'Tis down in yonder garden green,
  Love, where we used to walk,
The finest flower that ere was seen
  Is withered to a stalk.

'The stalk is withered dry, my love,
  So will our hearts decay;
So make yourself content, my love,
  Till God calls you away.'

ANON

446

Ute Mountain

'When I am gone'
the old chief said
'if you need me, call me',
and down he lay, became stone.

They were giants then
(as you may see),
and we
are not the shadows of such men.

The long splayed Indian hair
spread ravelling out
behind the rocky head
in groins, ravines;

petered across the desert plain
through Colorado
transmitting force
in a single undulant unbroken line

from toe to hair-tip: there
profiled, inclined away from one
are features, foreshortened, and the high
blade of the cheekbone.

Reading it so, the eye
can take the entire great
straddle of mountain-mass,
passing down elbows, knees and feet.

'If you need me, call me.'
His singularity dominates the plain
as we call to our aid his image:
thus men make a mountain.

CHARLES TOMLINSON

447

The Vacuum

The house is so quiet now
The vacuum cleaner sulks in the corner closet,
Its bag limp as a stopped lung, its mouth
Grinning into the floor, maybe at my
Slovenly life, my dog-dead youth.

I've lived this way long enough,
But when my old woman died her soul
Went into that vacuum cleaner, and I can't bear
To see the bag swell like a belly, eating the dust
And the woollen mice, and begin to howl

Because there is old filth everywhere
She used to crawl, in the corner and under the stair.
I know now how life is cheap as dirt,
And still the hungry, angry heart
Hangs on and howls, biting at air.

HOWARD NEMEROV

Vergissmeinicht

Three weeks gone and the combatants gone,
returning over the nightmare ground
we found the place again, and found
the soldier sprawling in the sun.

The frowning barrel of his gun
overshadowing. As we came on
that day, he hit my tank with one
like the entry of a demon.

Look. Here in the gunpit spoil
the dishonoured picture of his girl
who has put: *Steffi. Vergissmeinicht*
in a copybook gothic script.

448

We see him almost with content
abased, and seeming to have paid
and mocked at by his own equipment
that's hard and good when he's decayed.

But she would weep to see today
how on his skin the swart flies move;
the dust upon the paper eye
and the burst stomach like a cave.

For here the lover and killer are mingled
who had one body and one heart.
And death who had the soldier singled
has done the lover mortal hurt.

KEITH DOUGLAS

The Villain

While joy gave clouds the light of stars,
 That beamed where'er they looked;
And calves and lambs had tottering knees,
 Excited, while they sucked;
While every bird enjoyed his song,
Without one thought of harm or wrong—
I turned my head and saw the wind,
 Nor far from where I stood,
Dragging the corn by her golden hair,
 Into a dark and lonely wood.

W. H. DAVIES

Vision by Sweetwater

Go and ask Robin to bring the girls over
To Sweetwater, said my Aunt; and that was why
It was like a dream of ladies sweeping by
The willows, clouds, deep meadowgrass, and river.

Robin's sisters and my Aunt's lily daughter
Laughed and talked, and tinkled light as wrens
If there were a little colony all hens
To go walking by the steep turn of Sweetwater.

Let them alone, dear Aunt, just for one minute
Till I go fishing in the dark of my mind:
Where have I seen before, against the wind,
These bright virgins, robed and bare of bonnet,

Flowing with music of their strange quick tongue
And adventuring with delicate paces by the stream,—
Myself a child, old suddenly at the scream
From one of the white throats which it hid among?

JOHN CROWE RANSOM

The Visitant

I

A cloud moved close. The bulk of the wind shifted.
A tree swayed over water.
A voice said:
Stay. Stay by the slip–ooze. Stay.

Dearest tree, I said, may I rest here?
A ripple made a soft reply.
I waited, alert as a dog.
The leech clinging to a stone waited
And the crab, the quiet breather.

2

Slow, slow as a fish she came,
Slow as a fish coming forward,
Swaying in a long wave;
Her skirts not touching a leaf,
Her white arms reaching towards me.

She came without sound,
Without brushing the wet stones,
In the soft dark of early evening,
She came,
The wind in her hair,
The moon beginning.

3

I woke in the first of morning.
Staring at a tree, I felt the pulse of a stone.
Where's she now, I kept saying.
Where's she now, the mountain's downy girl?

But the bright day had no answer.
A wind stirred in a web of appleworms;
The tree, the close willow, swayed.

THEODORE ROETHKE

The Vixen

Among the taller wood with ivy hung,
The old fox plays and dances round her young.
She snuffs and barks if any passes by
And swings her tail and turns prepared to fly.
The horseman hurries by, she bolts to see,
And turns agen, from danger never free.
If any stands she runs among the poles

451

And barks and snaps and drives them in the holes.
The shepherd sees them and the boy goes by
And gets a stick and progs the hole to try.
They get all still and lie in safety sure,
And out again when everything's secure,
And start and snap at blackbirds bouncing by
To fight and catch the great white butterfly.

JOHN CLARE

A Walk

Animals have no names—
Who said they should be given them?
Their unseen lot
Is uniform suffering.
The bull, conversing with nature,
Moves off into the meadow,
White horns planted
Over lovely eyes.
The stream like a plain girl
Lies gently amidst pastures,
Laughing, moaning,
Thrusting its limbs into the earth.
Why does it weep? Why is it sad?
For what reason does it ail?
The whole of nature smiles,
Like a looming prison.
Each little flower
Diminutively waves.
The bull sheds grey tears,
Stands in its splendour, scarcely stirring.
A weightless bird circles
In the deserted sky,
Its throat labouring
Over an ancient song.
Before its eyes the waters sparkle,

The great forest sways,
And the whole of nature laughs,
Dying with every instant of the day.
NIKOLAI ALEKSEEVICH ZABOLOTSKY
From the Russian (trans. Daniel Weissbort)

Walking West

Anyone with quiet pace who
walks a grey road in the West
may hear a badger underground where
in deep flint another time is

Caught by flint and held forever,
the quiet pace of God stopped still.
Anyone who listens walks on
time that dogs him single file,

To mountains that are far from people,
the face of the land gone grey like flint.
Badgers dig their little lives there,
quiet-paced the land lies gaunt,

The railroad dies by a yellow depot,
town falls away toward a muddy creek.
Badger-grey the sod goes under
a river of wind, a hawk on a stick.

WILLIAM STAFFORD

The Wanderer

Doom is dark and deeper than any sea-dingle.
Upon what man it fall
In spring, day-wishing flowers appearing,
Avalanche sliding, white snow from rock-face,
That he should leave his house,
No cloud-soft hand can hold him, restraint by women;
But ever that man goes
Through place-keepers, through forest trees,
A stranger to strangers over undried sea,
Houses for fishes, suffocating water,
Or lonely on fell as chat,
By pot-holed becks
A bird stone-haunting, an unquiet bird.

There head falls forward, fatigued at evening,
And dreams of home,
Waving from window, spread of welcome,
Kissing of wife under single sheet;
But waking sees
Bird-flocks nameless to him, through doorway voices
Of new men making another love.

Save him from hostile capture,
From sudden tiger's leap at corner;
Protect his house,
His anxious house where days are counted
From thunderbolt protect,
From gradual ruin spreading like a stain;
Converting number from vague to certain,
Bring joy, bring day of his returning,
Lucky with day approaching, with leaning dawn.

W. H. AUDEN

The Wandering Spectre

Wae's me, wae's me,
The acorn's not yet
Fallen from the tree
That's to grow the wood,
That's to make the cradle,
That's to rock the bairn,
That's to grow a man,
That's to lay me.

ANON

War

With the open eyes of their dead fathers
Toward other worlds they gaze ahead—
Children who, wide-eyed, become
Periscopes of the buried dead.

ANDREI VOZNESENSKY
From the Russian (trans. William Jay Smith and Vera Dunham)

War God's Horse Song

I am the Turquoise Woman's son.
On top of Belted Mountain
beautiful horses—slim like a weasel!
My horse with a hoof like a striped agate,
with his fetlock like a fine eagle plume:
my horse whose legs are like quick lightning
whose body is an eagle-plumed arrow:
my horse whose tail is like a trailing black cloud.

455

The Little Holy Wind blows thru his hair.
My horse with a mane made of short rainbows.
My horse with ears made of round corn.
My horse with eyes made of big stars.
My horse with a head made of mixed waters.
My horse with teeth made of white shell.
The long rainbow is in his mouth for a bridle
          and with it I guide him.
When my horse neighs, different-colored horses follow.
When my horse neighs, different-colored sheep follow.
         I am wealthy because of him.

      Before me peaceful
      Behind me peaceful
      Under me peaceful
      Over me peaceful—
      Peaceful voice when he neighs.
I am everlasting and peaceful.
I stand for my horse.

ANON

From the Navajo (version by Louis Watchman)

'Was it for this'

                Was it for this
That one, the fairest of all rivers, loved
To blend his murmurs with my nurse's song,
And, from his alder shades and rocky falls,
And from his fords and shallows, sent a voice
That flowed along my dreams? For this, didst thou,
O Derwent! travelling over the green plains
Near my 'sweet Birthplace', didst thou, beauteous stream,
Make ceaseless music through the night and day
Which with its steady cadence, tempering
Our human waywardness, composed my thoughts
To more than infant softness, giving me

456

Among the fretful dwellings of mankind
A knowledge, a dim earnest, of the calm
That Nature breathes among the hills and groves.
When, having left his mountains, to the towers
Of Cockermouth that beauteous river came,
Behind my father's house he passed, close by,
Along the margin of our terrace walk.
He was a playmate whom we dearly loved.
Oh, many a time have I, a five years' child,
A naked boy, in one delightful rill,
A little mill-race severed from his stream,
Made one long bathing of a summer's day;
Basked in the sun, and plunged and basked again
Alternate, all a summer's day, or coursed
Over the sandy fields, leaping through groves
Of yellow groundsel; or when crag and hill,
The woods, and distant Skiddaw's lofty height,
Were bronzed with a deep radiance, stood alone
Beneath the sky, as if I had been born
On Indian plains, and from my mother's hut
Had run abroad in wantonness, to sport
A naked savage, in the thunder shower.

WILLIAM WORDSWORTH
From *The Prelude*, Book I

Watch Your Step—I'm Drenched

In Manchester there are a thousand puddles.
Bus-queue puddles poised on slanting paving stones,
Railway puddles slouching outside stations,
Cinema puddles in ambush at the exits,
Zebra-crossing puddles in dips of the dark stripes—
They lurk in the murk
Of the north-western evening
For the sake of their notorious joke,
Their only joke—to soak

The tights or trousers of the citizens.
Each splash and consequent curse is echoed by
One thousand dark Mancunian puddle chuckles.

In Manchester there lives the King of Puddles,
Master of Miniature Muck Lakes,
The Shah of Slosh, Splendifero of Splash,
Prince, Pasha and Pope of Puddledom.
Where? Somewhere. The rain-headed ruler
Lies doggo, incognito,
Disguised as an average, accidental mini-pool.
He is as scared as any other emperor,
For one night, all his soiled and soggy victims
Might storm his streets, assassination in their minds,
A thousand rolls of blotting paper in their hands,
And drink his shadowed, one-joke life away.

ADRIAN MITCHELL

The Weapon

Scots steel tempered wi' Irish fire
Is the weapon that I desire.

HUGH MACDIARMID

Weathers

I

This is the weather the cuckoo likes,
    And so do I;
When showers betumble the chestnut spikes,
    And nestlings fly:
And the little brown nightingale bills his best,
And they sit outside at 'The Travellers' Rest',
And maids come forth sprig-muslin drest,
And citizens dream of the south and west,
    And so do I.

II

This is the weather the shepherd shuns,
    And so do I;
When beeches drip in browns and duns,
    And thresh, and ply;
And hill-hid tides throb, throe on throe,
And meadow rivulets overflow,
And drops on gate-bars hang in a row,
And rooks in families homeward go,
    And so do I.

THOMAS HARDY

The Well Rising

The well rising without sound,
the spring on a hillside,
the ploughshare brimming through deep ground
everywhere in the field—

The sharp swallows in their swerve
flaring and hesitating
hunting for the final curve
coming closer and closer—

The swallow heart from wing beat to wing beat
counselling decision, decision:
thunderous examples. I place my feet
with care in such a world.

WILLIAM STAFFORD

'When I set out for Lyonnesse'

When I set out for Lyonnesse,
    A hundred miles away,
    The rime was on the spray,
And starlight lit my lonesomeness
When I set out for Lyonnesse
    A hundred miles away.

What would bechance at Lyonnesse
    While I should sojourn there
    No prophet durst declare,
Nor did the wisest wizard guess
What would bechance at Lyonnesse
    While I should sojourn there.

When I came back from Lyonnesse
    With magic in my eyes,
    All marked with mute surmise
My radiance rare and fathomless,
When I came back from Lyonnesse
    With magic in my eyes!

THOMAS HARDY

'When lilacs last in the dooryard bloom'd'

When lilacs last in the dooryard bloom'd,
And the great star early droop'd in the western sky in the night,
I mourn'd, and yet shall mourn with ever-returning spring.

Ever-returning spring, trinity sure to me you bring,
Lilac blooming perennial and drooping star in the west,
And thought of him I love.

WALT WHITMAN
From *Memories of President Lincoln*

'When old corruption first begun'

1

'When old corruption first begun,
    'Adorn'd in yellow vest,
'He committed on flesh a whoredom—
    'O, what a wicked beast!

2

'From then a callow babe did spring,
    'And old corruption smil'd
'To think his race should never end,
    'For now he had a child.

3

'He call'd him surgery, and fed
    'The babe with his own milk,
'For flesh and he could ne'er agree,
    'She would not let him suck.

4

'And this he always kept in mind,
    'And form'd a crooked knife,
'And ran about with bloody hands
    'To seek his mother's life.

5

'And as he ran to seek his mother
    'He met with a dead woman,
'He fell in love and married her,
    'A deed which is not common.

6

'She soon grew pregnant and brought forth
    'Scurvy and spott'd fever.
'The father grin'd and skipt about,
    'And said, "I'm made for ever!

' "For now I have procur'd these imps
  ' "I'll try experiments."
'With that he tied poor scurvy down
  'And stopt up all its vents.

'And when the child began to swell,
  'He shouted out aloud,
' "I've found the dropsy out, and soon
  ' "Shall do the world more good."

'He took up fever by the neck
  'And cut out all its spots,
'And thro' the holes which he had made
  'He first discover'd guts.'

WILLIAM BLAKE

'When the rain raineth'

When the rain raineth
  And the Goose winketh,
Little wotteth the Gosling
  What the Goose thinketh.

ANON

'The wicked who would do me harm'

The wicked who would do me harm
May he take the throat disease,
Globularly, spirally, circularly,
Fluxy, pelley, horny-grim.

Be it harder than the stone,
Be it blacker than the coal,
Be it swifter than the duck,
Be it heavier than the lead.

Be it fiercer, fiercer, sharper, harsher, more malignant,
Than the hard, wound-quivering holly,
Be it sourer than the sained, lustrous, bitter, salt salt,
Seven seven times.

Oscillating thither,
Undulating hither,
Staggering downwards,
Floundering upwards.

Drivelling outwards,
Snivelling inwards,
Oft hurrying out,
Seldom coming in.

A wisp the portion of each hand,
A foot in the base of each pillar,
A leg the prop of each jamb,
A flux driving and dragging him.

A dysentery of blood from heart, from form, from bones,
From the liver, from the lobe, from the lungs,
And a searching of veins, of throat, and of kidneys,
To my contemners and traducers.

In name of the God of might,
Who warded from me every evil,
And who shielded me in strength,
From the net of my breakers
        And destroyers.

ANON
From the Gaelic (trans. A. Carmichael)

The Wife of Usher's Well

There lived a wife at Usher's Well,
    And a wealthy wife was she;
She had three stout and stalwart sons,
    And sent them o'er the sea.

They hadna been a week from her,
    A week but barely ane,
Whan word came to the carline wife
    That her three sons were gane.

They hadna been a week from her,
    A week but barely three,
Whan word came to the carline wife
    That her sons she'd never see.

'I wish the wind may never cease,
    Nor fashes in the flood,
Till my three sons come hame to me,
    In earthly flesh and blood.'

It fell about the Martinmass,
    When nights are lang and mirk,
The carline wife's three sons came hame,
    And their hats were o' the birk.

It neither grew in syke nor ditch,
    Nor yet in ony sheugh;
But at the gates o Paradise,
    That birk grew fair eneugh.

'Blow up the fire, my maidens!
    Bring water from the well!
For a' my house shall feast this night,
    Since my three sons are well.'

And she has made to them a bed,
    She's made it large and wide,
And she's ta'en her mantle her about,
    Sat down at the bed-side.

Up then crew the red, red cock,
　　And up and crew the gray;
The eldest to the youngest said,
　　' 'Tis time we were away.'

The cock he hadna craw'd but once,
　　And clapp'd his wings at a',
When the youngest to the eldest said,
　　'Brother, we must awa'.

'The cock doth craw, the day doth daw,
　　The channerin' worm doth chide;
Gin we be mist out o' our place,
　　A sair pain we maun bide.

'Fare ye weel, my mother dear!
　　Fareweel to barn and byre!
And fare ye weel, the bonny lass
　　That kindles my mother's fire!'

ANON

Wild Iron

Sea go dark, dark with wind,
Feet go heavy, heavy with sand,
Thoughts go wild, wild with the sound
Of iron on the old shed swinging, clanging:
Go dark, go heavy, go wild, go round,
　　Dark with the wind,
　　Heavy with the sand,
Wild with the iron that tears at the nail
And the foundering shriek of the gale.

ALLEN CURNOW

Willy Wet-Leg

I can't stand Willy wet-leg,
can't stand him at any price.
He's resigned, and when you hit him
he lets you hit him twice.

D. H. LAWRENCE

'The wind blows out of the gates of the day'

The wind blows out of the gates of the day,
The wind blows over the lonely of heart,
And the lonely of heart is withered away;
(While the faeries dance in a place apart,
Shaking their milk-white feet in a ring,
Tossing their milk-white arms in the air;
For they hear the wind laugh and murmur and sing
Of a land where even the old are fair,
And even the wise are merry of tongue;
But I heard a reed of Coolaney say—
'When the wind has laughed and murmured and sung,
The lonely of heart is withered away.')

W. B. YEATS
From The Land of Heart's Desire

'The wind suffers of blowing'

The wind suffers of blowing,
The sea suffers of water,
And fire suffers of burning,
And I of a living name.

As stone suffers of stoniness,
As light of its shiningness,
As birds of their wingedness,
So I of my whoness.

And what the cure of all this?
What the not and not suffering?
What the better and later of this?
What the more me of me?

How for the pain-world to be
More world and no pain?
How for the old rain to fall
More wet and more dry?

How for the wilful blood to run
More salt-red and sweet-white?
And how for me in my actualness
To more shriek and more smile?

By no other miracles,
By the same knowing poison,
By an improved anguish,
By my further dying.

LAURA RIDING

'A Wind that rose'

A Wind that rose
Though not a Leaf
In any Forest stirred
But with itself did cold engage
Beyond the Realm of Bird—
A Wind that woke a lone Delight

Like Separation's Swell
Restored in Arctic Confidence
To the Invisible—

The Windhover:

To Christ our Lord

I caught this morning morning's minion, king-
    dom of daylight's dauphin, dapple-dawn-drawn Falcon, in
        his riding
    Of the rolling level underneath him steady air, and striding
High there, how he rung upon the rein of a wimpling wing
In his ecstasy! then off, off forth on swing,
    As a skate's heel sweeps smooth on a bow-bend: the hurl
        and gliding
    Rebuffed the big wind. My heart in hiding
Stirred for a bird,—the achieve of, the mastery of the thing!

Brute beauty and valour and act, oh, air, pride, plume, here
    Buckle! AND the fire that breaks from thee then, a billion
Times told lovelier, more dangerous, O my chevalier!

    No wonder of it: shéer plód makes plough down sillion
Shine, and blue-bleak embers, ah my dear,
    Fall, gall themselves, and gash gold-vermilion.

GERARD MANLEY HOPKINS

468

'Witches' Chasm'

The owl is abroad, the bat and the toad,
    And so is the cat-a-mountain;
The ant and the mole both sit in a hole,
    And frog peeps out o' the fountain.
The dogs they do bay, and the timbrels play,
    The spindle is now a-turning;
The moon it is red, and the stars are fled,
    But all the sky is a-burning:
The ditch is made, and our nails the spade:
With pictures full, of wax and wool,
Their livers I stick with needles quick;
There lacks but the blood to make up the flood.
Quickly, dame, then bring your part in!
Spur, spur, upon little Martin!
Merrily, merrily, make him sail,
A worm in his mouth and a thorn in's tail,
Fire above, and fire below,
With a whip i' your hand to make him go!

BEN JONSON

'With fairest flowers'

With fairest flowers
While summer lasts and I live here, Fidele,
I'll sweeten thy sad grave; thou shalt not lack
The flower that's like thy face, pale primrose, nor
The azur'd hare-bell, like thy veins, no, nor
The leaf of eglantine, whom not to slander,
Out-sweeten'd not thy breath: the ruddock would,
With charitable bill,—O bill! sore-shaming
Those rich-left heirs, that let their fathers lie

Without a monument,—bring thee all this;
Yea, and furr'd moss besides, when flowers are
    none,
To winter-ground thy corse.

From *Cymbeline*, Act 4 Scene 2

The Woodlark

Teevo cheevo cheevio chee:
O where, what can thát be?
Weedio-weedio: there again!
So tiny a trickle of sóng-strain;

And all round not to be found
For brier, bough, furrow, or gréen ground
Before or behind or far or at hand
Either left either right
Anywhere in the súnlight.

Well, after all! Ah but hark—
'I am the little wóodlark.
The skylark is my cousin and he
Is known to men more than me.
Round a ring, around a ring
And while I sail (must listen) I sing.

To-day the sky is two and two
With white strokes and strains of the blue.
The blue wheat-acre is underneath
And the corn is corded and shoulders its sheaf,
The ear in milk, lush the sash,
And crush-silk poppies aflash,
The blood-gush blade-gash
Flame-rash rudred

470

Bud shelling or broad-shed
Tatter-tangled and dingle-a-danglèd
Dandy-hung dainty head.

And down ... the furrow dry
Sunspurge and oxeye
And lace-leaved lovely
Foam-tuft fumitory.

I ám so véry, O só very glád
That I dó thínk there is not to be had
[Anywhere any more joy to be in.
Cheevio:] when the cry within
Says Go on then I go on
Till the longing is less and the good gone,
But down drop, if it says Stop,
To the all-a-leaf of the tréetop.
And after that off the bough
[Hover-float to the hedge brow.]

Through the velvety wind V-winged
[Where shake shadow is sun's-eye-ringed]
To the nest's nook I balance and buoy
With a sweet joy of a sweet joy,
Sweet, of a sweet, of a sweet joy
Of a sweet—a sweet—sweet—joy.'
GERARD MANLEY HOPKINS

'Would you hear of an old-fashion'd sea-fight?'

Would you hear of an old-fashion'd sea-fight?
Would you learn who won by the light of the moon and stars?
List to the story as my grandmother's father, the sailor, told it to
 me.
Our foe was no skulk in his ship, I tell you, (said he;)
His was the surly English pluck—and there is no tougher or
 truer, and never was, and never will be;

471

Along the lower'd eve he came, horribly raking us.
We closed with him—the yards entangled—the cannon
    touch'd;
My captain lash'd fast with his own hands.
We had receiv'd some eighteen pounds shot under the water;
On our lower-gun-deck two large pieces had burst at the first
    fire, killing all around, and blowing up overhead.

Fighting at sun-down, fighting at dark;
Ten o'clock at night, the full moon well up, our leaks on the
    gain, and five feet of water reported;
The master-at-arms loosing the prisoners confined in the
    afterhold, to give them a chance for themselves.

The transit to and from the magazine is now stopt by the
    sentinels,
They see so many strange faces, they do not know whom to
    trust.

Our frigate takes fire;
The other asks if we demand quarter?
If our colors are struck, and the fighting is done?

Now I laugh content, for I hear the voice of my little captain,
We have not struck, he composedly cries, *we have just begun our
    part of the fighting.*

Only three guns are in use;
One is directed by the captain himself against the enemy's
    mainmast,
Two, well served with grape and canister, silence his musketry
    and clear his decks.
The tops alone second the fire of this little battery, especially the
    main-top;
They hold out bravely during the whole of the action.
Not a moment's cease;
The leaks gain fast on the pumps—the fire eats toward the
    powder-magazine.

One of the pumps has been shot away—it is generally thought
    we are sinking.

Serene stands the little captain;
He is not hurried—his voice is neither high nor low;
His eyes give more light to us than our battle-lanterns.

Toward twelve at night, there in the beams of the moon, they
    surrender to us.

Stretch'd and still lies the midnight;
Two great hulls motionless on the breast of the darkness;
Our vessel riddled and slowly sinking—preparations to pass to
    the one we have conquer'd;
The captain on the quarter-deck coldly giving his orders
    through a countenance white as a sheet;
Near by, the corpse of the child that serv'd in the cabin;
The dead face of an old salt with long white hair and carefully
    curl'd whiskers;
The flames, spite of all that can be done, flickering aloft and
    below;
The husky voices of the two or three officers yet fit for duty;
Formless stacks of bodies, and bodies by themselves—dabs of
    flesh upon the masts and spars,
Cut of cordage, dangle of rigging, slight shock of the soothe of
    waves,
Black and impassive guns, litter of powder-parcels, strong
    scent,
Delicate sniffs of sea-breeze, smells of sedgy grass and fields by
    the shore, death-messages given in charge to survivors,
The hiss of the surgeon's knife, the gnawing teeth of his saw,
Wheeze, cluck, swash of falling blood, short wild scream, and
    long, dull, tapering groan;
These so—these irretrievable.

WALT WHITMAN
From *Song of Myself*

'Yon island carrions desperate of their bones'

Yon island carrions desperate of their bones,
Ill-favour'dly become the morning field;
Their ragged curtains poorly are let loose,
And our air shakes them passing scornfully:
Big Mars seems bankrupt in their beggar'd host,
And faintly through a rusty beaver peeps:
The horsemen sit like fixed candlesticks,
With torch-staves in their hand; and their poor jades
Lob down their heads, dropping the hides and hips,
The gum down-roping from their pale-dead eyes,
And in their pale-dull mouths the gimmal bit
Lies foul with chew'd grass, still and motionless;
And their executors, the knavish crows,
Fly o'er them, all impatient for their hour.

WILLIAM SHAKESPEARE
From *Henry V*, Act 4 Scene 2

You're

Clownlike, happiest on your hands,
Feet to the stars, and moon-skulled,
Gilled like a fish. A common-sense
Thumbs-down on the dodo's mode.
Wrapped up in yourself like a spool,
Trawling your dark as owls do.
Mute as a turnip from the Fourth
Of July to All Fools' Day,
O high-riser, my little loaf.

Vague as fog and looked for like mail.
Farther off than Australia.
Bent-backed Atlas, our traveled prawn.
Snug as a bud and at home
Like a sprat in a pickle jug

474

A creel of eels, all ripples.
Jumpy as a Mexican bean.
Right, like a well-done sum.
A clean slate, with your own face on.

SYLVIA PLATH

Glossary

a sghembo: crooked, oblique, on the slant, askew
aboon: above
ane: one
atomies: atoms, tiny creatures

ban: law, restriction
barton: farmyard
beaver: vizor
birk: birch
blea: bleak
bouse: booze
braid: broad
brinded: marked with spots or stripes
butt and ben: two-roomed house

cachaça: rum, a spirit made from sugar cane
carle: husbandman
carline: an old woman, a witch
ceilidh: an informal evening of song and story
channerin': scolding
chanticleer: cockerel
chaparral: dense, tangled brushwood
chaudron: entrails
chined: back-boned
chippies: loose women, prostitutes
chuck: food
churl: husbandman
contos: tales, stories
comb: crest
coombe: deep little wooded valley
coop: hollow place
corbie: carrion crow
corse: body
craking: squeaking

cran: a measure of herrings, 37.5 gallons (168.75 litres)
crawing: crowing
crowse: sharp-tempered, conceited, elated, valiant
cruse: earthen pot
culvers: doves, pigeons

danegun: an old firearm, fairly primitive
darkling: in the dark
daunton: frighten, cast down
degged: sprinkled
diddering: shaking
dight: adorn, equip
dimute: demure
dint: blow
dottle: tobacco tar
dought: could bring myself
doughty: brave
dureless: transient, temporary

fashes: troubles
ferlie: marvel
flitches: tufts, clumps

gang: go
gingle: jingle
glebe: a field, land attached to parish church
glim: a glimpse, an eye
goneys: albatrosses
graybacks: vermin
grot: cave
gullies: seagulls

habergeon: a sleeveless coat of mail
hame: home
harp and carp: make music and sing
hause-bane: neck bone

heathpacks: heather
helves: alarmed lowing of cattle, moans
hooker: single-masted fishing smack
huntly: searchingly
huzzing: buzzing, humming noise

ilka: each
isinglass: mica in thin sheets

jades: horses
jiggers: West Indian or South American fleas

kens: knows
kirtle: a sort of gown or outer petticoat

laith: loath, unwilling
lazybeds: a trench dug over potatoes
lee: lie
leven: lea
lily: lovely
lists: wants, chooses
louted: bowed

machair: a low-lying sandy beach
mane: moan
maun: must
mead: meadow, usually beside stream
metes: measures
mickle: much, great
micuçu: folk name of a deadly snake
moidered: murdered, exhausted
mollies: fulmar petrels
mosey: proceed leisurely

nary a: not a
near: never

nipperkin: small quantity of alcoholic spirit
nubbing chit: gallows

ony: any
ope: open
orisons: prayers
ousel: blackbird
oxsters: armpits

pawl: a catch engaging with the teeth of a ratchet wheel to prevent backward movement
piccolo: juke box
pinnace: small boat
pismire: ant
poke: pouch
upon prank: frolicsomely
prig: to ride
progs: prods
progged: poked
pullen: poultry
punk: prostitute

rack: cloud in upper air
rieving: bereavement
ruddock: redbreast
rut: copulation

sained: blessed
sair: sore, very
sall: shall
saws: sayings
scrowed: streaked
scut: hare, hare's tail
sere: dry
sheugh: ditch, drain
sicca: such a
sike: slim
siller: silver
sillion: furrow
skilly: experienced
slab: thick

snigged: cut unevenly
solan: gannet
spraggle: sprawl, clamber
sprauchly: teetering, uncertain
sperrits: spirits
stark: strong
sturts: darts, starts
sward: grass
syke: trench
syne: then

tares: weeds
tent: heed
tett: tuft
thole: to endure
tib-cat: she-cat

tilly: bonus, something extra
tourney: tournament
trochilus: crocodile bird (of
   humming-bird family)
twindles: twirls and dwindles

vergissmeinicht: forget me not

wae's me: woe's me
water-pudge: puddle
weird: fate
welkin: sky
wight: a man
wot, wotteth: know, knows
wracks: wrecks

Los muertos abren los ojos que viven
The dead open their eyes, which live.

Que tiene, amigo?
Leon.
Hermoso es.
What have you got, friend?
A lion.
It's very fine.

repos donnez a cils
Give eternal peace to him.

Soyez muette pour moi, Idole contemplative . . .
Be silent for me, (o my) contemplative Idol . . .

Index of Poets and Works

480

485

486

489

490

492

493

494

Acknowledgements

The editors and publishers acknowledge with gratitude the co-operation and assistance of Jonathan Barker and Jennifer Insull at the Arts Council Poetry Library and of Mrs Barbara Ellis.

For permission to reprint copyright material the publishers gratefully acknowledge the following:

Faber & Faber Ltd and Random House Inc. for 'As I walked out one evening', 'Carry her over the water', 'Epitaph on a Tyrant', 'I cannot grow', 'Stop all the clocks', 'This lunar beauty', 'The Wanderer' from *Collected Poems* by W. H. Auden; Duckworth & Co. Ltd and Alfred A. Knopf Inc. for 'Ha'nacker Mill', 'Tarantella' from *Complete Verse* by Hilaire Belloc; John Murray (Publishers) Ltd for 'Death in Leamington', 'Meditation on the A30', 'Senex' from *Collected Poems* by John Betjeman; Farrar, Straus & Giroux Inc. for 'The Bight', 'The Burglar of Babylon', 'The Fish', 'Manners', 'Sandpiper', 'Songs for a Colored Singer' from *Elizabeth Bishop: The Complete Poems*, copyright © 1940, 1944, 1955, 1962, 1964, 1969 by Elizabeth Bishop, copyright renewed 1972 by Elizabeth Bishop; Eyre Methuen Ltd and Methuen Inc. for 'Of Poor B. B.', trs. Michael Hamburger, from *Poems 1913–1956* by Bertolt Brecht; Harper & Row Inc. for 'The Ballad of Rudolph Reed' from *The World of Gwendolyn Brooks* by Gwendolyn Brooks; the author and The Hogarth Press for 'Shroud' from *Fishermen with Ploughs* and 'The Hawk' from *Selected Poems*, both by George Mackay Brown; The Hogarth Press for 'The Compassionate Fool', 'She and I' from *Collected Poems* by Norman Cameron; David Higham Associates Ltd for 'Ballad of a Bread Man' from *Underneath the Water* and 'Timothy Winters' from *Union Street* by Charles Causley; the Literary Estate of C. P. Cavafy, Chatto & Windus Ltd and Deborah Rogers Ltd for 'As Much as You Can' from *The Collected Poems of C. P. Cavafy*, trs. Edmund Keeley and Philip Sherrard; the Estate of the late G. K. Chesterton and Dodd Mead & Co. for 'The Donkey', 'Lepanto' from *Collected Poems* by G. K. Chesterton; Curtis Brown Ltd for 'The Badger', 'The Flood', 'Hares at Play', 'Song: I Hid My Love' from *Selected Poems and Prose of John Clare*, eds. Eric Robinson and Geoffrey Summerfield, Copyright © 1967 by Eric Robinson; J. M. Dent for 'Little Trotty Wagtail', 'Mouse's Nest', 'The Vixen' from *The Poems of John Clare*, eds. J. W. and Anne Tibble; George Allen & Unwin Ltd for 'The Scholar', 'A Strong Wind' from *Collected Poems* by Austin Clarke; Mr Emmet M. Greene for 'The Drover' from *Collected Poems* by Padraic Colum; Granada Publishing Ltd and Harcourt Brace Jovanovich Inc. for 'anyone lived in a pretty how town' (copyright 1940 by E. E. Cummings, renewed 1968 by Marion Morehouse Cummings), Granada Publishing Ltd and Liveright Publishing Corp. for 'Buffalo Bill's', Granada Publishing Ltd and Harcourt Brace Jovanovich Inc. for 'maggie and milly and molly and may' (© 1956 by E. E. Cummings), Granada Publishing Ltd and Liveright Publishing Corp. for 'nobody loses all the time', all four poems from *Complete Poems 1913–1962* by E. E. Cummings; Ohio University Press for Epigrams 18, 43, 58, 59 from *Collected Poems and Epigrams* by J. V. Cunningham; the author and Curtis Brown (Australia) Pty for 'Wild Iron' from *Collected Poems* by Allen Curnow; Carcanet Press Ltd for 'Anger lay by me' from *Selected Poems* by Elizabeth Daryush; Jonathan Cape Ltd and Wesleyan University Press for 'The Black Cloud', 'A Child's Pet', 'The Inquest', 'The Moon and a Cloud', 'Sheep', 'The Villain' from *Complete Poems* by W. H. Davies; the Literary Trustees of Walter de la Mare and the Society of Authors as their representative for 'An Epitaph', 'John Mouldy', 'Napoleon' by Walter de la Mare; The Belknap Press of Harvard University Press and the Trustees of Amherst College for 'How the old Mountains drip with Sunset', 'Like Rain it sounded till it curved', 'A narrow Fellow in the Grass', 'There came a Wind like a Bugle', 'There's a certain Slant of Light', 'A Wind that Rose' from *The Complete Poems of Emily Dickinson*, ed. Thomas H. Johnson, Copyright 1951, © 1955, 1979 by the President and Fellows of Harvard College;